Introducing criminology

Introducing criminology

Clive Coleman
Clive Norris

WILLAN
PUBLISHING

Published by

Willan Publishing
Culmcott House
Mill Street, Uffculme
Cullompton, Devon
EX15 3AT, UK
Tel: +44(0)1884 840337
Fax: +44(0)1884 840251
e-mail: willan.publishing@virgin.net

Published simultaneously in the USA and Canada by

Willan Publishing
c/o ISBS, 5804 N.E. Hassalo St,
Portland, Oregon 97213-3644, USA
Tel: +001(0)503 287 3093
Fax: +001(0)503 280 8832

First published 2000
Reprinted 2001

ISBN 1-903240-10-7 (cased)
ISBN 1-903240-09-3 (paper)

British Library Cataloguing-in-Publication Data

A catalogue record for this book is available from the British Library.

Set in Palatino and Gill Sans

Printed by TJ International Ltd, Trecerus Industrial Estate, Padstow, Cornwall, PL28 8RW

Contents

Preface

When we asked friends and colleagues for advice on writing an intro-
ductory book on criminology, some of them said 'don't do it'. While they
may simply have been taking a dim view of our abilities, we prefer to think
they had in mind the difficulties involved in doing the task well. Perhaps
they were right. Overviews of the discipline, especially in a short volume,
often seem superficial, failing to give a full appreciation of the issues. In
attempting to provide depth, however, comprehensiveness is usually
sacrificed. We have attempted a mix of overview and in-depth examination of particular areas. Inevitably, some areas have not been covered at all,
such as victims, and prisons and punishment. We hope, however, we have
given a clear indication of the subject matter of criminology, the diversity
of approaches within it and the way in which criminologists go about their
work.

In the chapters that follow, Clive Norris was mainly responsible for the
content of chapters 5 and 6, and Clive Coleman for the remainder. We have
benefited from the advice of others, who kindly read and made comments
on draft sections when they had better things to do. We are very grateful to
Gerry Johnstone, Dave Metcalf, Jason Ditton, Keith Bottomley and Mike
McCahill. They must not, of course, be held responsible for the outcome.
Finally, we must thank our publisher, Brian Willan, who has been helpful,
constructive and supportive throughout.

Clive Coleman and Clive Norris
September 2000

Introduction

Crime and criminology were two of the growth industries of the second half of the twentieth century. Crime and how to respond to it are major issues of today. Many universities now offer degree courses in criminology, and it is often taken as an element in other degree programmes. In addition, there is significant interest on the part of the general public. There seemed to be a need for a relatively short book that would welcome people to the subject, being suitable for those who were just interested in it, those thinking of taking it up, or those who have already embarked on a course of study. There are plenty of big American-style textbooks that attempt a comprehensive coverage. This book does not try to do this. The first three chapters are broadly based, taking an overview of some major themes and approaches. The second half of the book provides a more detailed insight into the way in which criminologists go about their business by looking in depth at three topics, selected to illustrate work that has been done in different areas of criminology. We like to think that what we are doing is rather like inviting readers to a party, at which they will meet some key figures in the subject, eavesdrop on some of their conversations and arguments, and learn how they go about their work in terms of actual research.

This book, then, invites the reader to a party, given to celebrate the birthday of criminology, although there is some dispute about the date of this. Many of the guests will have claims to be called criminologists. They may surprise you by the diversity in their backgrounds and interests. Among the guests you will meet: an Italian Professor with a fascination with your bodily measurements, for whom size *is* important, and who claims to be the father of criminology; a rather challenging person who tells you that it is necessary to change the nature of our greedy capitalist society before we can make real progress in dealing with crime; someone who wants to improve the conditions in our prisons and limit their use to the smallest number of cases; a civil servant who works for a big government department, which is concerned with the running of the criminal justice system. Finally, a rather troublesome gatecrasher, who regrets that criminology was born at all. Still want to come? Then read on...

Parties can be fun; they can also be tense but revealing occasions. The world of criminology is not so very different from this. As we shall see, criminologists seem to form themselves into identifiable groupings, which do not always communicate easily with each other, almost as if they speak different languages. Indeed, they often *do* speak different languages, and criminology can develop in different ways in different countries (see Nye 1984 on the conflict between the 'French' and 'Italian' schools). The occasional skirmish is to be observed, the reasons for which are not always clear to outsiders. When criminologists are gathered together, it is not all sweetness and light, for big questions are asked by them, to which there are no easy answers. Since criminology raises issues about human nature and social order, and connects with the world of human suffering, it deals with questions that matter to people's lives. It is therefore not surprising that heat is often generated.

Birthday parties are often occasions for reminiscence. Guests tell stories that illustrate the character of the person whose big day is being celebrated. Some of the older guests are able to recall the very early history of the person, and even how they were first contemplated (or not) and conceived. This book will begin by asking such basic questions about the character of criminology: what is it about? It will attempt to trace its history and origins from the earliest times, when it may have been a mere twinkle in someone's eye. Who were the parents, and what were they like? What impact did they have on the development of their offspring? Did others have an influence on the development of criminology in ways that the parents did not contemplate? Has there been dispute over the parentage of the subject, and over the way in which its life and career should develop?

Indeed, we may even find those at the party who, far from celebrating the birth and continued existence of criminology, are essentially critical of its fundamental character and concerns: has it spent much of its time on the 'wrong' subject matter and asking the 'wrong' questions? Does it need to change in a radical way or even be abolished altogether? The basic nature of criminology, its origins and its subject matter are the focus of the first chapter of this book.

Parties are also occasions where games are often played. What kinds of games are played by criminologists? In chapter 2 we begin to look at a game which has consistently been played by criminologists over the years: 'spot the difference' between offenders and non-offenders. The intention has been to discover how offenders and non-offenders differ from each other. If differences could be found, it was thought that these would provide vital clues to the causes of offending. Some have suggested that the place to look for such differences is in the biological make-up of individuals – that their genetic or physical characteristics, for example, hold at least some of the clues to understanding crime and the criminal. Others took the view that, while not necessarily discounting some role for biological differences, the important differences between individuals with regard to the causes of crime are psychological. Chapter 2 therefore looks at the various perspectives within psychology which have attempted to understand crime, with special reference to the game of 'spot the difference'.

Chapter 3, entitled 'A broader vision of crime', is mainly concerned with the sociological approach to understanding crime. For much of its history, sociologists who have attempted to study crime have played their own version of 'spot the difference'. For them, the biological and psychological approaches were either looking in the wrong place, or at least their work needed to be supplemented by an understanding of the social background and circumstances of offenders in order to explain crime. Chapter 3 also documents a growing disenchantment with the game of 'spot the difference'. The game had not only proved to be more difficult than initially expected, but some came to regard the whole exercise as a fruitless quest. While some argued that the game should be abandoned altogether, others took the view that it should at least be supplemented by other activities and questions. It is clear that criminologists have become less preoccupied with playing 'spot the difference' than they used to be.

For readers who have got this far and are still not convinced that this is a party worth attending, we try a different tack in the three chapters that follow. Having provided broad overviews of some key issues and perspectives in criminology in the first three chapters, we move on to examine three topics from different key areas of criminology. The first of these topics is serial murder.

At parties and other social gatherings with 'normal' people, we find that our trade as criminologists (if exposed) is often the source of great curiosity. Some of the most frequently asked questions are about serial killers, for there seems to be great interest in this topic and a demand for material on it, as a visit to the crime section of any book shop will show. It is sometimes assumed that criminologists are people like the character Fitz in the TV series *Cracker*, who spend their time getting inside the minds of serial killers and constructing profiles that will enable the forces of law and order to track them down.

While criminologists might, quite rightly, try to distance themselves from this narrow and rather misleading (but apparently glamorous) view of their role, the serial killer does present a legitimate challenge to the criminologist. Surely this type of offender is a good candidate for 'spot the difference'? If theories of crime in general are difficult to construct when crime is such a varied category, ranging from the theft of milk from doorsteps to serial rape, surely such a specific crime as this should be a good candidate for constructing a criminological theory? We therefore give the experts pencils and paper, and ask them to come up with their theoretical 'profiles' of the serial killer. Which, if any, is the most convincing in terms of contributing to our understanding – that produced by biology, psychology or sociology? The chapter serves as an illustration of some of the procedures and problems involved in constructing a theory of a particular type of crime.

While for many years the quest to understand and explain crime has been a major preoccupation of criminology, a rather more recent focus has been the workings of the criminal justice system. Rather than attempting to give an overview of this area, we take an example of one important agency within it – the police. Often seen as playing a key role as gate-keepers in the criminal justice process, placed as they are at the entry point of the formal process, the police are also the agency with which most readers are likely to be familiar. Even if readers have not had their collars felt, they are likely to have had some contact with the police, and to have consumed a rich diet of representations of the police and policing through the mass media.

We focus on some key issues that have preoccupied criminologists in their study of the police. Firstly, what is their role? Are they solely respon-sible for policing, or are other agencies involved? What do the police actually do? Is their main role best seen as the control of crime, as is often suggested? Secondly, we introduce two concepts that are important in the study of criminal justice: discretion and discrimination, which we discuss in the context of the police and policing. What is discretion and why does it exist? Does police discretion result in discrimination against certain groups in the population? Here we introduce the concept of police culture, which has often been used to explain the way in which police discretion is exercised. Finally, we outline a framework which has been commonly used in the study of criminal justice: the distinction between due process and crime control models of criminal justice. We discuss these models in relation to policing, and ask how police practice in violation of 'due process' might come about.

Another area that has received increasing attention in recent years is crime prevention. Our final main chapter provides a brief introduction to this area, before examining in depth a highly topical example of crime prevention activity – closed circuit television (CCTV) systems. After examining the reasons behind the popularity and growth of CCTV, we look at a key question that criminologists are often expected to answer about such initiatives: does it reduce crime? As an illustration of the attempt to evaluate policy measures to see if they actually 'work', it demonstrates some of the difficulties involved in answering by research such an apparently straightforward question. Finally, we raise some broader issues raised by CCTV. Criminological research which merely concentrates on the technical evaluation of such measures has often been criticised for its narrow focus. Our position throughout this book is that criminology should locate its studies in a broader political and social context. We therefore raise some of the broader issues about CCTV. Is it a technology that benefits all (apart from the potential criminal) or can it lead to discrimination and social exclusion for certain groups in the population?

Chapter 1

Crime, the criminal and criminology

Having invited you to the party, it is now time to find out more about the guests and their activities. The starting point is to introduce you to two key terms: crime and the criminal. Although the meaning of these terms may initially seem obvious, there have long been arguments about the definition of them. These arguments are important, for they raise key issues about criminology and its scope, and the way in which societies identify and respond to actions as criminal. This leads into a consideration of the nature and focus of criminology itself. There are different ideas about its nature and aims, which will be explained. The final part of the chapter attempts to contribute to our understanding of criminology by taking a brief overview of its history, particularly in its early days. When was it born, and do those early years help to explain its nature and development in the years to come?

What is crime? Who is the criminal?

The legalistic position

For most of us, these do not appear to be particularly difficult questions. Crime is that action which is prohibited by the criminal law, and the criminal is the agent who carries out that action. Michael and Adler (1933: 2) are often cited as an example of the legal definition of crime: 'the most precise and least ambiguous definition of crime is that which defines it as behaviour which is prohibited by the criminal code'. They recognised that the definition of the criminal was rather more difficult, for although any person who breaks the criminal law is a criminal, how are such persons to be identified by criminologists? They conclude that 'the most certain way ... to distinguish criminals from non-criminals is in terms of those who have been convicted of crime and those who have not. ... The criminologist is therefore quite justified in making the convict population the subject of his studies as he does' (Michael and Adler 1933: 3). In practice, for many years criminologists conducted studies of prisoners; the prison provided a convenient captive sample for researchers and a context within which their specialism could develop with a particular focus – the individual criminal. However, prisoners are only a sample of those convicted of crime, who in their turn are only a sample of those who have broken the criminal law; it cannot be assumed that such samples are representative of all law-breakers.

Conduct norms and their violation

Not everyone was happy with such a focus on crime and the criminal. One of the dissenters was Thorsten Sellin, a famous sociologist of his day, who put forward an argument which has been heard in a number of different versions over the years. Sellin (1938) pointed out that the criminal law often reflected the values of powerful interest groups, even in democracies, rather than the moral standards within the general population. What is defined as criminal could vary over time and between different societies, making crime and the criminal a very slippery subject matter for the scientist, who should be using concepts that had a 'universal' nature, rather than ones which had a different meaning depending upon the particular society and historical time.

Rather than using 'ready made' terms and subjects of study defined by non-scientists, Sellin argued, scientists should be free to define their own terms, to reflect the nature of the subject matter and its 'universal' properties. Since all social groups in any society had rules or norms, a better basis for scientific investigation would be the study of these conduct norms. The more complex the society, the more likely that norms would come into conflict, such as where individuals are members of groups with different norms, or where one group has power over another with different conduct norms. These conduct norms, how they develop and relate to each other, and violations of them would be the focus of study, rather than crime and criminal as defined by the criminal law and the criminal justice system.

Many of these points were to be reiterated in years to come. The point about the relationship between criminal law and power rang a few bells in the USA, a country which had experienced Prohibition. This involved legislation that prohibited the manufacture, sale and transportation of 'intoxicating liquor' and represented a political victory for the moral code of one segment of American society at the expense of others. Sellin's view that we should study the origins and violations of conduct norms was increasingly taken up by those who began to speak of 'deviant behaviour' as the focus of study, rather than crime. Most difficult to grasp is his idea that conduct norms could somehow be identified and classified into 'universal categories, transcending political and other boundaries, a necessity imposed by the logic of science' (Sellin 1938:31). This is an example of the attempt to imitate the way in which the natural sciences operated: to develop concepts and terms which would be equally applicable whether you found yourself in Tipperary or Timbuctoo (in the way that those such as velocity, density, gravity are in natural science). Most important for current concerns is that Sellin did not argue that the concept of crime should be extended to all violations of conduct norms, perhaps aware of the confusion this would create: 'extension of the meaning of the term crime is not desirable. It is wiser to retain that term for the offenses made punishable by the crimincl law ...' (Sellin 1938: 32). Others came to a different conclusion.

Extending the concept of crime

Like Sellin, Edwin Sutherland was concerned about the narrow focus of much criminology. He, however, was interested in the offences committed by business and professional people in the course of their occupations (what he called white-collar crime), and the way in which these were virtually ignored by criminologists and their theories of criminal behaviour. Sutherland (1940) therefore conducted a study of the decisions made by courts and commissions of the USA against the seventy largest business corporations in such matters as false advertising, anti-trust activity, labour relations, and infringement of patents, copyrights and trademarks (types of white-collar crime now frequently referred to as corporate crime). He found that 547 such adverse decisions had been made, an average of 7.8 per corporation, with each having at least one made against it. However, only 49, or 9 per cent of these decisions were made by criminal courts. Undaunted, Sutherland attempted to show that the remaining decisions were that the behaviour was 'actually' criminal. He did this by extending somewhat the definition of crime, which he claimed involves two things: 'legal description of an act as socially injurious and legal provision of a penalty for the act' (Sutherland 1945: 132). Note that this definition still takes the law as its yardstick, but not just the criminal law. In a sense, therefore, he was still clinging to a legalistic definition. According to this definition the remaining actions of the corporations were therefore 'crimes', although they were in practice treated as if they were not crimes. They thus avoided the usual stigma (and some of the harshest punishments) which were attached to offences treated by the criminal law, an example of what he termed the differential implementation of the law. He saw three main reasons for this relative leniency: the higher status of the offenders; the trend away from punitive responses; and the relatively undeveloped public hostility towards such offenders.

Sutherland was pointing to what he saw as class bias in the usual definition of crime and bias towards the respectable in the operation of the legal system. Not only were 'white collar' persons treated more leniently when they were caught, but also many such offenders were never prosecuted in the first place. Futhermore, if criminologists confined their attention to crime as usually defined, a kind of class bias would be introduced into their study, with a concentration on those from the poorer and less powerful sections of society. If so, the theories of crime likely to develop from such a blinkered vision would be correspondingly partial. Finally, since these sorts of offenders and offences rarely found their way into the official crime statistics (produced by the agencies of the *criminal* justice system), they were even more likely to be ignored by criminologists and not seen by the public as being part of the 'crime problem'. If taken seriously, the implications were momentous, requiring us to revise our ideas about crime and the criminal, the way to get information on them, and the kinds of theories we need to explain them.

The legalistic position restated

The sorts of arguments put by people like Sellin and Sutherland clearly got up the noses of some other criminologists, particularly those with a legal background, for whom 'crime' had a very precise meaning, and for whom the term 'criminal' should only be applied after the operation of the due process of criminal law. To take any other approach would lead to confusion and unethical branding of those who should be regarded as innocent until proven guilty. Paul Tappan is a good example of someone whose nostrils were particularly affected. Tappan (1947) accepted that it was quite legitimate for sociologists to study all sorts of 'conduct norms' and their violation. But for him criminal law provides us with an important, and fortunately very precise, type of these conduct norms: 'crime is an intentional act in violation of the criminal law (statutory or case law), committed without defense or excuse, and penalized by the state as a felony or misdemeanor' (Tappan 1947: 100). In addition, Tappan accepted that convicted criminals were not necessarily representative of all offenders, because of the selective processes of the discovery, detection, prosecution and adjudication of offenders. Nevertheless, 'ajudicated offenders represent the closest possible approximation to those who have in fact violated the law, carefully selected by the sieving of the due process of law' (Tappan 1947: 102), and should be the focus of study. It would be wrong to identify someone (or a business corporation) as a criminal unless they had been convicted of a crime.

In some ways, Tappan's background as both lawyer and sociologist appears to be pulling him in different directions. It is, however, easy to see the force of his concerns. But if his definition of crime is accepted and criminology is simply the study of violations of criminal law, there remain objections to a discipline which limits itself to a subject matter defined by the state (and, by implication, powerful interests which may influence the law-making process). Disciplines such as sociology could take a broader view of a wide range of different rules and violations of them. Questions had also been raised about the nature of criminal law and the interests it represented. Why not study the law in this way, rather than simply behaviour that violates it? As we shall see, sociologists gradually took up these questions. Unfortunately, those who attempted to extend the concept of crime to cover various kinds of misbehaviour not presently covered by the criminal law found themselves getting bogged down in acrimonious debates about definitions and terms, as happened with Sutherland (1945) and his work on 'white-collar crime'. As for the 'criminal', Tappan's views raise a key issue: if it is possible that adjudicated offenders are not representative of those who have broken even the criminal law, this represents a serious problem for those trying to make generalisations about criminals. This was enough to make some researchers attempt to find out about those who had broken the law but had not been caught (such as by the use of *self-report studies*, which ask people directly about their involvement in offending: see Coleman and Moynihan 1996: chapter 3). It was also a powerful impetus to look at those processes of law enforcement and criminal justice to see in what ways they were selective.

Crime as the violation of human rights

If Tappan was disturbed by the ideas of Sellin and Sutherland, he would have been dismayed by those of Herman and Julia Schwendinger (1970) some years afterwards. These writers were concerned with the attempt to identify basic human rights (such as personal security) rather than legal rules as the way to define crime. As such, forms of social organisation, as well as individuals, which violate such rights are criminal:

> individuals who deny these rights to others are criminal. Likewise, social relationships and social systems which regularly cause the abrogation of these rights are also criminal. If the terms imperialism, sexism and poverty are abbreviated signs for theories of social relationships or social systems which cause the systematic abrogation of basic rights, then imperialism, racism, sexism and poverty can be called crimes according to the logic of our argument.
> (Schwendinger and Schwendinger 1970: 148)

Although it is difficult to do justice to the 'logic of their argument' here, their position is that the definition of crime is inescapably political. Those accepting the legalistic approach of state-defined crime run the risk of becoming subservient to that particular state, the status quo, and the interests it serves. For example, consider the position of a criminologist in Nazi Germany of the 1930s, where certain groups in the population had their human rights attacked, with the support of the state and its legal apparatus. From the human rights perspective, the state can be seen as a perpetrator of crime, rather than simply the authority that defines crime. For the Schwendingers the role of the criminologist should be to engage in the stuggle for those basic human rights so that criminologists become guardians of those rights rather than defenders of the current order of things (consider again the predicament of our criminologist in Nazi Germany). What the human rights approach shares in common with that of some earlier writers is the attempt to identify certain basic standards, any deviation from which is 'crime'.

Crime as a social construction

What was clear from previous debates was that the contents of the category of crime, as defined by the criminal law, varies over time and place. Sutherland and Cressey (quoted in Rock 1973: 20) produced a list to illustrate the variety of acts which had been defined as crimes at some point, which included 'printing a book, professing the medical doctrine of circulation of the blood, driving with reins, selling coins to foreigners, having gold in the house, buying goods on the way to market or in the market for the purpose of selling them at a higher price, writing a cheque for less than a dollar'. So various are the things that have been defined as crimes that some took the view that the only thing they have in common is the fact that they have been defined as crimes by the criminal law. One reason why some scholars had spent so much time trying to identify the 'essential' nature of crime was that they were concerned with developing a theory (a systematic explanation) of criminal behaviour. If crime was in fact a rag-bag of assorted acts with very little in common between them, the chances of developing a general theory of crime seemed pretty slim indeed. Some researchers tried to reformulate their subject matter as deviant behaviour, anti-social conduct or the violation of conduct norms. At least these, defined by the researcher rather than the state, might have enough in common to make generalisations possible.

As we shall see, the years of effort in attempting to develop such theories took their toll. Eventually, some gave up the quest altogether and explored other avenues. If crime was simply that which has been designated as such by the criminal law, why not study how this comes about? Why not look at the criminal law itself as socially created, in particular social, economic and political circumstances? The variability and the political nature of criminal law were no longer problems hampering progress, but something to be investigated. From this perspective, crime was defined in particular historical circumstances, as a result of the activities of agents with varying degrees of power. Here were new processes and topics for investigation. In this view, criminal law was a social construction (rather than a set of given rules, violation from which was the principal topic for study). According to one version of this perspective it can be viewed as a collection of 'negative ideological categories with specific historical applications ... categories of denunciation or abuse lodged within very complex, historically loaded practical conflicts and moral debates ... these negative categories of moral ideology are social censures' (Sumner 1990: 26, 28).

If criminal law was a social construction ripe for investigation, so were crime and the criminal. How do some acts and persons come to be designated as criminal by the criminal justice system, out of a pool of possible candidates? Here we are speaking of social processes that produce recorded crimes, suspects, charged persons, prosecutions and various outcomes, such as discharges or prison sentences. These processes can be studied to see precisely how crimes and criminals are 'produced'. Seen in this way, crime and the criminal are the focus for investigation, but in a very different way from the traditional approach with its search for the causes of crime. For example, it asks such questions as what impact do race, class and gender have on whether an individual becomes a suspect for crime? The approach described briefly here is concerned with the processes of *criminalisation*. Such an approach focused attention on who made the rules, and who enforced them, rather than merely on who broke them; as we shall see in Chapter 3, it began to take on increasing importance in the study of crime, largely as a result of that body of work which came to be known as the labelling perspective, particularly through the writings of its best known proponent, Howard Becker (1963).

Taken to extremes, such an approach can result in an equally blinkered approach to that found in traditional criminology. With its primary focus upon the process of criminalisation, it can lead to a neglect of the original action of the offender, its meaning and the reasons behind it. It is also important that the study of criminalisation should be supplemented by study of those areas that frequently escaped the attention of the conventional criminal justice system and often criminology too, such as child abuse, domestic violence, corporate/white-collar 'crime', and crimes of the state such as torture, 'disappearances', ethnic cleansing and genocide. Perhaps it is helpful to distinguish three questions which have frequently been confused in debates:

- what is crime?

- what should be criminal?

- what should criminologists study?

These questions are still important in contemporary criminology, and are frequently revisited, especially by those working from a politically radical position and those working on areas such as corporate crime (see, for example, Slapper and Tombs 1999: chapter 1). Such debates about the definition of crime and the subject matter of criminology do not preoccupy all criminologists in their everyday work; many criminologists have taken the definition of crime and the criminal as *given*, whereas others see them as *problematic*, that is something to be questioned and investigated.

What is criminology?

One basic definition of criminology is that it is the study of crime and the criminal. As we have seen above, however, criminologists are not necessarily agreed on the definition of these two basic terms; rather than being taken for granted, some criminologists insist that these very terms should be seen as *problematic*. What this means is that we should ask the sorts of questions that were raised in the last section. Whenever the terms crime and criminal are used, we must be aware that there are alternative uses of these key terms. This is not to be pedantic (although it may seem like it), but is rather a recognition that different uses of the terms carry all sorts of implications and baggage with them. So, if we take the position that crime is violation of criminal law, criminals are those who have been convicted of a criminal offence, and that these are what criminologists should study, all sorts of implications and consequences follow from this. On the other hand, if we say that the subject matter of criminology should be the violation of human rights, a rather different conception of the discipline comes into view. The terms 'crime' and 'criminal' should not be accepted at face value, and consideration of the definition of them is for us a key part of the subject matter of the discipline.

Having made this basic point, it is possible to specify other aspects of the subject matter of something that could be called 'criminology' in its widest sense.

- the attempt to describe and analyse the extent, nature, and distribution of the various forms of 'crime' and 'offenders'.

- the analysis of the 'causes' of crime, including the attempt to develop theories which will help us to explain and understand it.

- the study of the formulation of criminal laws. Although this area is often said to be part of the sociology of law rather than criminology itself, our discussion above indicates the value of such study to criminology.

- the study of the various processes of law enforcement and criminal justice, such as policing, sentencing, etc. The term 'criminal justice' is often used to refer to the rather narrower field of the study of policy and practice in relation to crime by various agencies, but such work is frequently regarded as part of criminology.

- following on from the last point, the analysis of the various forms of policy and practice in punishment. This might range from looking at the effectiveness of different penal measures to the relationship of different regimes of punishment to the wider society in which they are located. This area of study is often referred to as penology.

- the study of attempts to control, reduce or prevent crime, by, for example, altering aspects of the situations in which it occurs, 'treating' individual offenders, or implementing broad social policies. There is clearly some overlap here with the study of criminal justice processes and punishment listed above.

- investigation of the victims of crime – the extent, distribution and nature of victimisation; their role in crime and criminal justice and policy issues concerning them. This area is frequently referred to as victimology.

- attitudes and reactions to, and representations of, crime on the part of groups not already mentioned, such as the general public, politicians and the mass media.

This list is not exhaustive, but does give an indication of the range of possible areas of study. In addition, there has been increasing recognition that the study of crime and the criminal often cannot be easily separated off from the other elements. This was one implication of our discussion of definitions. Those who use official statistics of crime, for example, have to take on board that those statistics are the product of the actions of suspects, victims, members of the public, and the police as agents of criminal justice. In order to do this, the actions of those agents have to be understood, together with any interaction between them (Coleman and Moynihan 1996). To focus on only one of these produces a partial criminology (Young 1997: 485).

However, it is important to note that people engaged in some of the activities listed above will not necessarily see them as 'criminology', or describe themselves as criminologists. They might prefer to see themselves, for example, as sociologists or psychologists with an interest in crime and associated areas; they identify themselves with that discipline rather than with criminology. In addition, perhaps because of the history of criminology and its traditionally rather narrow focus (see below), many are anxious to avoid being identified too closely with it. We now look briefly at relationships between criminology and a range of academic disciplines and at that history.

A multi-disciplinary discipline?

Criminology is often described as a multi-disciplinary enterprise (Garland 1997: 19; Lanier and Henry 1998: 5). What this means is that 'criminologists draw upon a variety of other disciplines, most notably sociology, psychology, psychiatry, law, history, and anthropology – indeed, one of the major dynamics of modern criminology is the incessant raiding of other disciplines or ideologies for new ideas ...' (Garland 1997: 19). To these disciplines could be added those of biology, geography, economics, and political science, all of which have made forays into the subject or have been raided in the way that Garland suggests. Two points follow from this. One is that this promiscuity – the frequent intercourse with a variety of partners – can make life both interesting and difficult. Variety may be the spice of life, but each of these disciplines tends to have its own assumptions, basic ideas and concepts, a bank of shared knowledge, a particular focus of inquiry, favoured methods of investigation, and a view of the world which leads to particular kinds of policy implications. Disciplines are also internally diverse, harbouring different perspectives within them (see, for example, the various approaches in psychology and sociology discussed in Chapters 2 and 3). All of this makes for a very diverse but intellectually challenging subject. Few criminologists are equally at ease with all of these disciplines.

The second point concerns criminology's claim to be a discipline at all. Is the enterprise so parasitic upon those other disciplines that it has no right to be called one itself? Is it merely the application of a number of other disciplines to a particular subject matter – one largely defined by the state as a problem? Is it better seen as a field of study, rather than a discipline as such? (Lea 1998)

While it has often been argued that criminology is not, or should not be seen as, a discipline at all, others have taken the view that the existence of a discipline is not merely about such matters as having a distinctive and defensible subject matter or methods of enquiry, but also about institutional foundations and structures:

> its claim to be an empirically grounded, scientific undertaking sets it apart from moral and legal discourses, while its focus upon crime differentiates it from other social scientific genres, such as the sociology of deviance and control, whose objects of study are broader and not defined by the criminal law. Since the middle of this century, criminology [in Britain] has increasingly been marked off from other discourses by the trappings of a distinctive disciplinary identity, with its own journals, professional associations, professorships and institutes. ...such a discipline came to exist as an accredited specialism, supported by universities and governments alike.
>
> (Garland 1997: 11)

15

Garland's argument is that the reasons for the existence of criminology are to be found in particular historical circumstances, and that its coming into being was by no means inevitable. It is also a history that tells us a great deal about the nature of criminology today. For one thing, this may help us to understand why many working on studies of crime and justice do not adopt this disciplinary identity, do not necessarily belong to the professional associations or publish in the specialist journals.

Criminology through the ages? Lombroso and all that

Garland (1997) has suggested that criminology grew out of a convergence between two projects – the governmental and the Lombrosian. The first refers to 'the long series of empirical enquries, which, since the eighteenth century, have sought to enhance the efficient and equitable administration of justice by charting the patterns of crime and monitoring the practice of police and prisons' (Garland 1997: 12). The other, the Lombrosian project, had a differerent objective – to build a science of causes, 'based on the premise that criminals can somehow be scientifically differentiated from non-criminals' (Garland 1997: 12). This distinction captures well two major emphases in terms of aims and objectives of the subject. The first is primarily concerned with applied, practical matters, with policy and governance (not necessarily by government agencies) of the population in the widest sense, with its management and control. The other is a more 'academic' theoretical enterprise, the search for the 'causes of crime', which in Garland's account is tied to a particular assumption that is said to have emerged in the work of Lombroso, and is correspondingly 'deeply flawed' (Garland 1997: 12).

We begin looking at the attempt to identify differences between criminals and non-criminals in the next chapter. The two projects, governmental and Lombrosian, create a particular tension in the discipline, with different criminologists according differing weights to them in their work. But 'the combination of the two seems essential to criminology's claim to be sufficiently useful and sufficiently scientific to merit the status of an accredited, state-sponsored, academic discipline' (Garland 1997: 12). Although both projects have experienced significant changes since, the discipline continues to be structured by them.

Garland's detailed and stimulating account cannot be reproduced here. It does, however, provide a useful corrective to textbook histories, which can be so brief and sweeping that they often seem to do for criminology what *1066 And All That* (Sellar and Yeatman 1930) did, but tongue in cheek, for history (e.g. the industrial revolution was described as a wave of gadgets sweeping across the country). His account, which stresses particular, historically specific features, has a number of consequences.

First, although some have attempted to write a history of the discipline by going back through history and searching for assorted writings about law-breakers and punishment (see Drapkin 1983), these writings are not necessarily criminology. Second, although most textbooks begin their discussion of the subject rather later (in the eighteenth century), with what is usually called the 'classical school' of criminology, this for him makes little sense

> given that they made no general distinction between the characteristics of criminals and non-criminals, and had no conception of research on crime and criminals as a distinctive form of enquiry. To use such a term to characterise eighteenth century thought seriously misrepresents the character of these writings and forcibly assimilates them to a project that was not invented until a century later.
>
> (Garland 1997: 15–16)

By this analysis, although we seem to be closer to locating a birthday for criminology, the classical school becomes the criminology that never was; according to Garland's definition of criminology, the classical school does not qualify. For others, however, the classical school can be seen as 'the first clearly identifiable school of criminology in retrospect' (Hughes 1998: 26). For Hughes, Garland's defintion of criminology is too restrictive in its emphasis on the attempt to identify the characteristics of the criminal by scientific means. It is certainly true that criminology has made constant reference to the classical school throughout its short history and that its ideas continue to appear in thinking and practice. In that sense at least, it is certainly a perspective that we need to consider here.

The classical school

The classical school (not that they knew themselves as such) grew out of the work of a group of 'Enlightenment' philosophers of the eighteenth century, who argued that human problems should be tackled by the application of reason, rather than tradition, religion or superstition. Their appearance was no coincidence, but related to the social context: a Europe in which a rising middle class was seeking to free itself from the shackles of regimes in which the monarchy, the aristocracy and the church were very much dominant. Some of these Enlightenment thinkers turned their attention to the nature of the criminal law and punishment, putting forward radical ideas for its reform. They opposed the unpredictable, discriminatory, inhumane and ineffective criminal justice systems that were to be found in their day, systems that often left much to the discretion of the judges (including the frequent use of 'mercy' and pardons), employed barbaric, cruel methods of punishment (and torture for extracting confessions), and seemed to any intelligent observer to be very ineffective in preventing crime.

The programme for changing this state of affairs was to produce a system in which law and punishment were predictable, non-discriminatory (treating all who had broken a particular law alike), humane and effective. Thus punishment should avoid unnecessary suffering, should be proportionate to the crime committed, follow as certainly and quickly as possible after the offence, and be just sufficient to act as a deterrent to the crime. As one of the most famous members of what came to be known as the classical school put it: 'in order for punishment not to be, in every instance, an act of violence of one or of many against a private citizen, it must be essentially public, prompt, necessary, the least possible in the given circumstances, proportionate to the crimes, dictated by the laws' (Beccaria 1963: 99; first published 1764).

A number of writers have attempted to distil the various ideas and assumptions thought to underlie the approach of those considered to be members of the classical school and to arrange them under certain headings that allow comparisons to be made with other approaches (see, for example Young 1981; White and Haines 1996; Lanier and Henry 1998). The story goes something like this:

Human nature
People are seen as self-interested, rational creatures (able to weigh up competing courses of action), able to make and act in accordance with personal choices (often described as 'free will').

Conception of society or social order
Left to their own devices, people will follow their own selfish interests, which will often conflict, resulting in a war of all against all. Because people are rational creatures, they can see the advantages in giving up part of their freedom to do as they please, accepting a set of laws in exchange for protection of life and property from a sovereign or state. Thus comes into being what was called the social contract, a basis for social order. A violation of law is a violation of this contract and justifies the right to punish.

Causes of crime
Since people are normally rational creatures, it seems to follow that either the pleasure or gain from the crime outweighs the pain of punishment associated with it, or that people are making irrational decisions for some reason (e.g. the institutions of law or education may be sending out 'wrong' or confusing messages, so that people do not have the appropriate information to make rational decisions).

Implications for policy
Criminal justice should be subject to strict rule of law (due process) and punishments should be known, fixed and just severe enough to deter. Discretion of judges should be minimised as far as possible in sentencing.

Other headings for comparison are often included. Such frameworks are invaluable in getting a grasp of the various perspectives and their basic concepts. There are, however, one or two limitations. First, such outlines are the product of a great deal of simplification; complexity and variety is often lost. We must not expect all of the thinkers who are grouped together under such labels to subscribe to identical ideas. Furthermore, the attempt to provide satisfying contrasts between classicism and its opponent in the nineteenth century (positivism) sometimes goes too far. For example, Beirne (1993) has argued that, contrary to popular belief, Beccaria (the most frequently given example of a 'classical' thinker), did not subscribe to a view of humans as endowed with 'free will' and 'rational choice', but was concerned with 'the application to crime and penal strategies of the "science of man," a deterministic discourse implicitly at odds with the conventional assumption about ... "classical criminology" ' (Beirne 1993: 5). Beirne suggests that Beccaria was involved in a very rudimentary attempt to forge some key concepts of an embryonic criminology. These concepts include "crime," "criminal," and "causes of crime" ' (Beirne 1993: 44). Perhaps unborn as yet, but the embryo was in place?

There is little doubt that the ideas of the classical school were very influential in the field of law, criminal justice and penal strategies. Criminal justice systems, especially those of western societies, often incorporated elements of the classical programme. Putting such principles into practice raised some problems, however. One concerned the assumption that all people were equal before the law and able to make equally rational decisions. What about, for example, children and those suffering from mental illness? Pure classicism, with its focus upon the crime rather than the offender, seemed to be oblivious to the differences between individuals which might influence notions of their culpability for a crime. Revisions to the classical scheme were therefore made in various legal systems, such as provision for the consideration of 'mitigating circumstances' (elements from the history and current situation of the person), that could be seen as affecting the operation of free will and rationality on the part of the individual. The resulting amalgam of classical and other principles is often referred to as neo-classicism.

A second main problem concerns the nature of society. Classical theory urges that all are equal before the law, but how is this to work when society itself is characterised by major inequalities? First, we might ask whether inequalities in the wider society are themselves involved in the origins of crime – a possibility that is not fully considered by the framework.

Secondly, it is often remarked that people with resources of various kinds (such as education, or access to the best legal representation) are more able to benefit from a criminal justice system which in principle treats all as equal before the law. Finally, if a poor person is to be punished with equal punishment as a rich person for the same offence (e.g. by a fine), this attempt to treat individuals equally may have more serious consequences for the former, who may thus be punished disproportionately. In an unequal society, the promise of equality before the law is very difficult to deliver in practice.

The moral statisticians

The main focus of the classical school was upon the reform of the criminal law according to certain principles. A rather different focus was taken up by the group of scholars who emerged early in the nineteenth century, and attempted to apply the methods and techniques which had mostly been developed in the natural sciences to 'moral' (social) phenomena. Their work was facilitated by the publication of national crime statistics in France, which first appeared in 1827. The appearance of such statistics was an aspect of the development of the 'governmental project' referred to earlier, a project which concerned itself with the governance (managing and regulating) of the people, especially what were often described as the 'dangerous classes' (Hacking 1990). Such statistics can be seen as a way of assessing the nature and extent of the 'problem' and monitoring the reponse to it. Adolphe Quetelet was one of the best known of the moral statisticians, and conducted extensive analyses of those statistics, including the influence of the seasons, climate and sex, on the 'propensity to crime'. His work revealed a remarkable consistency in patterns of recorded crime, suggesting that crime was subject to the same kinds of laws that were being established in the natural sciences:

> every thing which pertains to the human species considered as a whole, belongs to the order of physical facts: the greater the number of individuals, the more does the influence of individual will disappear, leaving predominance to a series of general facts, dependent on causes by which society exists and is preserved ... we shall determine their influence on society, just in the same way as we determine effects by their causes in physical science
> (Quetelet 1842, in Muncie *et al* 1996: 27–28)

Quetelet came to the conclusion that the causes of crime were to be found in aspects of social organisation, and that it was up to 'legislators' to identify and remove them as far as possible. In their attempt to use methods modelled on the natural sciences, and to identify causes of crime that could be stated in the same manner as the laws of those sciences, the moral statisticians have some claim to have been founders of a 'scientific' study of crime. However, they had no conception of a scientific specialism that could be separated off from other areas of study. The accolade of founder of 'scientific' criminology has usually been awarded to Cesare Lombroso. Very different from the moral statisticians, Lombroso's focus was upon the individual criminal, whom he thought could be the object of study for a new discipline.

The Italian positive school

While equally determined to place his studies on a scientific basis, Lombroso's (1876) early work owed most to biology, especially the work of Charles Darwin on the evolution of species. Through extensive measurements of convicted criminals, he claimed to have discovered physical differences in their anatomical make-up. These he likened to features to be found in 'savages' and apes. Lombroso concluded that criminals were 'throw-backs' to an earlier stage of human evolution; they were *atavistic*. These sorts of ideas gave the criminal a new social significance. If criminals were lower in the evolutionary scale, they – along with others – raised the spectre of *degeneration*, and could be seen as a threat to the evolutionary process and candidates for such measures as isolation, prevention from breeding and so on (Nye 1984; Pick 1989). Lombroso's ideas were in many ways consistent with those of others of his time, who drew attention to the study of the ancestry of offenders and the notion that physical features were an indication of a person's character or 'type' (see also Jayewardene 1963, for the view that certain English prison doctors anticipated some of Lombroso's ideas).

Lombroso's intial ideas and research studies were heavily criticised in his own lifetime, and he had modified his views considerably by the end of his career. His colleagues, Ferri and Garofalo, stressed the idea that crime has many causes, and that it is important to look at psychological and social causes as well as biological ones. The work of the Italian Positive School should be seen in a broader context. It sought to distinguish itself from the classical school in particular, stressing the superiority of its 'scientific' approach to what it claimed was the pre-scientific approach of the classical school, which was to some extent caricatured. Here is a debate between not only two sets of ideas, but two interest groups – judges, legislators, lawyers in the classical camp, and a new breed of scientific experts in the positivist camp – vying for dominance. For the positivists:

- The idea that people were endowed with free will was mocked as being untenable. Human behaviour was *determined* by a range of factors.

- The ideas of the classical school were derided as being rooted in metaphysical speculation, while positivism was rooted in the search for evidence, using the methods of scientific investigation, such as observation and measurement.

- Punishments for crime, based on the principles of the classical school, were outdated and barbaric (since people could no longer be seen as responsible for their actions in the way envisaged by that school). The new experts could be far more humane and effective in crime control. Policy and practice would therefore involve the application of science, aimed at the prevention and treatment of criminality.

If Lombroso's work on attempting to identify human 'types' was part of an already established tradition of research, the idea of a distinctive science of the criminal was new:

> His conception of the criminal as a naturally occuring entity – a fact of nature rather than a social or legal product – led Lombroso to the thought of a natural science which would focus on this entity, trace its characteristics, its stigmata, its abnormalities, and eventually identify the causes which make one person a criminal and another a normal citizen.
>
> (Garland 1997: 30)

What was remarkable was how, from such initial ideas, there grew an international movement, calling itself criminology, in order to distinguish its broader vision from the criminal anthropology of Lombroso himself, the specific notions of which were soon discredited. Garland (1985, 1997) suggests that among the reasons behind its popularity and growth towards the end of the nineteenth century are the following:

- the development of various forms of statistical data, such as the kind that had already been exploited by the moral statisticians;

- the advances in, and increasing prestige of, the discipline of psychiatry;

- it connected with, and gave scientific respectability to, prejudices and fears about the 'dangerous classes' in the expanding cities;

- it offered new possibilities for the scientific, expert and seemingly humane regulation of the population for governments and administrators, when existing strategies were perceived as failing;

- the development of the prison in the nineteenth century provided a context within which it could develop as a practical form of knowledge, with the individual criminal a readily available and 'obvious' object of study.

The British context

According to Garland (1997), the new movement initially had relatively little impact in Britain. More significant in the context of Britain was the work of the developing discipline of psychiatry and that of certain prison doctors, whose work was also focused on criminals as objects of study, but set in a very practical context (the everyday demands of the criminal justice system and the prisons) compared to the more ambitious endeavours of Lombroso and his colleagues. Although they were concerned with the range of psychological conditions that criminals (and others) could exhibit, there was by this time generally resistance to the idea of the criminal as a distinctive type of person (Garland 1997: 35) and to the criminology that had emerged on the continent that initially had this notion as its justification. Rather than consciously trying to give birth to a new science or discipline, they were more concerned with some pressing practical problems, such as how to classify offenders and how to make sense of those who would not respond to prison discipline. Only after the extravagant claims of Lombroso had been undermined, in the period leading up to the First World War, did such researchers begin to describe their work as criminological – in the wider sense of scientific research on crime and criminals – work that was nevertheless still largely moulded by medical and legal concerns.

One major exception to the early British tradition is the study by Goring, *The English Convict* (1913), which illustrates well the application of methods that would be approved by the new positivism, such as large samples, use of control groups, meticulous measurement, and advanced statistical techniques well beyond those used by Lombroso. Whilst refuting the precise notions of Lombroso's physical criminal type, Goring concludes that there is a 'physical, mental, and moral type of normal person who tends to be convicted of crime' (quoted in Pick 1989: 187) – a person of poor physique and mental capacity. Not departing so dramatically from Lombroso as often thought, Goring's book also contains a case against the idea that crime is largely due to environmental factors, as argued by Quetelet and others. Goring's affinity with the ideas of the eugenics movement, and its concern with improving the 'stock' of humankind, was consistent with his view that key factors could be inherited and that policies should take this into account (see Beirne 1993: chapter 6).

Much criminological research that was to follow can be seen as an attempt to find to what extent crime was due to nature (inherent properties of the individual) or nurture (environmental factors). In particular, there were sustained attempts to find biological, psychological and social causes for crime, an enterprise that we examine in the next two chapters. What seemed to be agreed was that scientific methods were the route to take in discovering these causes. Although contested, especially in the second half of the twentieth century, the claim (or the quest) to be a science has frequently been a key element in criminology's attempt to distinguish itself from other discourses on crime.

Conclusion

It seems agreed that the infant discipline was with us at least by the fourth quarter of the nineteenth century, but there has been some confusion over both its birthday and parentage. Many commentators have suggested that Lombroso was the father of the infant, a sickly child who was nursed into relative health by others. But the child needed a name. Lombroso's own preference was eventually brushed aside – he was increasingly seen as a suspect guardian for the infant discipline – and the name criminology emerged, probably, it now seems, the idea of one of its godfathers, Garafalo in 1885 (Beirne 1993: 235). The kind of academic enterprise favoured by the Italian positive school was certainly the first to bear the name of criminology. While the classical school, the moral statisticians and the practical efforts of psychiatrists and prison doctors had already produced offspring with rather different perspectives, which still have some resonance in contemporary criminology, Lombroso was certainly influential in moulding the character of a criminology at the end of the nineteenth century as a separate scientific discipline with a particular focus on the criminal.

There is one history of criminology which portrays it as a succession of perspectives, usually beginning with the classical school, through the work of the moral statisticians, to the work of Lombroso and his col-leagues and beyond. This view suggests that there has been a long connected sequence of reflections on a given topic. In a loose definition of the subject, these are all forms of 'criminology'. Alternatively, criminology proper is seen as emerging as these reflections shift from the speculative to the scientific. For others, such as Garland (1997), these histories will not do at all. For him, the development of criminology as a specialised form of enquiry, engaged in the scientific study of 'the criminal', an object of study that was not given but constructed in a particular way, was the product of particular historical circumstances. The study of crime and justice could have been continued by a wide range of parties, from different disciplines and agencies, without the formation of a criminology as such (the argument that a separate discipline of criminology is neither necessary nor desirable is still to be heard). Instead, the idea of a specialist discipline, focused on the study of the criminal, emerged in Europe at the end of the nineteenth century. Although based on a notion of the criminal that was to be discredited, this did not stop its rapid development.

In Britain, however, although research on criminals had been established in the nineteenth century, a university-based discipline did not exist before the mid-1930s, and it was not until the late 1950s and early 1960s that the conditions existed for its consolidation and development – primarily in the form of government decisions (driven by their own particular concerns) to fund criminological research both in the Home Office and in the university. For Garland (1997), it is when we see a coming together of the governmental, administrative project and the academic, scientific project (allied with the view that the latter can contribute to the former) that we begin to see the emergence of criminology as a viable independent discipline here.

There was an extraordinary growth in the discipline in the last three decades of the twentieth century – both in the teaching of the subject in the universities, where there are now many degree programmes, departments, professorships and specialist journals, and in research, within and outside the universities. This growth has taken place within a context of an expanding higher education sector, but also within a social and political context where there are pressing concerns about crime, victims, the criminal justice system, prisons, and so on. Criminology is shaped by such concerns and by its relationship with government, its policies and institutions.

This close relationship with the governmental project has clearly been not only a major source of growth for the discipline, but has also fundamentally affected its nature over the years. This is a major reason why some scholars are fundamentally critical of much criminology. For them, that close relationship with the governmental project is too narrow and restrictive, and leads to what is often rather dismissively called 'administrative criminology' – in which the main concern is with policy-relevant research aimed at controlling and reducing crime and improving the effectiveness of the criminal justice system. According to such critics, there is also a need for a broader, critical perspective on crime and justice that is not limited in this way (see Muncie 2000, for a recent example, arguing that criminology should focus on 'social harms' rather than crime, and social justice rather than criminal justice).

This chapter began with some apparently straightforward questions: what is crime? who is the criminal? what is criminology? what is its history? We have seen that there is more than one possible answer to each of these questions. Furthermore, the answers are interlinked, for the answer to one question has implications for the others. Considering such questions is not a waste of time, but raises key issues about criminology today and its future.

Chapter 2

Offenders and non-offenders: spot the difference?

Since the early days of their discipline, many criminologists have played the game of 'spot the difference' between offenders and non-offenders. If differences could be found, it was thought that these would hold the key to developing a theory (a systematic account of the causes) of crime, as well as opening up the possibility of an intervention before a crime is committed. We have seen how Lombroso became famous, and then infamous, for his attempts to find biological differences between the two groups. Although Lomboro's specific ideas were largely discredited, this did not stop the attempt to continue the broad tradition of searching for biological differences in the twentieth century. Others have looked for differences in terms of psychology; here the differences sought may be, for example, in terms of types of personality, one or more of which may be suggested as having a propensity to crime in general, or to a certain kind of crime.

In their extreme form, approaches which concentrate on characteristics of the person (whether they are biological or psychological in their focus) are what Albert Cohen (1966: 43) called 'kinds of people theories' of crime or deviance. They lead to the question 'How did they get that way?' The answer to this may be, for example, in terms of heredity, or some accident resulting in brain damage, or a distinctive form of personality development or learning. At the other extreme, there are those approaches that seem to suggest that people who commit crime are not special kinds of people at all, but that we should look to the situation or circumstances in which people are located in order to explain crime. The key differences to spot, such as various kinds of stresses or frustrations, the presence of significant opportunities to commit crime, pressure to conform to group expectations, or the absence of effective sanctions to deter crime, lie in the context, rather than in the person. Sociological approaches to crime, which are considered in the next chapter, frequently take this view.

Such a neat division between approaches which focus on the person and those that focus on the situation merely gives us two extreme types. In practice, there is frequent overlap. First, some theories suggest that the causes of crime lie in a *conjunction* of a particular kind of person with particular sets of circumstances; for example, some people might respond to extreme frustration by violence against others, but some will not. Second, a moment's reflection should reveal that the division between person and circumstances cannot be a rigid one; circumstances and experiences in the past are frequently seen as having a way of getting 'inside' the person, leaving an imprint that affects their future conduct. Finally, many researchers now take the view that the search for a simple theory of crime (as in some earlier attempts to 'spot the difference') is a misguided quest; what we call crime is a varied phenomenon and the result of a highly complex process of *interaction* between a multiplicity of elements. The objective should therefore be to understand the complex processes that seem to result in an increased probability of crime. The identification of 'risk factors' that seem to be more common among groups of offenders is an important, but modified, version of 'spot the difference'. Bearing this in mind, we begin by looking at attempts to identify biological factors in crime, before moving on to efforts at the level of psychology.

Biological approaches

Physical characteristics and crime

There has been an enduring search for the causes of crime from the discipline of biology in the twentieth century. First, there has been a continuing interest in the possibility of a link between physical characteristics and crime. Researchers have therefore continued to measure the bodily characteristics of 'criminals' (usually convicted persons) and compared them with control groups of the 'normal' population (on the assumption, of course, that these would be largely people who had not committed crime). Hooton's (1939) study along these lines was very much like Lombroso's early work in its notion that criminals were an 'inferior' type of person who could be identified by certain measurable bodily characteristics. Others introduced the idea of body types (somatotypes), which were thought to be linked to temperament (Kretschmer 1936), and then to the propensity to commit crime (Sheldon 1949). A number of studies which explored these ideas came up with the finding that the 'criminal' group tended to cluster within a certain body type – in the mesomorphic grouping, the lean and muscular type said to have an assertive temperament. Such a correlation (a statistical association between body type and crime) is open to rather different interpretations,

27

such as that muscular individuals would be more likely to be attracted to and better equipped to participate in activities that reward strength and toughness.

Twin studies

There was also an attempt to explore the genetic contribution to crime. This was done in two main ways: twin studies and adoption studies. Twin studies are a classic way of attempting to assess the relative contribution of heredity and environment to a trait or behaviour. There are two sorts of twins: monozygotic and dizygotic. Monozygotic twins (commonly referred to as identical twins) come from the same egg and share the same genetic makeup. Dizygotic twins, on the other hand, are from different eggs, fertilised in the womb at about the same time. They share less of their genetic makeup with each other. It is known that certain traits (such as hair or eye colour) tend to be shared by monozygotic twins, but not so frequently by dizygotic twins. The reason for this is that such traits are under the control of the genetic make-up, which monozygotic twins have in common, thus creating a high degree of correspondence (called concordance) for such traits.

If it could be shown that there are higher concordance rates for criminality in monozygotic twins than in dizygotic twins, wouldn't this suggest that there was a strong genetic component to crime? A number of studies conducted over the years, some of them much more sophisticated than others, have come up with the finding that the concordance rates for crime (usually measured by official convictions) are higher for identical twins than those for other twin pairs (see, for example, the overview in Raine 1993). Contemporary researchers do not claim that there is a 'crime gene', but this evidence does lead some to suggest that a genetic factor is influencing the propensity to crime. Again, this is a correlation, and an interesting one at that. Alternative interpretations have been suggested, such as that identical twins may be more alike in this way and in other forms of behaviour because, on the whole, they may be treated more alike in their upbringing. That is, the explanation for the higher concordance could be environmental rather than genetic. Researchers in this tradition have sometimes conducted a slightly different type of study in order to provide more evidence.

Studies of adoptees

Studies of adoptees track the development of siblings who have been separated at an early age. Identical twins would be ideal for such research, but separations of these are unusual and such studies are therefore rare. Siblings share a genetic make-up to a significant degree, but are thus exposed to different environments. The researchers then examine the relationship between the criminal convictions of the adoptees and the convictions of the biological and adoptive parents. For example, one Danish study (Mednick *et al* 1987) found a stronger relationship between the criminal convictions of biological parents and their adopted-away children than that between the adopting parents and the children. The relationship was particularly strong for chronic offending and was found to hold in the face of a variety of methodological criticisms and alternative interpretations, which had bedevilled many earlier studies of this type. They conclude that some factor is being transmitted from the biological parents to their children, and that this factor must be biological, although accepting the important interaction with social factors.

Similar findings were reported by a Swedish study (Bohman *et al* 1982). If the conclusions made are well founded, there needs to be detailed investigation of what exactly is being genetically transmitted and the processes through which it influences behaviour such as crime, difficult issues that are not tackled by such studies. Perhaps for this reason, another tradition of research in this area has attempted to explore the physiological processes and mechanisms, especially those involved in the functioning of the nervous system, that might help us to understand criminal and 'anti-social behaviour'.

The new biology of crime

Researchers have investigated the EEG (electroencephalogram) readings of offenders; examined their emotional responsiveness by measuring their heart rate, blood-pressure, breathing patterns and sweat secretion; charted their hormone, neurotransmitter and blood sugar levels. Others have attempted to forge a link between defects in the functioning of the brain and offending, focusing, for example, on:

- epilepsy and its possible link with offending;
- the role of head injuries in possibly producing such syndromes as 'hyperactivity' (attention deficit disorder) and delinquency;
- the possibility that offenders are deficient in certain skills, especially those related to language, which happen to be controlled by a certain part of the brain.

Although this list may seem rather a rag-bag of topics, recent research has been more clearly directed to explore the role of such processes in creating differences in personality, learning, motivation and the processing of information and thus in impulsivity, aggression, emotional responsiveness and stimulus-seeking behaviour, with a particular focus upon the 'psychopathic personality' (see chapter 4) and the notion that this may have a biological basis.

A recent book on this area of study ends with what Rutter *et al* (1998: 127) describe as 'over-the-top' claims:

> the evidence is overwhelming that crime is in large part due to problems in the brain, that these problems are what distinguish the criminal few from the mischievous many and that they can be identified early on and, to an as yet unknown degree, treated. Many will protest that our new understanding of the brain's biology takes a drably determinist view of human nature. It doesn't ... . Biology dictates destiny only if it is ignored.
>
> (Moir and Jessel 1995: 332)

By contrast, another text, which looks carefully at the research studies conducted in this area with a much greater awareness of methodological and other limitations, suggests that 'the role played by biological processes in crime is likely to be relatively modest and indirect ... [but] the evidence to date is sufficient to indicate that criminology cannot ignore the relevance of a biological level of analysis' (Blackburn 1993: 137).

What is most striking is the way in which some sociological texts give very little attention and credibility to the biological perspective. One possible reason is the technical nature of many of the studies: the literature can be difficult to fathom. There is a natural preference for one's own discipline. Psychology, on the other hand, has an important interface with this material (often referred to as psychobiology) and most texts include a discussion of biological factors in crime (see, for example, Feldman 1993; Hollin 1989). But the stance taken by some sociologists is grounded in philosophical, methodological and other objections. One argument is that such work has been *positivist* in nature:

- that it is determinist in its assumptions, giving no role to human purpose and meaning;

- that it claims to use the methods akin to those of the natural sciences, methods that are inappropriate to the study of social life;

- that conflicts of value and interest in society are ignored and a consensus model of society is assumed, in which, for example, the definition of crime or anti-social behaviour is not seen as problematic (on these points see, for example, Taylor, Walton and Young 1973: 31–40).

Furthermore, it is often suggested that a biological perspective takes attention away from the wider social, economic and political context and its importance in understanding crime. Despite the claims of biologists to accept interaction between the biological and the social, there is still sometimes resistance from sociologists to their individually-based, clinical approach, which seems to turn social problems into medical issues and leaves such matters as the structure of inequalities in the wider society unexamined. This may suit established interests in that society very nicely indeed, but runs counter to the perspectives of many sociologists, who also frequently adhere to egalitarian principles. Finally, concerns are often expressed about the way that such ideas might be used, especially given past history, in which, for example, ways of preventing 'criminals' (and others) from reproducing themselves have frequently been advocated. The use of drugs, surgery and, perhaps in the future, genetic screening to identify 'risky' individuals in this and other areas, raises many complex and controversial issues. As such, the new biology of crime is a body of work that criminologists need to engage with on an informed basis.

Psychological approaches

There is sometimes confusion about the nature and scope of psychology and its relationship to psychiatry and psychoanalysis. While psychology is a discipline which seeks an understanding of all human behaviour and mental processes, psychiatry has been concerned with the more special-ised understanding and treatment of those with mental illnesses or disorders. Psychiatry in Britain has its roots in the 'psychological medi-cine' or 'alienism' of the middle of the nineteenth century. It maintained its links with medicine, and psychiatrists in Britain still receive a foundation in medicine before proceeding to train in the discipline. As Garland (1985) makes clear, the emerging discipline of psychiatry had a close relationship with criminology. Although it was accepted from an early date that most prisoners were not mad or insane in the popular sense, much early research on crime and offenders was carried out in Britain by psychiatrists and prison physicians, who commonly held the view that many offenders suffered from mental illness or abnormality when those terms are given a broader meaning to include 'moral disorders' (Johnstone 1996), and who tailored their work to the administrative needs of the system in which they worked. The result was an 'institutionally based, medico-legal crimin-ology, which predominated in Britain for much of the nineteenth and the first half of the twentieth century' (Garland 1997: 38), concerned with practical tasks, such as 'the giving of evidence before courts of law, or the decisions as to classification, diagnosis, and regimen which prison medical officers made daily' (Garland 1997: 36). This focus contrasted with the broader, theory building ambitions of criminology on the continent of Europe and in the USA.

According to Blackburn (1993: 32), early academic psychology took little interest in crime. Most psychological research was done by those prison doctors we have just encountered, until the very influential work by Cyril Burt (1925), published as *The Young Delinquent*. This work, based on extensive statistical analysis of the characteristics and background of 400 schoolchildren, took the view that delinquency was the outcome of various combinations of factors, from a long list of possibilities, operating in each case (a multi-factor approach). He concluded that poor discipline, poor relationships in the family, and particular types of temperament were especially important.

Reflecting a rather different tradition was the establishment of the Institute for the Study and Treatment of Delinquency (ISTD) in 1931, and its associated Psychopathic Clinic in 1933 (later renamed the Portman Clinic). What was significant about these developments was the influence within them of psychoanalytic ideas. Psychoanalysis represents one particular perspective within psychology which by no means has been subscribed to by all psychologists. It is therefore time to briefly survey the major perspectives in the discipline which have attempted to aid the understanding of crime. As ever, the divisions between them are never entirely clear cut, and there is considerable diversity within each. What is presented here is a little like a set of quick sketches of some old friends.

Atkinson *et al* (1993: 7) suggest that there are five major perspectives in modern psychology. Any topic in the discipline, such as learning or crime, can be approached by one or more of these.

- The **biological perspective** attempts to understand behaviour by reference to electrical and chemical processes taking place within the body, especially in the brain and nervous system. We have already encountered this approach in our consideration of the biological level of analysis above.

- The **psychoanalytic approach** takes the view that people have a complex inner mental life, much of which takes place at an unconscious level, and which holds the key to understanding behaviour. Phenomena as diverse as dreams and emotional problems can have deeper meanings which can be uncovered by the analyst.

- The **behavioural perspective**, most associated with the work of Skinner. The focus is primarily upon overt behaviour, its observable antecedents and consequences, rather than upon internal processes, as is the case with the first two approaches. Few psychologists today would describe themselves as behaviourists, but the influence of the approach has been considerable.

- The **cognitive approach** has developed strongly in recent years, and was partly a response to the narrowness of the behaviourist approach. It is explicitly concerned with mental processes, such as perception, memory, decision-making and problem-solving.

- The **phenomenological perspective** focuses upon describing the subjective experiences of people, rather than upon theories and prediction. Some of these approaches are called humanistic, in that they focus upon those features which are distinctive to people rather than animals (note that much research in psychology has been conducted on animals), and some of which are said to reject the use of 'scientific methods' to understand human nature. In stating that 'to assume that problems of mind and behaviour can be solved by discarding all that we have learned about scientific methods of investigation seems fallacious' (Atkinson *et al* 1993: 12), these writers are reflecting a very common view within psychology.

Unfortunately, it is not possible to find theories of crime that correspond exactly with these five perspectives. In fact, psychologists have taken relatively little interest in crime as such, preferring to concentrate upon such topics as aggression or sexual deviation. The most self-contained group of theories is the psychoanalytic, and we start with these. We then look at a number of attempts to see crime as a result of learning processes. It is here that we begin to see the different approaches adopted by behaviourist and cognitive perspectives.

Psychoanalytic approaches

Although these approaches trace their ancestry to Freud, we should not expect those under this heading always to agree with him, or with each other. Certain common ideas can be identified which seem relevant in the context of crime.

- Children are born with certain antisocial and pleasure-seeking impulses and successful socialisation depends upon the development of an internal agency (such as the 'superego') which will regulate conduct in line with group standards.

- For this socialisation to occur successfully depends on satisfactory parent–child relationships.

- Disturbed or unsatisfactory relationships with the parents at different stages of development will result in unconscious conflicts within the child, which will result in problems of various kinds in later life.

- The nature of the problem, one of which may be crime, depends on the nature of those problematic relationships and the stage of development in which they occurred.

Such ideas enjoyed considerable popularity in the first half of the twentieth century, before falling out of favour within criminology.

Aichhorn (1955, originally published 1925), Alexander and Staub (1931) and Alexander and Healy (1935) subscribed to the notion that criminals were those who had been unsuccessful in the movement from the infantile 'pleasure principle' to the 'reality principle' that normally governed the conduct of adults. Healy and Bronner (1936) saw crime as the result of inner dissatisfactions, with their roots in a failure to experience a strong emotional bond with another person, usually a parent. Delinquency was the acting out or the sublimation (channelling into another form) of these inner processes. Glover (1960) suggested that psychopaths are persons whose superego development has been prematurely arrested, with hostile identifications with parent(s), who have failed to satisfy the child's 'dependency needs'.

But probably the best known of those who were indebted to such ideas was John Bowlby (although there were other major influences on his work) and his theory of maternal deprivation. This was originally based on his study of 44 juvenile thieves who had been referred to a child guidance clinic; these were compared with a matched group of other children attending the clinic for whom there had been no reports of stealing (Bowlby 1944). The 'thieving' group were found to have much higher rates of separation from their mothers for six months or more in the first five years of life. This led Bowlby to conclude that a warm and unbroken relationship with a mother or permanent mother substitute was necessary for mental health, and that such separation was responsible for many of the more serious cases of delinquency.

Unfortunately, a larger and more ambitious study (Bowlby et al 1956) failed to come up with clinching evidence for the theory, and the earlier study in particular came in for some heavy criticism, especially over the methodology employed: the samples were not representative, the comparison group was poorly matched, and the assessment of the children may well have been unreliable (for example, it was conducted by people who were aware which children were 'delinquent' and which were not, knowledge which might well have affected those assessments).

However, these ideas helped to stimulate a body of research on the role of family background, focusing at first and rather narrowly on broken homes, but eventually broadening out into studies of a whole range of factors, such as those affecting the quality of upbringing and its impact on delinquency (see Feldman 1993: 184–205 and Blackburn 1993: 160–173) One expert in the field (Rutter 1972; 1981) concluded that the concept of maternal deprivation had outlived its usefulness, and that separation *per se* was not important for later delinquency, although a failure to form any attachment to the carer was.

Assessments of the contribution of psychoanalytic perspectives to the understanding of crime have ranged from the general to the specific. It has been remarked that these ideas do not help us much in understanding the age distribution of crime, particularly the way in which crime reduces after a peak in the mid or late teens. Similarly with the finding that women have much lower crime rates then men. Blackburn (1993: 115) notes that since Freud maintained that men resolve the oedipal complex more completely than women, they should have more developed superegos than women and thus lower rates of crime. Blackburn (1993: 116) also suggests that theories that rely on unconscious conflicts may be more useful in accounting for 'irrational' crimes, and that most offenders do not seem to be neurotic or 'psychopathic'. Thus such theories may be only useful for some crimes and offenders. Feldman (1964) has pointed out that neurosis may be the result of crime and the associated experiences that might accompany it, as much as its cause. Because such studies of offenders are usually retrospective, it is difficult to be sure which came first.

These are mainly points of detail. Much of the resistance to psycho-analytic ideas has been based on broader objections: 'the lack of scientific method in formulating the theories, the vague and untestable nature of many of the central concepts, and the reliance on the interpretive skills of the analyst in the understanding of any given behaviour' (Hollin 1989: 37). Many psychologists were resistant to such ideas as 'unconscious conflicts' and other mysterious and difficult to research concepts, such as the superego, and to a method that seemed to formulate and validate its theories through the retrospective interpretation of case materials by the analyst. How could he/she ever be wrong? It seems, however, that there is more interest in such perspectives in recent years:

> contrary to the somewhat overdone positivist critiques, the theory has proved to be falsifiable, and has withstood the test in certain respects ... . The resistance of psychologists to the notion of un-conscious processes has also begun to dissipate ..., and with the cognitive 'revolution' psychology has begun to move closer to psychoanalysis.
>
> (Blackburn 1993: 116)

We shall clarify the last point made a little later. The view expressed seems a little different from that when Rutter and Giller (1983: 257) concluded some years ago that psychoanalytic theories 'have not proved to be particularly useful either in furthering our understanding of crime or in devising effective methods of intervention'.

Learning theories

Differential association
One of the earliest attempts to view crime as a product of learning was developed by the famous criminologist, Edwin Sutherland, whom we

have already met in the context of his 'discovery' of white-collar crime. Sutherland was keen to develop a general theory of criminal behaviour, especially one that could accommodate white-collar crime as well as the crimes of the less powerful and prosperous (Sutherland and Cressey 1960). One part of his theory was concerned with explaining how individuals came to be involved in crime. This contrasted with the more sociological component which was more concerned with explaining variations in the incidence of crime in different parts of the social structure.

The individual-level explanation was called the theory of differential association. It claims that criminal behaviour is learned in a process of communication with other people, mostly in small intimate groups. The learning includes techniques for committing crime, but, more important, particular kinds of attitudes, motives and rationalisations. A person becomes criminal because the definitions favourable to violation of law they hold outnumber definitions unfavourable to violation of the law. The impact of differential associations varies according to their frequency, duration, priority (how early in life they occur) and intensity (how significant the source of definitions is to the individual concerned). In terms of 'spot the difference', note that Sutherland is suggesting that the learning *process* involved is no different from any other learning: it is the *content* of the learning that is important. In addition, no assumptions are made in the general theory about individual differences, such as in biological make-up or personality. Individuals differ in terms of the number and nature of the definitions they have learned.

The theory has enjoyed a great deal of attention, especially among sociologists, and is still being discussed in the literature of criminology. Over the years, however, it received considerable criticism, including the view that the theory was vague and untestable in its original form, and therefore not a 'scientific' theory. The 'obvious' solution was to try to reformulate the theory in a more testable form. Others suggested that there were exceptions to the theory, perhaps undermining its claim to be a theory of all criminal behaviour. Box (1971: 121) complained about the silence of the theory on the contribution of the person to the process of learning: a passive and empty vessel into which various cultural norms and values are poured. Are we simply the imprint of a kind of balance sheet of our learning experiences? Others commented that the theory needed to take account of research and theory on learning in psychology (see below).

Classical conditioning
The name of Ivan Pavlov will always be remembered in connection with his dogs. Pavlov conducted one of the most famous experiments into the way in which organisms learn. The salivation of dogs was measured, and, as you might expect, the dogs would begin to salivate on the appearance

of food. The food is referred to as an unconditioned stimulus, which produces an unconditioned response, for no learning is involved in this sequence. If, however, some other stimulus were to occur consistently before the appearance of the food, such as a buzzer being sounded, the dogs would come to salivate when experiencing this stimulus on its own. The dogs had learned that one stimulus follows another. In technical terms, in this instance a conditioned stimulus (such as the buzzer) is producing a conditioned response (the salivation).

Although there is more to this body of experimentation than we can present here, the basic idea of Pavlovian or classical conditioning should be clear. Although there is no theory of crime today based entirely on such principles, for human learning is clearly more complex than this alone, they do feature as one element in a number of theories (e.g. Eysenck 1977; Wilson and Herrnstein 1985). One example is the idea that children must be conditioned not to offend, and that this can be achieved by consistently creating unpleasant sensations in the child whenever it misbehaves, or is about to do so. In time, the child will come to associate misbehaviour with the unpleasant feelings, such as fear and anxiety, that have accompanied it in the past. These feelings have thus become a conditioned response, which, it is argued, serves to control the behaviour of the individual.

Hans Eysenck (1977) has formulated a theory of crime (or rather, of antisocial behaviour) that employs this idea among a number of themes. The first is the approach to personality, a concept which suggests that people tend to behave consistently in different situations and at different times. It proposes that this can be described according to three dimensions or scales, with most individuals falling somewhere in the middle of the two extremes of each: extroversion–introversion; neuroticism–stability; and a third scale which attempts to measure something called psychoticism. Extroverts are said to be sociable, active, optimistic, but impulsive and sometimes unreliable, whereas introverts are seen as quiet and reserved, tending to plan ahead and be pessimistic. Neurotics are moody, anxious, restless and rigid in their attitudes; at the other extreme are those who are emotionally stable. Various descriptions of psychoticism have been offered; it seems that the person high on this scale has such characteristics as being cruel and inhumane, hostile to others and aggressive, lacking in feeling and insensitive, and troublesome.

The second theme is that personality has a biological basis, which has a large inherited component. In particular, because of biological differences, extroverts are said to condition less quickly and less strongly than introverts, need more intense stimulation to achieve pleasurable states of consciousness, and be less responsive to pain. Neuroticism too is said to have a biological basis, with high levels of resulting anxiety also interfering with the conditioning process. Eysenck maintains that psychoticism also has a biological basis.

The third element is an account of the socialisation process. In this, the view is taken 'that antisocial behaviour, being obviously egocentric and orientated towards immediate gratification, needs no explanation' (Eysenck 1987: 30); instead, the theory seeks to explain how egocentric and aggressive impulses are controlled in a way that results in conforming conduct. The answer lies in Pavlovian (or classical) conditioning. Antisocial behaviour is punished by parents, teachers and others; if done consistently, the behaviour and even the contemplation of it is accompanied by a conditioned anxiety response, so that the behaviour is avoided. Thus a 'conscience' is formed which is a 'conditioned reflex'. The degree of socialisation in any individual is therefore dependent on a combination of the biological make-up of the child (which affects its conditionability) and the nature of conditioning experiences of the individual. According to the theory, we should expect to see offenders scoring high on the three personality factors (extroversion, neuroticism and psychoticism). The theory is therefore sometimes called 'the three factor theory'.

There have been many attempts to test Eysenck's theory (for summaries see, for example, Eysenck 1987, Hollin 1989, Blackburn 1993). These mostly involve comparing the scores on the three personality factors, singly or in combination, of groups characterised by official convictions or self-reported offences, with the scores of groups of non-offenders. While Eysenck's (1987) review of the evidence is optimistic, Feldman (1993: 435) concludes that the theory's predictions 'while poorly supported in incarcerated populations of offenders, are consistently well supported by self-report studies in the general population'.

The reasons for this difference in the findings according to how criminality is measured are not entirely clear. Hollin (1989) concludes that overall '[t]he weight of empirical evidence lends support to Eysenck's thesis that there is a relationship between personality (as he defines it) and crime'. However, as Feldman (1993: 169) points out, these results are only correlations. These do not necessarily show that the causal processes specified in the theory are at work, and he suggests some alternative explanations for the correlations between the personality scores and measures of offending. In addition, the factor of psychoticism is open to dispute: although it produces some of the strongest correlations with offending, this is hardly surprising since the scale measures such items as aggressiveness and antisociality, which are hard to distinguish from the characteristics of what needs to be explained. Blackburn (1993: 127) makes the point that there is no explanation which might link this factor to socialisation, thus weakening the power of the theory.

Other ideas upon which the theory is based have also been disputed. The theory focuses only upon the role of punishment in the training of children. The role of parental affection and the use of positive reinforcement for approved conduct are important but are ignored in the framework (Feldman 1993: 169). Hollin (1989: 58) makes the point that Eysenck's approach to the study of personality is only one of several approaches, and has been criticised (Mischel 1968), and that other personality dimensions may prove to be linked to criminality. Although Feldman (1993: 169) concludes that the approach is likely to play a role in the explanation of criminal conduct, it is not comprehensive in its approach, ignoring such items as the role of instigating events and many social factors in explaining crime. The theory of Trasler (1962) was an attempt to incorporate a range of social factors, such as child-rearing practices, in a similar approach. Overall, there is clearly some diversity of opinion on the theory. While some appear to see some merit in the approach, others are more critical, such as Blackburn (1993: 127) who concludes that it 'is not well supported'.

Operant learning
This perspective upon learning originates from the work of B.F. Skinner, the famous psychologist associated with that approach in psychology called behaviourism. In this view, behaviour can be seen to operate on the surrounding environment to produce consequences which may be rewarding or aversive for the individual concerned. In the first case the behaviour is said to be reinforced and will tend to be repeated, whereas in the second the behaviour is said to be punished and will become less frequent. Cues in the environment signal to the individual when particular behaviours are likely to be reinforced or punished in these terms. The individual thus has a learning history which explains the 'acquisition' of particular patterns of behaviour.

Crime has been analysed in these terms as an operant behaviour, with the criminal to be understood in terms of a particular background of reinforcement and punishment experiences. Jeffery (1965) attempted to reformulate differential association into a theory of differential reinforcement, as did Burgess and Akers (1966: 137), for whom criminal behaviour is said to be 'learned according to the principles of operant conditioning'. For some critics, these attempts to improve on differential association were hardly an improvement. For Taylor, Walton and Young (1973: 133) such an approach may be well founded on studies of rats (the original Skinner studies were also conducted with pigeons), but human purpose, choice, and the development of what people find rewarding is actually much more complex than this framework allows. For many psychologists, the focus on events external to the individual produced an unduly restricted analysis, neglecting the role of processes within the individual, processes that were the focus of a developing cognitive psychology.

Social learning theory

Some psychologists sought to follow in the footsteps of operant theory, but to improve upon it by incorporating additional dimensions. Bandura (1977) included 'external' reinforcement in his approach, but noted that behaviour could equally be learned by observing the behaviour of others (especially those with status, success and/or the ability to control rewards) and its consequences in terms of reinforcement or punishment, and can also be reinforced or punished by the self (such as in reflecting on achievements and failures), thus making its repetition more or less likely. If behaviour has been reinforced in the past, this generates an expectancy that it will be in the future. These additions reflect a cognitive element in the theory, in the sense that they involve mental processes on the part of the individual, and not just 'external' reinforcement or punishment. Bandura has increasingly come to incorporate cognitive elements into his approach, stressing the way in which the individual processes and structures experience. His more recent work is now called social cognitive theory (Bandura 1986).

Akers (1977) has developed his own version of social learning theory. To the main ideas of Sutherland's original theory, and his own earlier notion of differential reinforcement, is added the notion of imitation, a process that is affected by the characteristics of persons who are models, the observed behaviour, and the observed consequences of it (as in Bandura's approach outlined above). As a sociologist, Akers stresses that the social structure has an impact on the process of learning, and thus on behaviour. Differences in learning contexts may be created by the individual's family, peer group and school; by their age, sex, race and class; and finally by the wider community and society in which they are located. Akers claims that most research relevant to this theory has provided evidence which is supportive of the approach, and has been involved in some of this research himself (Akers *et al* 1979). Social learning theories of various kinds have enjoyed a certain popularity over recent decades and are often included in attempts at integrating various separate theories in order to achieve a more comprehensive approach that is intended to combine the strengths but counter the weaknesses of any single theory on its own (see, for example, Elliott *et al* 1985 on delinquency and drug use).

Overview

Learning theories have received a considerable amount of attention over the years from psychologists and sociologists in the quest to understand crime. In terms of 'spot the difference', they suggest that criminal be-haviour is to be understood by reference to differences in the learning experiences of individuals. However, while some suggest that pre-existing differences between individuals (e.g. in their biology or personality) are important in understanding the impact of those experiences (e.g. Eysenck), others ignore or give far less attention to this possibility in their framework.

Learning theories have come in for some criticism, particularly differential association, and those which are based on the more behaviouristic accounts of learning which rely most heavily on classical and operant conditioning. These are criticised as putting forward an over-simplistic view of human nature and the learning process, conceiving it in an over-mechanical way, making the individual a passive receptor of that process. As such, they do not allow for human purpose and meaning, or recognise that some individuals may not be receptive to the learning process, or that the same event can be experienced very differently by different people.

An approach which gives more attention to the actor's creative and interpretive contribution to learning and action as a whole has therefore been advocated by some psychologists. It has long been a criticism within psychology that behaviouristic accounts are deficient in that they do not give sufficient attention to 'internal' mental processes, focusing as they do on 'external' events. This is why there has been an increasing focus upon cognitive processes within psychology and the study of learning, in the hope that these will help us to understand the complexity of human behaviour. Learning theories of crime have therefore often moved in this direction, increasingly incorporating cognitive elements. The boundary between learning theories and our next topic, cognitive theories, is therefore not clear cut.

Cognitive approaches

The criminal personality?

In 1976, Yochelson and Samenow made a remarkable claim – to have discovered the distinctive thinking patterns of the criminal, with styles and 'errors' of their very own. Over 40 such errors of thinking are described, including pervasive fearfulness, especially of a state in which the individual feels worthless, the 'power thrust' – a need for power and control, 'fragmentation' – inconsistencies in thinking, a failure to empathise with others, perceiving themselves as victims, poor decision-making, and extensive fantasies of antisocial acts.

Although this study is clearly cognitive in its focus upon thinking processes, it is open to considerable criticism. The study is based on a sample of 240 male offenders, many of whom had been committed to a psychiatric hospital for assessment, or because they had been found 'not guilty by reason of insanity'. This is hardly a representative sample of offenders to make generalisations about the 'criminal mind'. Second, no attempt was made to compare this sample with a comparison group of non-offenders, to see how distinctive the findings were. Third, the interviews conducted for the study have been criticised as unsystematic, with insufficient attention to validity and reliability (Hollin 1989: 47). Fourth, the study produces an arbitrary list of patterns and errors, which does not relate to any broader theory of cognitive functioning (Blackburn 1993: 203). We do not fully understand how the patterns originated, neither can we be sure that they 'cause' criminal behaviour. According to Blackburn (1993: 203), it seems likely that the patterns described approximate to those of a particular personality disorder, rather than to some 'criminal mind'.

Kohlberg's theory of moral development

Kohlberg (1964, 1978) has suggested that the cognitive process of moral reasoning in people develops through a number of levels over time. The pre-conventional or pre-moral stage (level 1) is characteristic of pre-adolescent children and some adolescents and adults. The conventional level (level 2) is attained by most adults and adolescents, while the post-conventional or principled level 3 is only reached by a minority of adults. Each level has two stages within it, making six stages altogether. For example, whereas the reasoning for doing the 'right' thing at stage 1 is simply to avoid punishment, at stage 6 it is commitment and belief in moral principles. Movement to a higher stage depends on intellectual capacity and experiences, particularly role-taking opportunities. Kohlberg attempted to develop an approach in which people actively construct moral judgements rather than passively learn them from the external environment.

We clearly cannot do full justice to the theory here. However, it is important to note that it is a theory of moral reasoning rather than of criminal behaviour as such. We should not expect a perfect correspondence between the nature of people's reasoning and their actual behaviour. It is, however, reasonable to suggest from it that offenders may tend to be characterised by 'underdeveloped' moral reasoning. Researchers have therefore attempted to compare the moral judgements of delinquents and non-delinquents. Blackburn (1993: 132) concludes that the evidence from research indicates 'a correlation between moral development and delinquency, but pre-conventional reasoning seems most evident in younger and in more psychopathic delinquents', but there are certain important qualifications.

- These findings relate only to 'official' delinquents; no clear relation has been established with self-reported delinquency.

- There appear to be differences according to type of offence or offender. Thornton and Reid (1982), for example, found that those convicted of offences involving personal material gain were less 'mature' in their moral judgements than those convicted of assault for no material gain.

- The studies conducted in this area, which involve presenting respondents with hypothetical situations about which they are asked to make moral judgements have been criticised as having doubtful relevance to thinking about crime in real concrete situations.

- Hollin (1989: 52) suggests that the concept of moral development needs clarifying. While research studies have concentrated on the *content* of moral codes in terms of beliefs and attitudes, this is different from the *process* of moral reasoning. Furthermore, we should not expect behaviour necessarily to correspond with either of them, knowing as we do the capacity of people to behave in ways they believe to be wrong.

Hollin (1989: 53) concludes that a 'direct causal link between moral functioning and criminal behaviour remains to be established'. Research continues, and if elements of the theory survive the test, they will certainly need to be complemented by other factors and approaches, such as aspects of situations which are known to influence behaviour in the 'real' world.

Attempting to identify some key variables
The two examples of the cognitive approach we have considered both took a broad approach in attempting to identify overall differences between offenders and non-offenders. Others have taken a more specific approach in that they try to take more specific variables which frequently appear in theories and endeavour to assess their relationship with crime, antisocial behaviour, etc. Perhaps more progress can be made by taking a more focused approach, picking off targets one by one? We take a number of variables and consider them in turn.

Intelligence It has long been pointed out that samples of offenders score lower on average than non-offenders on measures of intelligence. This finding was often treated with scepticism or even dismissed. Critics pointed out that the studies producing this finding were conducted with officially convicted offenders, who might be a biased sample, and even surmised that less intelligent offenders would be more likely to get caught. More recent studies, which take class and race into account, and use self-reported rather than simply official measures of offending, still find a small but significant correlation, especially for verbal ability (Blackburn 1993: 187). This finding is open to a number of interpretations, such as that low intelligence affects the ability to think in an abstract way, foresee the consequences of actions and appreciate the feelings of victims – all cognitive processes (Farrington 1997: 386). Another is that its effect is via low school attainment (which is also a predictor of offending), which may set in train a process of disengagement from school, truancy, and association with other 'problem' children. This interpretation is consistent with a number of sociological theories.

Impulsivity and low self-control   A number of theories of crime suggest that offenders are characterised by impulsivity (Eysenck 1977, Wilson and Herrnstein 1985) or by low self-control (Gottfredson and Hirschi 1990). Other similar or related concepts which are used are low impulse control, inability to delay gratification and low tolerance for frustration. Such variables are measured in a variety of ways, including: by self-report questionnaire items such as 'I generally do and say things quickly without stopping to think'; by using the assessments of teachers or others of individuals' degree of daring, concentration or restlessness; by psycho-motor tests, such as the Porteus Mazes, which attempt to assess speed and inaccuracy in completing tasks.

Both Hollin (1989) and Blackburn (1993) take overviews of the research conducted and suggest that the results are mixed and inconsistent. They suggest two possible reasons for this. One is that there appear to be a range of different measures and definitions being employed in this area, an indication that we are not dealing with a single phenomenon, but something more complex. Secondly, offenders are a pretty mixed bunch (what is often referred to as 'the heterogeneity of the offender population'), so it should not surprise us if some groups of offenders score more highly on this while others do not. Farrington's (1997: 384–5) more recent brief overview, on the other hand, presents only evidence which supports the link between impulsivity and offending, and draws attention to research on 'hyperactivity-impulsivity-attention-deficit' (HIA), a cluster of personality factors, its link with offending, and the suggestion that this may have a biological basis. This is a reminder that more attention needs to be paid to 'impulsivity' itself, including its theoretical significance, for it can be employed in different ways by different theoretical perspectives – biological, psychoanalytic, behavioural, and cognitive – for it to constitute an explanation.

Self-concept   Some attention has been given by psychologists to the idea that offenders may differ in terms of their self-concept from non-offenders. Research studies indicate that offenders, on average, have lower levels of self-esteem than non-offenders (Blackburn 1993: 198). A number of theories have employed the idea of self-concept. In Reckless's (1961) containment theory, a favourable self-concept is one insulator against deviant behaviour. One strand of the labelling perspective (of which more later) is that stigmatising and in other ways negative social reactions to a rule-breaker may result in shifts in self-concept, or a 'symbolic reorganisation of self' (Lemert 1967), which makes further deviance more likely. For Kaplan (1980) delinquency is a way of enhancing self-esteem, a way of restoring a sense of self-worth which has been lacking in conventional spheres of the person's life. Blackburn's (1993: 199) review of the evidence concludes that the research evidence for any of these specific views is weak and inconsistent and 'has not established any consistent causal relationship between self-concept and delinquency' and that the correlation between them may be the result of the operation of other variables. He also suggests that temporary changes in self-esteem rather than the relatively stable self-concept may be more relevant to particular deviant acts.

Values, beliefs and attitudes   Perhaps offenders differ from others in their values, beliefs and attitudes to an extent which would make their offending easier to understand? This would be consistent with various learning theories, and also with sociological subcultural theories, which suggest that delinquents hold alternative sets of norms and values, which result in law-breaking conduct (see, for example, Cohen 1955, for whom the delinquent subculture was the opposite of middle-class values). This is a huge topic, and what research has been conducted has mainly been with reference to juveniles. With gang delinquents, there seems to be some evidence of differences in values, beliefs and attitudes, but the similarities to conventional norms and values are more striking (see, for example, Short and Strodtbeck 1965).

Matza (1964) came to the rescue, pointing out that delinquency was mostly episodic in nature, so that various theories which saw delinquents as having been programmed into an alternative set of norms and values would predict too much delinquency. For him, delinquents largely subscribe to conventional values, and his account stresses the situational, interactional context of delinquency, suggesting that individuals drift into delinquency, partly through the episodic release from the moral bind of law through *techniques of neutralisation*. These are invocations of extenuating circumstances for breaking rules that are claimed to neutralise the guilt that would otherwise be felt in breaking the law, such as a denial of responsibility ('I couldn't help it'), or appeal to higher loyalties ('I know it's wrong, but I can't let down my mates'). Since these are essentially situational processes, it has proved difficult to test them out, as some have tried to do, by the use of questionnaires and interviews away from those situations, and it remains unclear to what extent these techniques precede acts or are rationalisations/excuses after the event.

This material is primarily sociological, but similar concerns can be found in psychology. For example, in Bandura's (1983) theory of aggression, personal and social standards of behaviour can be neutralised by 'cognitive distortions' such as dehumanising or blaming the victim. Abel *et al* (1984) found seven types of such distortion among child molesters (such as 'children don't tell because they enjoy the sex').

Attribution theory examines how individuals explain unwelcome or unexpected events, and it seems accepted that such cognitive attributions are important in anger and aggression (Blackburn 1993: 223). However, the suggestion that offenders differ from non-offenders in terms of their 'locus of control' (Rotter 1975) – a general belief that events are controlled by factors external to the individual rather than by one's own actions – has not received consistent support in research studies (Blackburn 1993: 202; Hollin 1989: 48), although Werner (1989) found that 'internality' was a significant protective factor among those at risk for criminality.

Skills that relate to relationships with other people There has also been some interest in those skills that relate to relationships with other people. Role-taking – seeing things from the point of view of others – is a key element in Kohlberg's theory outlined above, and research studies indicate that offenders have a tendency to see things from their own viewpoint (egocentrism) rather than that of other people (Hollin 1989: 49; Blackburn 1993: 205), but also that skills in role-taking might be employed in certain sorts of manipulative offending behaviour – a further reminder of the varied nature of crime and offenders. Findings are rather inconsistent on empathy – the capacity to appreciate the feelings of others and, perhaps, to respond to them – partly, perhaps, because there are a number of different concepts and measures of this (Blackburn 1993: 205).

Interpersonal problem-solving skills have also been investigated, with some evidence emerging that offenders are less thorough and capable in such problem situations, suggesting that they may act in real situations on the basis of limited or misleading information (Blackburn 1993: 207). Rutter, Giller and Hagell (1998: 151–2) draw attention to recent research studies which suggest that aggressive individuals have a distorted way of processing information in social encounters, including wrongly perceiving negative intentions in others, misinterpreting social interactions and concentrating on the aggressive behaviour of others: this may be the result of their own past experiences. Finally, there is the linked area of social skills. It is often assumed that offenders are deficient in such skills, and indeed, training in such skills is often used in the treatment of offenders. Unfortunately, Blackburn (1993: 207) suggests that the evidence on this score is limited, partly because of the lack of agreement on the definition, measurement and identification of such skills, and concluding that delinquents are probably varied in this respect.

Rational choice perspectives

Rational choice perspectives are cognitive in the sense that they focus upon the decisions people make in different situations of opportunity and in relation to particular types of crime. Rational choice theories grew out of the concern with situational crime prevention – attempting to reduce crime by altering aspects of the situations in which crime occurs, such as by changes in the layout of housing estates or the provision of locks and bolts. Although such studies helped to show which measures had an impact and which did not, they did not look at offenders and the decisions they made when confronted with such preventive measures. For example, did they give up altogether, choose another target, a different location, or even a different kind of crime (the last three are forms of what is called displacement, in which crime is not prevented in an absolute sense)? While situational crime prevention had an immediate policy relevance, rational choice perspectives held the promise of filling these gaps in its framework for preventing crime.

There is a variety of approaches that come under this heading. Some have adopted the approach of classical economic theory, with its assumptions of the rational actor seeking to maximise returns and minimise costs in crime as in economic behaviour. This approach has had limited usefulness in looking at the complexity of crime. More realistic is the framework developed by Cornish and Clarke (1986). There are three basic elements in their approach.

- *The image of a reasoning offender.* Offenders seek to benefit themselves by crime, and make decisions and choices, which are characterised by a degree of rationality. This is not full rationality as in some other approaches, but one limited by such factors as the time and information available for making a decision, and the cognitive abilities of the individual.

- *A crime-specific focus.* It focuses upon crime rather than the offender, and on specific kinds of crime, rather than attempting to tackle crime in general, as many theories did in the past.

- *They make a key distinction between criminal involvement and criminal events.* The first refers to 'processes through which individuals choose to become initially involved in particular forms of crime, to continue and desist' (Cornish and Clarke 1986: 2). These can clearly take place over long periods of time, and involve a variety of different sorts of information. Criminal event decisions, on the other hand, are usually processes that take place over much shorter periods of time, employing a more limited range of information, for example about the area and the particular house in the case of a decision to burgle.

From these three principles, four models are developed for the example chosen – burglary in a middle-class suburb.

- *An initial involvement model,* which includes the sorts of factors that other theories have focused upon, such as psychological characteristics, upbringing, social factors, and previous experience and learning, as well as those processes and information which lead the individual to a decision to commit burglary (needs, solutions evaluated and perceived, reactions to chance events).

- *An event model* involves those processes and information involved in the selection of a particular target in a particular location.

- *A continuing involvement model*, focusing upon increased professionalism, changes in life style and values, and changes in peer group, 'that influence the constantly re-evaluated decision to continue with this form of burglary' (Cornish and Clarke 1986: 6).

- *A desistance model*, which focuses upon external events and re-evaluation of readiness which may result in the decision to desist from the particular crime.

Similar models can be developed for other types of crime (see, for example, the studies of different types of crime in Cornish and Clarke 1986). Such an approach feels very different from some of the others we have considered. It touches the parts that other theories rarely reach, such as the immediate, situational aspects, and the processes of continuance and desistance in crime, viewed within a framework stressing choice and decision-making.

Whereas the traditional approaches we have looked at were almost exclusively concerned with the background factors and differences which may predispose individuals to become involved in offending, the image of the reasoning offender seems to stress the 'foreground' and features that offenders have in common with other people, implying 'the essentially non-pathological and commonplace nature of much criminal activity' (Cornish and Clarke 1986: 6). There have been other attempts in contemporary criminology, but in a very different way, to focus on the 'foregound' rather than on the traditional background factors in crime; in a controversial book, Jack Katz (1988) attempted to explore what he sees as the neglected 'lived realities' of crime, including the 'sensual' and other attractions of 'doing evil'.

Rational choice theory has attracted some criticisms. First, it is often said that rational choice theories are limited because offenders rarely act in a rational way. For example, Wright and Decker (1994: 197), in their fascinating study of active burglars in St Louis, Missouri, suggest that rational choice theories pay too little attention to 'the subjective influence of emotions on offender decision-making'. Their burglars typically made decisions in a hurried, emotional way, in contrast to the picture created through interviews of offenders in prison (on whom most of the research has been done), who may 'rationally reconstruct' their crimes well after the event. Although this may be a valid criticism of some versions of the approach, Cornish and Clarke do not assume full rationality, and accept that offences differ according to the extent of cognitive processing involved. The approach does, however, generally focus our attention on certain aspects of decision-making rather than others.

A related point is that although this approach may be helpful in looking at many property crimes, such as burglary, it is of little value with offences like murder, rape, and assault (Trasler 1986). Cornish and Clarke (1986) reply that violence is still chosen by the individual, and decisions, however rudimentary, are made about the victim, the location and timing, although they accept that 'special motivational theories' may be included in accounts of some crimes.

These first two points indicate that the approach is more a perspective into which a variety of ideas and findings can be incorporated, rather than a specific theory in the traditional sense. It tells us where to look, rather than what to expect when we get there.

The third point, also made by Trasler (1986) concerns the crime-specific focus. Since much crime is committed by a smallish group of offenders who do not specialise much, is this focus the best strategy? Cornish and Clarke deny that their framework assumes offenders tend to specialise, but concede that it may not be sensible to construct separate involvement models for those crimes which are largely perpetrated by the same sorts of offenders.

The fourth and final point concerns the narrow focus engendered by the approach. Wright and Decker (1994) conclude from their study that the approach fails to take account of the wider social and cultural context within which decisions are made; for example, street life culture, which stressed such features as self-reliance and spontaneity, had a considerable impact on their burglars' decisions, such as ill-gotten gains being spent on drugs, alcohol and status-enhancing goods. Although a wider perspective is allowable in the involvement models, this seems to fade from view in practice, where the concern is very much with situational elements that, hopefully, can be manipulated by immediate policy measures.

The dominance of policy relevance and situational factors leads to a neglect of wider social, economic and political contexts, which may be crucial in understanding crime and crime rates but which are deemed to be of little practical use. This is hardly surprising, given that these studies grew out of research sponsored by the Home Office in the wake of its concern with crime prevention; they have been designated by Jock Young (1994), rather unsympathetically, as examples of the 'new administrative criminology', tied to state interests in controlling and reducing crime, if possible by methods that are cheap, practicable and do not disturb the status quo. Few civil servants or politicians in office welcome research that calls for fundamental social change to prevent crime. Management of the crime problem takes priority over the understanding of underlying causes. For Young, the new administrative criminology is a major force in British criminology, and can be seen as the new establishment criminology, sponsored by the state, and a well resourced tradition compared to that which is practised elsewhere.

The revival of approaches locating the sources of crime in the individual

Rutter, Giller and Hagell (1998) note that research focusing on individual characteristics had become unfashionable by the 1970s. Self-report studies had revealed that delinquent acts were so widespread, it seemed unlikely that theories stressing individual differences would be useful in accounting for them. Sociological approaches, which we consider in the next chapter, were also much in vogue. It seems fair to say that the 1980s and 1990s have seen a resurgence of interest in theories and research on crime which locate the causes within the individual. This point has been made by a number of commentators, including Lilly, Cullen and Ball (1995: 196) and Rutter, Giller and Hagell (1998: 127). The reasons given for this revival by the two sets of authors are, however, very different. The revival of interest in individualistic theories, according to Rutter, Giller and Hagell, is due to five factors:

- The increasing influence of biological psychiatry in the study of behaviour, even though overstated claims are often made in this context, and it must not be forgotten that people are also social animals.

- More recognition of the heterogeneity of antisocial behaviour, with more focus on different types. For example, they suggest that antisocial behaviour that persists throughout the lifecourse in certain individuals is more likely to be explained in terms of individual differences than that which is more common, but limited to the adolescent phase.

- A clearer acceptance that individual factors operate in a probabilistic, not deterministic fashion and that there is a complex and dynamic interaction between the person and the environment.

- A recognition of the steps needed to distinguish causal relationships from mere correlations – something that was too rarely done in the past, a point we have frequently made in the course of this chapter.

- A strengthening of the research base on the characteristics of individuals in relation to antisocial behaviour.

However, such an account stresses the factors internal to criminology and its associated disciplines, what Jock Young (1994: 71) refers to as their 'interior' history. He adds that academic debate also has an exterior history – that it is also driven by events in the world outside, the world of politics and practice. This context is stressed by Lilly, Cullen and Ball (1995), who relate the revival of individualistic theories to the conservatism of the 1980s and early 1990s. Both the USA and Britain experienced long periods of conservative rule at this time, with Ronald Reagan and Margaret Thatcher and their governments springing to mind. Such a context, they suggest, was conducive to theories locating the roots of crime in the individual's will, mind or body, in the form of rational choices, psychological or biological differences, approaches which appeal to those who prefer not to consider fundamental social change, for they focus on the individual as the problem, leaving the wider social context unexamined. They also tend to lead to 'get tough' policies on crime, such as incapacitation of the wicked and deterrence for the calculating, rational offender, policies Lilly, Cullen and Ball view as expensive and of limited effectiveness. Altogether, these approaches are branded – crudely and misleadingly – as examples of 'conservative criminology'.

Elsewhere in the same discussion Lilly, Cullen and Ball say that not all individualistic theories are inherently conservative, nor are their authors necessarily to the right of the political spectrum, and neither are the policies that seem to arise from them necessarily right-wing (Lilly, Cullen and Ball 1995: 219). Although we can see that individualistic approaches might appeal to those reluctant to consider fundamental social change, there seems a good deal more diversity in this collection of ideas that any apparently persuasive labelling as 'conservative' seems to allow. Although it is true that individualistic accounts are (almost by definition) weak on the wider social context, this is at least partly due to the conventional academic division of labour, in which sociological approaches are often separated off from psychological and biological ones, and may in turn be weak in their consideration of the individual level.

Even the idea that 'conservatives' will prefer individualistic accounts is not a universal truth. Lilly, Cullen and Ball (1995: 201) state that a further conservative view suggests that the sources of crime lie in the breakdown or erosion of traditional social institutions, such as the family, schools, churches and stable employment. This kind of argument is clearly sociological in content, rather than individualistic. There are, then, a number of themes to be found in 'conservative' thinking about crime and policy, which are not fully clarified by this discussion. There are, for example, important differences between what might be called 'traditionalist' conservatism and the (now not so) New Right (Tame 1991).

Having said this, we must not forget Young's (1994) important point about the exterior history of academic debate. It is certainly true that there was an ascendancy of the right in Britain and the USA in the 1980s and early 1990s, and that crime was high on the agenda of the governments in both countries. While Britain saw the emergence of what Young calls the new administrative criminology with its focus on situational crime prevention and rational choice, he sees something rather different as the 'establishment' criminology in the USA, a creature he calls 'right realism'. This is based largely on the work of James Q Wilson, author of the best-selling *Thinking About Crime* (1975), and an advisor to the Reagan administration, and co-author of another highly influential book (Wilson and Herrnstein 1985). The latter work embodies some of the ideas we have discussed in this chapter, and its popularity is consistent with the increasing attention paid to individual differences in recent years.

Wilson and Herrnstein are said to be 'realist' by Young in the sense that they accept that crime is a real problem in American society, that it had grown rapidly over the years and needed to be taken seriously in terms of explanation and policy. This contrasted with those who seemed to suggest that concern about crime had been inflated by misleading statistics and the mass media. Unlike the exponents of the new administrative criminology in Britain, who had turned away from traditional theories of crime, Wilson and Herrnstein put forward a general theory of criminal behaviour – or at least of serious 'street' and 'predatory' crime. It is a theory based on the principles of behavioural psychology, including the work of Eysenck. It recognises that crime can be understood in terms of the immediate circumstances in which it occurs or in terms of enduring dispositions of the individual. The main elements can be summarised as follows:

- *Choice*: people choose actions in terms of the gains and losses that are associated with various alternatives. We therefore need to understand the way in which people evaluate those gains and losses.

- *Conditioning*: both classical conditioning, involving the autonomic nervous system as in Eysenck's theory, and operant conditioning have a key role to play. The susceptibility of the individual, and the effective-ness of the conditioning are therefore important factors. Some people are so resistant to classical conditioning that they are deficient in 'conscience'.

- *Impulsiveness*: some people have difficulty in seeing the likely future consequences of their behaviour, or discount those they can foresee to such an extent that they are resistant to the operant conditioning that might result in them choosing 'non-crime'. The rewards of crime are generally in the present, whereas the costs often occur in the future, whereas the opposite is the case for 'non-crime'.

- *Equity and inequity*: people evaluate situations in terms of the gains being received by people (e.g. income or material goods) relative to the contributions made (e.g. amount of work, degree of skill). Individuals differ in their evaluations of what is seen as fair or unfair because of a range of factors, including their level of understanding and social learning. People also differ in their responses to situations of perceived inequity, partly according to individual differences.

The theory can be summarised by the following quotation:

> The larger the ratio of the rewards (material and non-material) of non-crime to the rewards (material and non-material) of crime, the weaker the tendency to commit crimes. The bite of conscience, the approval of peers, and any sense of inequity will increase or decrease the total value of crime; the opinions of family, friends, and employers are important benefits of non-crime, as is the desire to avoid the penalties that can be imposed by the criminal justice system. The strength of any reward declines with time, but people differ in the rate at which they discount the future. The strength of any reward is also affected by the total supply of reinforcers.
> (Wilson and Herrnstein 1985: 61)

The book is an attempt to integrate a number of elements that we have come across into one framework: choice, conditioning or learning, individual (including biological) differences, and people's subjective evaluations of situations. But for many commentators, what is most striking about their approach is the role given to constitutional factors, including the endorsement of the study of body types mentioned earlier. Wilson and Herrnstein (1985: 103) are not unusual in their view that 'crime cannot be understood without taking into account individual predispositions and their biological roots'. For them, 'spot the difference' of this kind has an important part to play. They are, however, aware of the complex relationships between such variables and the social realm, suggesting that long-term trends in crime rates can be understood by reference to three main factors.

- the proportion of young males in the population – likely to be temperamentally aggressive and with short time horizons.

- changes in the benefits (e.g. more opportunities) and costs (e.g. risk of punishment, costs of being out of work) of crime.

- changes in society's degree of investment in inculcating self-control in individuals (e.g. through families and schools).

The theory has been subjected to criticism. Lilly, Cullen and Ball (1995), for example, mention the lack of clarity in the basic concepts, the selective use of evidence, concentrating on that which supports the theory, and the neglect of offending such as white-collar crime, which arguably can often be seen as predatory. It is, however, the wider implications of the work that they find most disturbing – the idea that biological differences between individuals (mainly among the poor, who seem to specialise in the type of crime upon which the theory concentrates), are the root of much crime, has particular implications about human nature and what policies should be implemented to reduce crime. This is a further example of resistance by sociologists to the biological approach to explaining crime (which is only one element in this theory) that we mentioned earlier in the chapter.

Conclusion

Playing the game of 'spot the difference' between offenders and non-offenders has proved more difficult than we might have first thought. Along the way, however, we have learned some lessons. First, there is the 'heterogeneity of the offender population' – that offenders and crime are varied in nature, so that we should not expect all offenders to be alike in certain respects, such as in their biological or cognitive functioning. We should therefore be sensitive to different types of crime and offender – from the serial sex offender through to the juvenile shoplifter, from the drugs dealer to the violent offender. Some might suggest that this diversity makes the task a fruitless one – that the only thing such persons and acts share is the fact that they are defined as criminal. Others have dedicated themselves to the game with renewed enthusiasm in recent years, determined to make a go of it by using more specific targets in their studies. Rutter, Giller and Hagell (1998: 166) suggest that individual characteristics are more likely to affect antisocial behaviour which begins early in childhood and carries on during the life of the individual, rather than the more common variety which seems to be limited to the adolescent phase.

Second, there is the plethora of possibly overlapping 'variables' which have been investigated in relation to offending, which have often been conceptualised and measured in a variety of ways. For example, are impulsivity and hyperactivity part of a single syndrome or separate factors? Rutter, Giller and Hagell (1998: 149), in their recent review, rate hyperactivity (or inattention) as having the most robust association with antisocial behaviour which begins early in childhood and tends to persist into adulthood, but say it is unclear whether this is separate risk factor or part of a broader one with impulsivity and 'cognitive impairment'. They conclude the best-supported risk factors are 'hyperactivity, cognitive impairment (especially with respect to verbal and executive planning skills), temperamental features (especially impulsivity, sensation seeking, lack of control, and aggressivity), and a bias in social cognitive information processing' (Rutter, Giller and Hagell 1998: 166).

Third, there is the variety of research methods used, ranging from artificial experimental settings to which subjects are asked to respond, through to long-term studies of the development of a group over time. Is offending measured by official convictions (as was traditionally the case) or by self-reports? Do different methods make a difference to the findings? If so, why? How applicable are some of these findings (for example, from experimental and survey research) to 'real' situations?

Fourth, we see that a correlation between two variables does not necessarily mean the relationship is a causal one: more sophisticated research is needed to take that further step. And to constitute an explanation, which helps us to understand how a variable produces the effects it does, we need a theoretical understanding of the processes at work. Given the various difficulties of the enterprise, it is not surprising that some have turned to a more modest approach, which promised to bring more immediate results, especially in relation to doing something about controlling crime, such as rational choice perspectives.

Fifth, it should be noted that some of the criticisms of the approaches we have considered here are concerned with some of the broader implications of this work: what do these studies imply about human nature, about policy, and about politics? Are some aspects ignored or neglected? For example, it has been a common complaint that the broader social context has been neglected, and that a conventional definition of crime is usually employed, with white-collar offenders, for example, rarely making an appearance. The next chapter looks at approaches that have attempted to deal with some of these sorts of issues.

Finally, in terms of 'spot the difference', this chapter has shown how we can identify two rather different emphases in this area of criminology. On the one hand, there is what Garland (1996) has called 'the criminology of everyday life', such as rational choice and situational perspectives, in which crime is seen as commonplace and offenders as not very different, if at all, from the rest of 'us'. It stresses the 'foreground' of offending and the possibilities for preventive action in that context. On the other hand, there is a criminology which still stresses, but in a softened, less ambitious form, the notion of difference, in that attempts are made to identify the risk factors which might distinguish offenders (or particular sorts of them) from non-offenders. This focuses on the 'background' and individual characteristics of offenders. The first has echoes of the 'classical school' that we considered in the first chapter; the second, buttressed by such developments as the new biology of crime, can trace its ancestry to the work of nineteenth-century positivism.

Chapter 3

A broader vision of crime

A major focus of the last chapter was the attempt to identify the causes of crime, primarily through the approaches of biology and psychology. At first, the discipline of sociology continued to play this traditional game but looked for causes elsewhere, in the social contexts in which individuals and groups were located – the sociological version of 'spot the difference'. Either the approaches considered in the last chapter were looking for those causes in the wrong place, or at least those approaches needed to be supplemented with a broader vision. We shall see how, eventually, some sociologists turned away from the search for causes, and began exploring other avenues. We look first at the approach which looked for the origins of crime in the urban environment, before reviewing some other major perspectives that have influenced criminology over the course of the twentieth century. Although many of these perspectives are sociological, others, such as feminism and postmodernism, cannot be neatly identified with any traditional discipline of this kind; their ideas, however, have implications for both sociology and criminology.

Environmental criminology

As we saw in chapter 1, the nineteenth century saw efforts to identify patterns in the new statistics of crime and to explain the distributions revealed. A. M. Guerry, for example, one of the 'moral statisticians', pioneered the use of maps in the study of crime. In the first half of the twentieth century, a group of sociologists at the University of Chicago undertook studies of the structure of the city and the social and cultural forms that developed within it. Two of these researchers, Shaw and McKay (1942), plotted data on where juvenile delinquents lived on a map of Chicago divided into concentric zones, radiating from the city centre to the outer commuter zone. They found that rates of delinquency declined as you moved out from the centre, a pattern that was also found in other American cities of the time and which came to be known as the *zonal hypothesis*. There was a particular focus upon one zone, the zone in transition, an area of the city characterised by low rents and physical deterioration adjacent to the city centre, where there was a concentration of delinquents. This concentration was found to persist over long periods of time, despite the fact that the composition of the population living in the area had changed frequently over time, since it was the area where the various new immigrant groups tended to live until they could afford to move elsewhere. This diverse and rapidly changing population, they argued, led to *social disorganization* – an absence of stable or common standards and a breakdown in community institutions – and a resulting failure to socialise or control children effectively. Social disorganization was seen as a key explanation for high rates of delinquency in such areas.

To the zonal hypothesis and social disorganization can be added a third key idea – *cultural transmission*. Shaw and McKay suggested that in such areas of the city, delinquent traditions could become established and passed on in play groups and gangs. Such ideas were taken up and developed by subcultural theory and by Sutherland in his theory of differential association. Overall, the Chicagoan perspective can be seen as being very different from many of those considered in the last chapter. The focus in understanding crime was not on the characteristics of individuals, but on the social circumstances brought about by rapid change in certain parts of the city. The policy implications involved the physical renewal of such areas and the attempt to redress social disorganization by community development.

More recent studies of the distribution of offender residence in the Chicago tradition have failed to confirm the universality of the original zonal distribution. In England, for example, planned development and the location of council housing on the periphery of cities, thus relocating higher risk populations away from the inner city, have led to more complex patterns (Morris 1957; Baldwin and Bottoms 1976). Even recent study of Chicago itself (Bursik 1986) has found the original model no longer applies.

The work of the Chicago School established a tradition of research into the spatial distribution of *offenders*, but more recent studies have also been concerned with the spatial distribution of *offences* (the two need to be carefully distinguished – see below). Although the Chicago School advocated the use of other sources of data, including participant observation, in the study of patterns of social life in the city, much of the early work conducted on spatial distributions has been criticised for its failure to treat official statistics of crime and offenders with caution, for these may be affected by such factors as different police practices between areas, and therefore give a misleading picture. Some researchers have therefore attempted to supplement official data with self-report data on offenders, and victim survey data on offences, intending to provide measures that are independent of the criminal justice process and possible biases.

The concept of social disorganization has also been subjected to considerable criticism. Some critics pointed out that some of the areas labelled in this way did have their own, if unconventional, forms of social organization. The more qualitative, first-hand research studies of the Chicago School, and even Shaw and McKay's concept of delinquent traditions, seemed to endorse this view. Sutherland (1947) suggested that the term 'differential social organization' was more open to such possibilities and thus preferable. Others criticised social disorganization for the way in which it seemed to concentrate solely on processes taking place within the zone in transition. This led to a neglect of processes in the wider society, especially the distribution and operation of power, such as in the form of decisions by politicians, officials and business corporations which have important consequences for such areas. Bursik and Grasmick (1993) claim that the concept of social disorganization is still useful, provided that we take this criticism on board: stability is needed for the processes of social control to operate, from those in the family through to those which are organised in the public sphere.

Studies in England, on the other hand, have found that social disorganization, at least when measured by high population turnover, does not seem to hold the key (see, for example, Baldwin and Bottoms 1976). Social class, an obvious alternative explanation, is inadequate on its own, for there are many differences in offender rates between areas with a similar social composition. Studies have pointed to the following factors in creating areas with especially high rates of offender residence:

- the importance of the local housing market in distributing crime-prone individuals to certain parts of the city, including the way in which council housing is allocated (e.g. some areas build up concentrations of those in most severe housing need, and likely to have other problems, in the difficult-to-let areas);

- the patterns of culture and social life in an area which influence such matters as the socialization of children and friendship patterns (for example, is there a criminal subculture on an estate?) (on these first two points, see Bottoms and Wiles 1997);

- the way in which a reputation as a 'problem area' can be generated (by, for example, media coverage focussing on an area's problems), and have real consequences, such as in terms of decisions made by existing and potential tenants, small businesses and so on – not to move in, or to move out (see, for example, Damer 1974), thus contributing to the neighbourhood's decline.

Explaining the distribution of *offences* is a rather different exercise from explaining the distribution of *offenders*. For example, offenders do not necessarily commit their offences in the areas where they live. The traditional pattern is that offences tend to be concentrated in city centres. This is not necessarily the case for all offences (for example, domestic violence), and this pattern may alter as opportunities arise elsewhere owing to major changes in the location of opportunities (such as out of town shopping centres). The concept of *opportunity*, which includes the density, attractiveness and accessibility of targets, is therefore a good starting- point when searching for an explanation.

Criminologists have also employed what is known as *routine activities theory*, which builds on the concept of opportunity in suggesting that crime is more likely to occur the more there is a 'convergence of likely offenders and suitable targets in the absence of capable guardians' (Cohen and Felson 1979: 590). For example, this approach suggests that rates of household burglary in the suburbs rose as more homes became unoccupied during the day, owing to changing 'routine activities' on the part of occupants. Illuminating attention has been given to such topics as decision-making by 'likely offenders' (which is by no means as rational as the opportunity model alone seems to suggest) and to the question of where such offenders commit offences (evidence suggests a preference for areas that present opportunities and with which they are familiar) (Bottoms and Wiles 1997). Wikstrom (1990) has attempted to bring a range of such factors together into a tentative model to explain variations in crime rates in the urban environment. As with the explanation of offender rates, it is important not to focus exclusively upon what is going on within the areas, and to look at the broader context of power and decision-making in the wider society that may influence such things as opportunities for crime and routine activities, and how areas can change fairly rapidly over time (Bottoms and Wiles 1997).

We have only scratched the surface of the field known as environmental criminology. There are other questions that have attracted attention because of the apparent policy relevance of any approach which promised to explore the relationship between the physical environment and crime. Is it possible to 'design out crime' by changes to the physical layout of the environment? Can we stop the process of neighbourhood decline into a 'problem area' by attention to the physical environment? Criminologists still ask some of the same sorts of questions as Shaw and McKay; in the next section we revisit the work of Edwin Sutherland, whose theory of differential association has much in common with their concept of cultural transmission.

Sutherland, differential association and white-collar crime

We have already met Edwin Sutherland in previous chapters. In chapter 1, we saw how he entered the debate about the definition of crime, when he argued that the definition should include what he called 'white-collar crime'. We then saw in chapter 2 how he therefore formulated a theory of criminal behaviour that would encompass these offences as well as those that made up the more traditional subject matter of criminology. Sutherland's theory stressed the origins of learning experiences in the company we keep, especially in small intimate groups. He is a good example of someone who was determined to formulate, as best he could, a general theory of criminal behaviour, that is a systematic explanation covering all criminal behaviour.

The quest for such a general theory has been the objective of some criminologists throughout the history of the discipline, and remains important for some today. Some have argued that this quest is pointless and doomed to failure, because, for example, of the sheer variety of crimes, which perhaps only share in common the fact that they have been labelled as such. Others suggest that any such theory will not tell us very much: it will need to be so flexible, broad and all-encompassing that it will end up as a collection of bland generalizations. Sutherland's own theory, according to Nelken (1997: 902) is 'now regarded as flawed and super-ficial, and the search for a universal theory of crime has lost its attractions'. Maybe so, but Sutherland's theory aroused enough interest to be the subject of research and debate for many years afterwards.

What of Sutherland's attempt to change the face of criminology by the 'discovery' of white-collar crime? Sutherland's (1949: 9) original defini-tion, 'crime committed by persons of high social status in the course of their occupations', has been criticised for failing to distinguish offences committed against the organisation from those committed on its behalf. Some have therefore suggested a distinction between occupational and corporate (or organizational) crime. Although attempting to render the original concept redundant, such reformulations lose something of the original force of Sutherland's concept, which was part of a wider critique of the narrow focus of criminology, and remains in use by some writers. We have seen in chapter 1 how a good deal of energy has been expended on whether white-collar crime is 'really' crime.

Research on white-collar crime has been made difficult by the paucity of good information on which to base generalizations (Nelken 1997: 891). Many such offences are not included in the official statistics of crime, often being dealt with, if at all, by specialist agencies, and self-report and victim surveys (victimization is often thinly spread among victims who often unaware of their own victimization) are of little use. Researchers have therefore often had to use such sources as newspaper reports, journalistic accounts and very patchy agency records, which are hardly a good basis on which to come to conclusions about the extent, nature, impact and trends in white-collar crime. Researching the relatively powerful is often difficult enough in any case: Sutherland's (1949) key text was originally published in a 'cut' version, because of the inflammatory nature of some of its findings. Little wonder, perhaps, that much work has involved attempting to demonstrate the seriousness of, and harm created by, such actions (Nelken 1997: 893), rather than the kind of work which has characterised 'ordinary' crime.

Those who have looked for explanations of white-collar crime have revisited the old questions: is it so different from other types of crime to merit its own theoretical approach, or should our theories of crime be able to accommodate it? Are explanations based on individual characteristics or structural considerations more appropriate, or some combination of the two? Finally, in terms of the response to white-collar crime, should it be treated (in terms of, for example, policing, prosecution and punishment) in the same way as ordinary crime, or is it so different that different treatment can be justified? The persistence of such basic questions underlines Nelken's (1997: 895) point that 'ambiguity about the nature of white-collar crime and the best way to respond to it, form an essential key to the topic'.

Slapper and Tombs (1999: 1) suggest that Sutherland's 'efforts to redirect the energies of academic criminology were, in the immediate term at least, a failure'. There has, however, been a clear growth in interest in the topic in more recent times, spurred on, perhaps, by the increasing concerns about the insidious activities of professionals and organizations, which have the capacity to affect so many lives, in local, national and, increasingly, global contexts. The environmental movement is but one example of this, and we now hear calls for a 'green' criminology, focusing on environmental violations and their control (South 1998). There can, however, be a tendency for the topic to become a 'specialism' within criminology, rather than being placed at the heart of research and teaching. As such, it can be somewhat marginalized, the more so because of its 'ambiguous' character and its capacity, even today, to raise awkward questions.

Merton, anomie and strain

One of the most enduring and influential attempts to provide a broad sociological framework for the understanding of deviant behaviour (including crime) is Robert Merton's theory of anomie. First outlined in 1938 and subsequently developed by Merton in a number of places, it has been a source of research and theory ever since, whether being praised, criticised, added to or modified by subsequent generations of criminologists. Borrowing and modifying the concept of anomie from the famous French sociologist Emile Durkheim, it was an attempt to explain why rates of deviant behaviour vary between societies, and between different groups in the same society, thereby tackling what was seen as the traditional sociological task. It was an explicit attempt to explore the sources of deviance within the wider society, rather than locating them in 'biological drives' or 'individual malfunction'. For Merton, deviant behaviour could even be seen as a normal (i.e. typical) response to an abnormal situation. Merton makes an important distinction between the cultural goals of a society and the institutionalized means (or legitimate avenues) for achieving those goals. The sources of high rates of deviant behaviour lie in a disjunction between these two elements. Merton suggested that the United States in particular (and other societies which were structured in similar ways) was characterised by such a disjunction.

American society places great stress on the cultural goal of success, usually in terms of money. The culture also includes an ideology of equality of opportunity – that success goals are open to all-comers, regardless of origins. In reality, access to the success goals through the institutionalized means is not an equal opportunity game: there is inequality of opportunity. Certain groups in particular find themselves often losing out the in race for success. They therefore experience the disjunction more acutely than others: 'it appears from our analysis that the greatest pressures towards deviation are exerted upon the lower social strata' (Merton 1957: 144). This, of course, concurred with the knowledge that, according to official statistics, offenders tended to come from the lower social classes. According to Merton, a number of different adaptations are open to those experiencing this disjunction between goals and means.

- Conformity: in spite of the disjunction, people still maintain allegiance to both cultural goals and means.

- Innovation: the cultural goals continue to be embraced, while the institutionalized means are replaced by technically more efficient means for achieving the goals, some of which may well be illegitimate.

- Ritualism: in response to the frustrations inherent in the quest for success, the cultural goals are no longer stressed, but the institutionalized means continue to be followed. There is a feeling of resignation, of 'playing safe'.

- Retreatism: the goals and the institutionalized means are abandoned, such as with heavy drinkers and drug addicts.

- Rebellion: allegiance is withdrawn from both cultural goals and institutionalized means and new ones substituted in their place.

Merton (1957: 157) thus speaks of a 'strain toward anomie' where the culture and the social structure do not mesh together, with anomie itself seen as normlessness, a breakdown of the norms, 'a breakdown of the regulatory structure' in which, at the extreme, 'calculations of personal advantage and fear of punishment are the only regulating agencies'. This idea of strain has resulted in commentators calling this an example of a sociological *strain theory*.

Despite its success, Merton's theory has received much criticism over the years. Much of it has suggested that the theory is incomplete and undeveloped as a theory of deviant behaviour – a limitation that Merton has readily accepted since the earliest statements of the approach (Merton 1938: 682). For example, it has often been said that it fails fully to account for different outcomes: why do some still conform when experiencing acutely the disjunction? how do we account for different kinds of deviant behaviour adopted? Albert Cohen (1965) pointed out that the framework was individualistic, neglecting group processes and their role in deviance, and ignored the role of the social reaction to deviance in shaping it. Cloward and Ohlin (1960) maintained that not only were legitimate opportunities unequally distributed in society, so too were illegitimate opportunities, making a difference in what kind of deviance, if any, the individual might turn to when subjected to strain. A further comment was that Merton perhaps gave undue weight to social class in his explanation. After all, any theory of rates of deviant behaviour might be expected to be able to account for the more dramatic variations in rates according to gender and age, but Merton is silent on these issues.

These and other criticisms failed to silence the theory, which, although subject to the changing fads and foibles in criminology and sociology, continued to appear in various forms over the years. Steven Box (1983) adapted Merton's concept of anomie for the study of corporate crime, arguing that such organizations are profit-seeking institutions in an uncertain environment, leading to the exploration of alternative, and perhaps illegal, means that will reduce that uncertainty. A similar argument is used by Passas (1990), also in relation to corporate deviance. Market capitalism, which promotes the pursuit of profit by the most technically efficient means, while encouraging appetites and consumption irrespective of the capacity for their fulfilment, does appear to be a recipe for the strain toward anomie in the way that Merton suggested.

Messner and Rosenfeld (1994) in their 'institutional anomie theory' broadly follow Merton's framework in accounting for high rates of crime in the USA, adding that economic institutions are so dominant in that society that people are less socialized or constrained by values, commitments and beliefs other than those of the market place. Agnew (1985), on the other hand, has pressed the claims for a strain theory which is more social psychological in approach, arguing that 'negative relationships' of various kinds create negative emotions in the person. Whether crime and delinquency or some other adaptation results from this strain depends on a variety of constraints. Some evidence seems to suggest that delinquent behaviours are associated with various negative relationships and life events (Agnew and White 1992).

Lea and Young (1984), in what they call their 'left realist' approach, stressed the role of relative deprivation in creating crime – a level of perceived unfairness in one's allocation of resources. More recently, Jock Young (1999) has argued that the rise in crime in the second half of the twentieth century is due to the combination of relative deprivation and rising individualism, in a society that has become more socially exclusionary, while culturally inclusionary (through the mass media) – thus fostering expectations that the society cannot satisfy in significant groups in the population, precisely what Merton had in mind.

In the global context, Rock (1997: 239) suggests that the concept of anomie, in the sense of chronic deregulation, is appropriate to a number of places around the world which are tottering on the brink of chaos and lawlessness, where the state is struggling or has withdrawn from the battle to maintain order. Merton's account of anomie, which was developed within the context of the USA at a particular time, will not necessarily apply there. Finally, Merton's theory became a major element in some subcultural theories of delinquency, to which we now turn.

Subcultures, gangs and delinquency

Albert Cohen (1955: 59) suggested that subcultures arise as collective responses to 'problems of adjustment' shared by people who are 'in effective interaction with one another'. In other words, they provide a set of shared solutions to the problems that a group faces. Cohen (1955) himself produced an account of the 'delinquent subculture', which he saw as originating in the status frustration experienced by the working-class boy in the middle-class institution of the school, an arena where he found himself at a disadvantage. One response to this was a rejection of middle-class norms and values and the development of a set that were their very opposite. This process explained the 'malicious, non-utilitarian and negativistic' nature of much delinquency, such as vandalism. Thus, for the working-class boy who is unsuccessful at school and therefore deprived of status in that context, the gang and the delinquent subculture become an alternative source of status, measured by criteria that the boy can meet. Such a subculture does not have to be reinvented by each cohort of youth in such a position, but is a 'ready-made' solution available for those experiencing such problems of adjustment.

Cloward and Ohlin (1960) developed a similar approach to the same subject matter – gang delinquency. While Cohen (1955) had reservations about Merton's anomie, Cloward and Ohlin imported it in more or less pure form as the problem of adjustment faced by many city boys of working-class origin in the USA, especially the more able and ambitious. They then attempted to account for the possible diversity in outcomes – addressing a weakness in anomie theory on its own. First, in areas of the city where there were established illegitimate opportunity structures, such as organized crime and rackets, criminal subcultures or gangs would tend to arise. Second, where no such illegitimate opportunities existed, conflict gangs would focus on fighting. Third, retreatist subcultures, focusing on drug use, were made up from those who failed to find a place in criminal or conflict subcultures.

We can see clearly that the object of attention at this time was the gang delinquency of lower-class boys in large cites, which was seen at that time as the problem in need of explanation and policy response. Gangs were seen as groups with a stable membership, a clear structure and leadership. Members were seen as committed to a distinctive set of norms and values, with delinquency a central activity in the gang. The gang was the carrier of the subculture; the one implied the other.

Finally, the subculture was seen as very different from the norms and values of the wider society; for Cohen (1955) it was the very antithesis of middle-class culture. These theoretical assumptions were rarely supported by research studies, even in the USA (see, for example, Short and Strodtbeck 1965). Delinquency did indeed tend to occur in groups, but these were typically loose-knit peer groups, or 'near-groups' (Yablonsky 1962) rather than structured gangs. Delinquents were not found to be committed to a delinquent set of norms and values and delinquency was not a central or required activity. As Matza (1964) pointed out, such assumptions would predict too much delinquency; a more appropriate image was that of the drifter between convention and crime, episodically released from the moral bind of law by techniques of neutralization (see previous chapter) and the desire to experience oneself as an active agent, able to make things happen.

Attempts to apply such theories in the British context were equally, if not more, disappointing. Downes (1966) found little evidence for status frustration or frustrated ambition among London delinquents. Instead, the typical response to lack of success in school and work was dissociation – opting out, or at least playing down their importance, turning instead to leisure, where a lack of satisfying opportunities might lead to attempts to generate a little excitement and sometimes illegal behaviour. In Parker's

(1974) study in Liverpool, stealing car radios was a way of buying yourself a 'good time', again a response to limited leisure opportunities. Although the original theories were found wanting, a great deal was learned about delinquency in the process of testing them out.

These theories, which attempted to tie together delinquency, sub-culture, gangs and the social predicament of the working-class boy, were eventually judged a failure, even though they had a major impact on social policy in the USA in the 1960s. Gangs continue to be studied, especially in the USA (see, for example, Huff 1996), although the lesson seems to be not to make too many assumptions about their nature and development without research evidence. Muncie (1999: 164) suggests that:

> American gang research has warned of imputing any uniformity to the processes of gang formation and development. Noting a rapid spread of street gangs in almost all cities of the United States, this research has come to argue that most gangs are neither stable in membership nor cohesive. Yet the age spread of gang members appears to have extended into the forties and their common characteristics remain criminality, drug use, drug trafficking and violence.

Subcultural theory did not wither and die, but reappeared in new guises. As we shall see, that group of criminologists called the 'left realists' draw extensively on subcultural theory. Another major development was the work produced on the range of youth leisure styles (or subcultures) which appeared in Britain from the 1950s onwards: teds, mods, rockers, skinheads, punks, rude boys, and so on (for a brief overview, see Muncie 1999). One of the best known books on the subject suggested that such subcultures could be seen as forms of 'resistance through rituals' (Hall and Jefferson 1976): that such youth styles were coded responses to the contradictions and conflicts faced by (especially working-class male) youth within the social, economic and historical context of post-war Britain. Such forms of 'resistance' were commonly seen as 'imaginary', symbolic or 'magical' rather than as real solutions to the problems faced by such groups.

Such approaches came under attack for their neglect of girls, especially in the earlier work, the overplaying of the political significance of such subcultures and the underplaying of their commercial aspects, and the concentration on the radical and spectacular aspects as opposed to their conservative and unremarkable features (Muncie 1999: 185–192).

Nevertheless, the structure of subcultural theory can still be clearly seen: subcultures as collective responses to problems arising from the wider social context for particular groups of people. There were, however, clear differences from the earlier American theories; for example, these theories did not see these particular subcultures as having crime or delinquency as their major activity. Even though law-breaking might occur (for example, illegal drugs) and such subcultures were often seen as 'deviant' in the wider society, their focus was said to be on leisure and style. The customary linking of subcultures, gangs and delinquency had been superseded: each should be examined in its own right. Even if the kind of scenario described by subcultural theories of gang delinquency existed at all, it was clear that these approaches provided no explanation for the great deal of 'mundane' delinquency that was being revealed by self-report studies. It seemed that a new kind of approach was needed.

Control theory

Most of the sociological approaches we have considered up to now seem to be suggesting that we need to explain why people deviate from conformity, in asking 'why do people break the law?' It is as if conformity itself needs no explanation; only deviation from it needs to be accounted for. Control theory suggests otherwise: it starts off by assuming that crime and delinquency need no special explanation, for they bring with them their own attractions and rewards, such as money, possessions, excitement and power over others. Instead, it is conformity that needs explanation, rather than being assumed. So control theory asks 'why don't we all break the law?' The answer lies in the idea of control or constraint: that people who conform do so because they are controlled or constrained. These controls can be inside or outside the person (internal or external controls). Those stressing the former tend to be classified as biological or psychological (such as Eysenck 1977, discussed in the last chapter), and the latter as sociological, although the division is not a hard and fast one. Here, we shall mainly be discussing the second approach, sometimes called social control or social bond theory. Control theories have a long pedigree and are often to be found lurking within other theories; the concept of social disorganization suggested conditions under which social control breaks down, and anomie is often seen as a lack of moral restraint or regulation, which allows individual ambitions, self-interest and appetites a free rein.

Although there are a number of examples, the sociological control theory that provided an influential outline was set out and tested by Travis Hirschi (1969) at the end of the 1960s. Hirschi sought to demonstrate the superiority of his version of control theory over competing explanations of delinquency, which were already beginning to look rather jaded, some reasons for which we outlined in the last section. Hirschi outlines four types of social controls (or elements of the social bond) that make up the theory.

- **Attachment**. This refers to the sensitivity of the individual to the opinions, concerns and feelings of others, such as parents, friends, teachers. Whether the person takes those into account will depend on the quality of the relationships with those people; if the relationships are strong, conformity is more likely; if they are weak, the individual becomes freer to deviate.

- **Commitment**. This suggests that a major reason for conformity is fear of the consequences of deviation. We spend time, energy and bits of our selves in certain activities with an eye to the future, such as an education, career, or just building a reputation as a certain kind of person. These can be put at risk by episodes of delinquency, as any young person who acquires a criminal record will testify. Aspiration, ambition and commitments of these kinds therefore play a part in producing conformity.

- **Involvement**. People who are kept busy doing 'conventional things' have less time or opportunity to get up to mischief. Adolescents with large amounts of unstructured time at their disposal, on the other hand, are a problem waiting to happen. This is a contemporary version of the old saying that 'the devil makes work for idle hands'.

- **Belief**. Whereas traditional subcultural theory suggested that delinquents held a different set of norms and values and asked how this situation arose, control theory asks how some individuals can break rules in which they basically believe. Hirschi suggested that there is variation in the degree to which individuals think they should abide by the rules of society, variation which may be due, for example, to differences in socialization. In some, there is therefore an absence of moral restraint that makes delinquency possible.

Control theory has had a relatively successful career. Research studies have fairly consistently supported certain elements, especially those of attachment and commitment. The evidence for the element called involvement was not convincing, even in Hischi's (1969) own study of over four thousand school students in California, which found that only some activities were particularly likely to induce conformity: these were studying and doing homework, which could be seen as indicators of another element, commitment. Elements from the theory have popped up in many places since Hirschi's original study, usually modified or combined with some other elements in order to overcome perceived weaknesses and gaps. For example, it has been said that the theory neglects group processes and the role of delinquent friends in delinquency. While Hirschi suggested that delinquents would lack social bonds to anyone, some researchers claim that bonding to delinquent peers is a key factor, if not the key factor, in delinquency (see, for example, Elliott *et al* 1985).

Hirschi (1979) is against the attempt to integrate elements of control theory with elements from other theories, such as strain and social learning (see, for example, Elliott *et al* 1985), when this involves taking elements from theories that are based on very different assumptions about human nature. He does, however, see that the approach is compatible with some others, such as rational choice theory (Hirschi 1986), with its calculative model of the actor. Steven Box (1971, 1981), although making substantial use of the approach in his work, nevertheless suggested that it had a rather narrow focus on the delinquent, rarely going beyond the family, the peer group and the school in its analysis. In the end we need to know why it is that some young people fail to become bonded to the 'conventional' social order. To answer that question surely needs a wider perspective that takes into account the wider structures and processes of society (such as those implied by the term 'racism'), that influence the lives and prospects of young people.

A further point often made is that the theory has been most used to account for 'ordinary' juvenile delinquency, rather then other forms of crime. Nelken (1997: 903), for example, suggests that it (at least in its original format) is a 'weak candidate for explaining white-collar crime' because such individuals often appear to have substantial commitments. However, the theory has been used extensively in attempting to account for the low rates of crime of women compared to men (Heidensohn 1985, 1996; Hagan *et al*, 1979, 1985; Hagan 1988), and frequently appears as a component in more broad-ranging theories of crime (see, for example, Braithwaite 1989). Meanwhile, Hirschi himself appears to have drifted away from his more sociologically inclined control theory, now pressing the claims of a general theory of crime that stresses the role of low self-control. This emphasises the importance of a relatively stable individual characteristic, for which the major cause is seen as ineffective child rearing (Gottfredson and Hirschi 1990) – a further example, perhaps, of the revival of approaches focusing on the individual discussed in the last chapter.

Interactionism, labelling and moral panics

For much of its history, as we have seen, criminology has concentrated on the question of aetiology: what are the original causes of crime and delinquency? The attempts to answers this question have varied; biological, psychological and sociological approaches in particular have been employed. Although control theory tried to ask the key question in a rather different way, it was still concerned with the causes of conforming and delinquent conduct. A rather different focus emerged from a group of sociologists (e.g. Becker 1963: Lemert 1951, 1967) who were working within the tradition of what is called symbolic interactionism, an approach which focuses upon the symbolic meanings and understandings which are developed in the course of social interaction. Complex social interaction was seen as a rich field for investigation, and deviance, rather than crime, became one of the objects of attention. Such an approach urged the study of social processes such as the definition of deviance, social reactions to it, and the emergence of deviant identity, which it felt had been much neglected in the study of crime and deviance. Perhaps because of some well known passages in the work of Howard Becker (1963), commentators began to speak of the emergence of something called labelling theory, even though the approach was not only concerned with labelling, and, on its own admission, was hardly systematic or grand enough to be called a theory in the strict sense. In addition, labelling could be, and was, analysed with the help of a range of perspectives in sociology, not just interactionism (Plummer 1979). The 'labelling' and interactionist perspectives on deviance were not, therefore, identical.

It was the concept of labelling that caught the imagination, perhaps because of a social context in countries like the USA and Britain of the late 1960s, which experienced such things as increasingly visible social diversity, social change, new radical social movements, protest and civil disobedience, with the power of the state and definitions of crime and deviance becoming more open to question. Becker's (1963: 9) statement has now become something of a cliché:

> social groups create deviance by making the rules whose infraction constitutes deviance, and by applying those rules to particular people and labelling them as outsiders. From this point of view, deviance is not a quality of the act the person commits, but rather a consequence of the application by others of rules and sanctions to an 'offender'. The deviant is one to whom the label has successfully been applied; deviant behaviour is behaviour that people so label.

As Schur (1971) suggested, labelling could take place at a number of levels. First, that of collective rule making. The study of law making and the origins of rules of various kinds had been much neglected in the past, but became a key area of study. Becker (1963) led the way with his study of the laws relating to drugs in the USA. Such studies raised questions about power and politics, for laws were the result of a political process, and helped to bring the study of power and the state to a more central position in the study of criminology.

Second, labelling was a routine activity by those agents and organizations which were responsible for the identification and processing of deviance. The perspective urged and undertook studies of the interaction between alleged rule-breakers and those agencies. They explored the possibility that such characteristics as social class, race, gender and demeanour could have a bearing on one's chances of acquiring a deviant label. Such studies cast the routine statistics produced by those agencies in a new light. For example, crime statistics were reconceived by some as indices of organizational processes, rather than as measures of criminal behaviour (Kitsuse and Cicourel 1963). If such statistics were 'socially constructed', what did this mean for all those criminological studies that had used officially registered crime and offenders to develop theories of crime?

Third, labelling could take place in interpersonal relations in everyday interaction. What cues do people use to recognise a person as deviant? Are stereotypes important in this? Once labelled, is there a tendency to reinterpret the past as evidence that the person was 'like that all along' (retrospective reinterpretation)? And what of the consequences of being labelled for individuals and groups concerned? Does the individual find conventional opportunities, such as employment, more restricted? Is the individual's sense of self, or personal identity affected – do they begin to think of themselves in a different way? And, finally, what are the consequences of these processes for the future conduct of the individual? Is further deviance more likely? Lemert (1967) introduced the concept of secondary deviation, which referred to that deviation which is a response to the problems created for the individual by the labelling process (or social reaction, as he called it). Overall, Lemert was raising the possibility that processes normally considered to operate as 'social control' could have the opposite effect.

Such ironic possibilities were taken seriously on this side of the Atlantic, but with a distinctive twist. Studies began to speak of a process of *deviancy amplification* resulting from the labelling of certain individuals or groups, such as drug-takers (Young 1971), or youth groups such as mods and rockers (Cohen 1973a). Often implicated in this process were the mass media, inflating concern about a particular problem and carrying powerful messages about it, including the production and transmission of stereotypes. Such processes might have a powerful impact on the group concerned, including the amplification of their deviance (Young 1971). In a distinctively British development of the labelling perspective, there arrived the concepts of the folk devil and moral panic, concepts that have been extensively used in criminology and sociology, with the latter entering journalistic and everyday use. They were used in an important study of the concern about 'mugging' in 1970s Britain, which suggested that this was a moral panic, based on a label imported from the USA without any firm basis in statistical trends, but which carried messages about law and order, race, crime and the condition of Britain, and served as a kind of scapegoat which drew attention away from the 'real' problems facing British society at that time. (Hall *et al* 1978; for a critique of their use of statistical data and the concept of moral panic, see Waddington 1986).

Plummer (1979) has summarised the labelling approach as being concerned with the nature, origins, application and consequences of deviancy labels. There is little doubt that it has had an enormous impact on the study of crime and deviance ever since, directing attention to new and neglected questions. From the 1960s onwards, a significant body of work began to focus upon the process of criminalization, rather than the traditional study of the causes of crime, about which serious reservations were being raised after many years of effort with fairly unimpressive returns. The approach did, however, harbour certain confusions and weaknesses.

First, there was confusion over whether it was a theory, providing us with a systematic explanation of something (such as 'career' or secondary deviance), or merely a perspective which raises distinctive questions and issues. Plummer's (1979) view is that only by regarding it as a perspective will we appreciate its value. As a theory it seems one-sided and simplistic; the idea that labelling may lead to further deviance may be useful as a hypothesis, but one that has not proved to be very fruitful. It is now thought better to ask under what circumstances labelling may have that consequence. Braithwaite (1989), for example, has argued that 're-integrative shaming' of offenders may avoid the counterproductive consequences that seem to follow from stigmatizing, exclusionary forms of justice.

Second, the approach was criticised from the very start for its neglect of the original causes or motivations for deviance. To some extent, this seems unfair, for the approach never intended to cover this, but to be a corrective to the overemphasis on this in the past. However, on its own, the perspective did have the consequence of ignoring such matters or seeing them as trivial. At the very least, a truly interactionist approach should be concerned with the meanings of action for the people concerned, even if the search for original causes is regarded as a fruitless quest.

Third, the approach is often said to be deficient in its analysis of power and structure. Gouldner (1975), for example, noted the concentration in practice on the 'local caretakers' of social control and their dealings with the deviant, rather than the sites of real power, such as in the state. Others, such as Taylor *et al* (1973), suggested the approach lacked a developed analysis of social structure and power, making it difficult to tackle such questions as law-making. Some of the reasons for this might lie in the interactionist foundations of key exponents, a framework better suited to the analysis of deviance in social interaction. As we shall see, others who felt they were better equipped for a broader structural analysis were happy to take up such questions (see the next section on radical criminologies).

Fourth, the overall image of the deviant created has been criticised: the image, for example, as a passive victim of the labelling process, who appears 'more sinned against than sinning' (Gouldner 1975: 38). This may romanticise the deviant, diverting attention from the original action and the suffering created for any 'real' victims, who seem to have been forgotten.

Radical criminologies

There is no single 'radical' criminology. It is not a unified and unchanging body of ideas. Better to speak of radical criminologies, which perhaps share in common a critique of 'orthodox', 'establishment' or 'mainstream' criminology, and a commitment to radical change, not only in the discipline and the way in which we respond to crime, but in the wider society, which is seen as intimately connected with crime and the response to it. Beyond this, there is some diversity: for example, radical criminologies can come from a variety of political positions (such as Marxism, anarchism, feminism – in all of which there can be divergent positions). Two developments justify separate sections: left realism (which some do not feel qualifies as truly radical, in any case) and feminist criminologies. In order to understand the origins and nature of radical criminology, we need to go back to the late 1960s and early 1970s. In this brief account, we shall concentrate on Britain.

The late 1960s saw the emergence of a group called the National Deviancy Conference, a loosely organized group of sociologists and activists who held a series of very well attended conferences, some of the papers from which were subsequently published (see, for example, Cohen 1971). The group had perhaps two basic things in common: a dissatisfaction with 'traditional' or mainstream criminology, and the fact that they were much influenced by the labelling perspective. According to its critics, British criminology had a distinctive character, with two features singled out for particular criticism (see Cohen 1973b).

First, it was felt to have a clinical or psychological bias, with a dominance of certain disciplines, such as psychiatry and psychology, which tended to look for the sources of crime within the individual, rather in the way described in the last chapter. Sociological questions were felt to be neglected.

Second, it was considered to be dominated by correctional interests, that is a concern with the causes of crime and ways of controlling and managing it, rather than in attempting to understand it. Part of the reason for this lay in the alliance between the Home Office and the Cambridge Institute of Criminology, with the former having control of much research funding and access to research sites. Understandably, the Home Office would prefer to sponsor research that would serve the needs of policy makers and practitioners, leading to a conservative, state-aligned discipline that failed to ask fundamental questions. Such questions were, to some extent, being raised by the labelling perspective: questions about the definition of deviance; questions about the way in which labels were applied and the possibly counterproductive effects of this. Here was a perspective that urged a shift in focus from crime to criminalization and harboured a critique of the state, rather than serving its interests.

Some of those sharing these ideas nevertheless became dissatisfied by some of the limitations of the labelling perspective which were outlined in the last section. In particular, some felt that a more developed political analysis of crime, law and social structure could be achieved. Taylor Walton and Young's *The New Criminology* (1973) is a key text in radical criminology, and attempts to provide a comprehensive framework for a 'fully social theory of deviance'. As such it shows the influence of both Marxism and the labelling perspective in including the study of the wider (in terms of 'political economy') and immediate (social psychological) origins of social reaction to deviance and its consequences, but also the study of the wider and immediate origins of the deviant action itself (neglected by a focus on labelling alone). As for what to do about crime, the punishment/treatment of individuals or piecemeal social reform would not deal with the problem: fundamental social change was necessary for that. The remarkable claim is made that the crime can be abolished under certain circumstances – a socialist society in which there would be:

- more toleration of diversity (and less inclination to criminalize);

- the abolition of inequalities of wealth and power, which would remove the motivation for much crime;

- the eventual withering away of the state, without which crime, which is defined by the state, would by definition disappear. New ways of dealing with any rule-breaking behaviour would have to be developed.

Despite some omissions and controversial claims, the book has remained an influence ever since, both as a rallying call for radical criminology and an agenda for criminological study (see Walton and Young 1998). Few can claim the capacity to cover all the required elements, but Hall *et al*'s (1978) study of the social reaction to law and order issues in the 1970s, which argues that moral panics do not occur randomly, but are related to fundamental economic, political and social crises in society, is often given as an example of an attempt to cover certain aspects of the agenda in the way suggested, in particular to provide a political economy of social reaction. In Taylor *et al*'s (1975) next book the emphasis was more firmly upon the need for a materialist (Marxist) analysis of crime and law in relation to capitalist society. Some of the comprehensiveness of the earlier framework seemed to have been lost, and the move towards Marxism was typical of radical writings during the 1970s. At the end of the decade, the National Deviancy Conference (1979) published a collection of papers with the symptomatic subtitle, *From Deviancy Theory to Marxism.*

Gradually, criticisms began to accumulate, especially of radical criminology in its more exclusively Marxist guise. One of the first came from within Marxism itself, when Hirst (1975) suggested that the quest for a Marxist criminology was a misguided one. Marx himself had very little to say about crime in his writings. This was not an oversight, for crime is not a particularly appropriate topic for Marxist analysis and peripheral to that framework. In Hirst's view, a Marxist criminology was just about as viable as a Marxist analysis of sport. To be fair, Marxism was able to provide answers (perhaps flawed or incomplete) to questions about the political economy of social control, the state and its structures of law, but it was less equipped to deal with the details of crime, except perhaps to suggest in a rather simplistic way that it represented a form of rebellion against the capitalist order, a means of survival, or an aspect of the class struggle. At the very least, the approach needed to be supplemented by other perspectives, but radical criminologists of this grouping were rarely interested in empirical research on crime itself, with their sights firmly fixed elsewhere.

A further criticism singled out what it saw as the undue utopianism of the approach. If only a transformation of the social order is worthwhile, with piecemeal reform seen as pointless, this may lead to a self-imposed exclusion from important policy debates about issues that have real consequences for people's lives. Such an outcome also has the effect of leaving the field open to one's political opponents, in this case those from the right. Indeed, during the late 1970s and early 1980s, 'New Right' conservatism in Britain and the USA seemed to have made the law and order issue its own, with socialism appearing to offer few 'realistic' proposals about how to tackle rising crime. Jock Young (1986) has since argued that the approach (with which he was previously associated) failed to take crime and people's fears of it seriously, including the real harm inflicted by poor people on other poor people. This could hardly be regarded as a redistribution of property, rebellion or aspect of the class struggle. An overly romantic image of the criminal was conveyed, seen as an embryonic class warrior, a present-day Robin Hood, redistributing private property, with victims and the harm they experience sorely neglected. It was in this context that Young and his colleagues argued for a more 'realistic' approach from the left, that would take crime and its victims seriously: left realism (see below p.79–82).

Further blows to the notion that a Marxist analysis would provide the answers to crime and other problems of contemporary life occurred in the form of the collapse of Marxist-inspired states and faith in its principles as a recipe for political and social organization, especially in Eastern Europe. The influence of Marxism has declined greatly since the 1970s in criminology as elsewhere. A final point to mention is that made by the emerging group of feminist scholars who began to take an interest in crime and criminal justice; although there are many references to class in radical criminology, issues of gender are much neglected in their studies. This is surprising, since it appears that gender is a better predictor of crime than class. We consider in more detail the feminist contribution below.

The impact of the radical programme has been enormous. Coupled with the labelling perspective, the questions it has raised continue to influence criminology in a profound way. It is now a very different discipline from that which existed in the 1960s. Not only have they influenced others, but the radical pioneers continue to produce work that is distinguished by its breadth of vision (see, for example, Taylor 1999, who has carried forward the study of the political economy of crime and the response to it). Of those who have been much influenced, it is worth mentioning those who still call for a 'critical criminology' (see, for example, Scraton and Chadwick 1991). The focus is still on the power of the state to criminalize, but the analysis of power has also been influenced by the French commentator Michel Foucault, with his views that power is exercised in many sites other than the state, and that knowledge and power are intimately connected. The vision is broader in other ways too: responding to some of the above criticisms, the focus is still upon class, but upon gender, race and sexuality too, and the institutionalized forms of discrimination and criminalization based upon them. Although referred to disparagingly by Young as remaining examples of 'left idealism', these developments are important in the picture of contemporary criminology.

Feminist perspectives

Following the rapid development of the feminist movement in the 1960s, various academic disciplines began to feel the impact of a new set of criticisms and ideas. It was the 1970s before this impact was much felt within criminology. At first, it took the form of a critique of mainstream criminology (see, for example Klein 1973; Smart 1976), which began by observing that women had been largely ignored in the discipline. The literature was based almost entirely on studies of men and boys. When women did occasionally make an appearance, they were treated in unsatisfactory ways, subject to biological and psychological assumptions of a stereotypical and sexist nature. Pollak (1961), for example, argued that the devious and deceitful nature of women led to their contribution to crime being much underestimated by official statistics. Although one of the most striking things about crime rates, however they are measured, is the way in which men far outnumber women in their rates of offending, gender was nevertheless given relatively little attention, even by the emerging radical criminology. Following this critique, a number of studies began to appear, as if to fill the gaps and deficiencies that had been identified. This work focused on a number of topics and areas, such as:

- the issue of whether theories of mainstream criminology could be adapted in order to explain the crimes of women, or, at least, their low crime rates? If not, what kinds of theories would be useful? (Leonard 1982)

- empirical research on women and girls and their involvement in crime, such as the study of delinquent girls in gangs (Campbell 1984);

- women as victims of crime, especially those often committed by men and involving actual or the threat of violence, such as rape, sexual abuse and harassment, and domestic violence (e.g. Stanko 1985). Most famously, Brownmiller (1975) put forward a new interpretation of rape, which saw it as power-based, the fear of which contributed to the subordination of women, affecting their lives and choices in subtle but pervasive ways;

- the treatment of women by the criminal justice system, as offenders and as victims (Eaton 1986; Edwards 1984). For example, are women offenders treated more harshly or more leniently than men?

- the role of women in social control, such as the study of women police officers (Heidensohn 1992).

Such studies, of which only a few examples have been given, were often conducted from a broadly feminist viewpoint, leading some to suggest that a feminist criminology had emerged (for far more comprehensive overviews, see Heidensohn 1985, 1996; Walklate 1995). As the title of Gelsthorpe and Morris' (1990) book indicated, however, it was more accurate to speak of feminist perspectives in criminology, for there were a number of differences in approach. It would be fair to say that, in the early days at least, feminists had a broad concern with exposing and working to free women from a broad range of limitations and oppressions that they experienced. The overall quest was in this sense a gendered one, that sought to emancipate women from those problems. In criminology and criminal justice, this might range from correcting the way in which women and gender had been ill-served by criminology, to attempting to rectify the way in which rape victims are treated by the criminal justice system.

There were, however, clearly important differences within feminism itself which manifested themselves in different emphases and approaches towards crime and criminal justice. There are a number of ways in which these differences can be considered. For example, we can identify differences in broad political ideas, which lead to different interpretations of the origins of the problem to be addressed, the strategy to be taken towards it, and the kind of ideal arrangements towards which to work.

- *Liberal feminism* is said to be concerned with equal rights and equality of opportunity for women (Gelsthorpe 1997: 512) and has concentrated on sex differentials in crime and discriminatory practices in the criminal justice system in its research (Walklate 1998: 73).

- *Radical feminism*, on the other hand, has focused on the oppression of women by men in particular, and has concentrated on women as victims ('survivors', a more positive term, is preferred) of 'date', marital and other rape, domestic violence, murder and child abuse (Walklate 1998: 75).

- *Socialist feminism* sees women's oppression as rooted in patriarchal capitalism, seeing the need to consider the interaction of gender and class in understanding crime (see, for example, Messerschmidt 1993) and for fundamental economic and social change to tackle the roots of women's oppression.

Smart (1990), following Harding (1986) has suggested that feminist perspectives can also be distinguished in terms of their views on the nature and status of knowledge (epistemology) and methodology. Much of the early work can be seen as *feminist empiricism* – the attempt to provide those studies on women, crime and criminal justice that were absent, studies that would provide the knowledge needed to argue for policies to address their oppression.

Standpoint feminism, on the other hand, argues that more research, more knowledge, will not necessarily serve the feminist cause; knowledge that conveyed the perspectives and experiences of women themselves, achieved through the struggle against oppression, would only be adequate to the task.

Finally, *'postmodern feminism'*, influenced by ideas we consider in more detail in a later section, questions our capacity to speak of 'women' as subjects with common experiences and rights; instead, diversity and change in women's experiences and identities are stressed. Its approach is broadly 'deconstructionist': it seeks to analyse bodies of 'knowledge', their construction, language, key concepts and their links with power. It is also suspicious of 'master narratives' – grand theories and their associated programmes for change. It can be seen that such a perspective is likely to engender antagonism from those more traditional feminists who have stressed the importance of a gendered emancipatory project in the interests of 'women' – from the postmodern perspective, a subject within a master narrative needing deconstruction? Smart (1990: 77) herself feels that it is time for feminism to abandon criminology – a discipline she sees as trapped within the modernist project (see later sections of this chapter), unable to deconstruct crime, for this would 'involve abandoning the idea of a unified problem [crime] which requires a unified response – at least, at the theoretical level'.

With such a variety of positions, it is difficult to provide an overall assessment. A starting-point might be to say that there has often been a neglect of important considerations other than gender in the study of crime, victimization and justice. Marcia Rice (1990) made the key point that *black* women were missing from such studies and writings. A similar point could be made about class, although socialist feminism is an exception here. The uncritical use of terms such as patriarchy, capitalism, oppression, and 'women' has tended to suggest that the predicament of women is pretty much the same everywhere, although, as Carrington (1998) suggests, we do not need to accept the whole postmodernist package to recognise diversity and change. A further point is that much of the early work focused, understandably, on women as offenders, victims and in the criminal justice system. A more recent development promises to contribute to a more fully gendered criminology (rather than a woman-centred one) by looking at the role of masculinities, including their relation to crime (Connell 1987, 1995; Messerschmidt 1993; Jefferson 1997), thus counteracting the rather one-dimensional view of men, masculinity and male power conveyed by some feminist writings.

Both Carlen (1992) and Gelsthorpe (1997) disagree with Smart's (1990) rejection of criminology. Carlen suggests that such a view fails to recognise the greater theoretical diversity and flexibility of some recent criminology, and that a deconstructionist approach can be used within it. She also feels that although postmodern ideas about knowledge and so on are difficult to link with political struggles, an abandonment of criminology would be to abandon women who are affected by crime and the criminal justice system to their fate. Better to work through such problems and to connect with political struggles for change. For Gelsthorpe (1997: 528), although there are useful insights to be had from postmodern approaches to discourse and knowledge, they have little to say about concrete practices and principles, such as visions of justice. For Naffine (1997), deconstruction on its own cannot change the institutional structures that keep traditional practices and meanings in place.

Left realism

Left realism as a collection of ideas came to prominence within the particular context of Britain in the early 1980s. A Conservative government appeared to have captured the law and order issue as its own, employing it as a major plank of its electoral strategy, and successfully convincing significant groups in the population that tough measures were needed to deal with a rising tide of crime and disorder (including industrial conflict). The opposition was in disarray, and seemingly unable to come up with policies that could compete. For Young, the existing radical criminology (what he came to call 'left idealism') was little help, with its reluctance to see crime as the problem or to enter into immediate policy debates, while the establishment criminology of the Home Office, with its focus on such matters as crime prevention and rational choice, had little regard to the wider structural context and its role in causing crime. The time seemed opportune for a framework coming from the left of the political spectrum (but nearer the centre than previous radical criminologies) that would 'take crime seriously' and come up with 'realistic' policies that would connect with the public and help the Labour Party to recover lost ground. It was therefore grounded in social democratic ideas, rather than those of the far left. There are a number of key components.

- In one of the earlier statements of the approach, Young (1986: 21) claimed that the 'central tenet of left realism is to reflect the reality of crime, that is in its origins, its nature and its impact'. A quest for comprehensiveness runs throughout, stressing the need to avoid the partial nature of other criminologies; for example, left idealism is said to focus upon criminalization, but rarely on crime or victims. More recent accounts of the perspective (Young 1994, 1997) have put forward 'the square of crime' as a framework, stressing the need to examine four elements and their relationships: victims, offenders, formal agencies of social control, and the public (informal control). Crime rates, for example, can only be understood in terms of the interaction between these four elements.

- The acceptance that crime is a problem, to be taken seriously, and that there is a rational core to people's fears of it. It is thought important to avoid the view conveyed by left idealism that concern about crime was a moral panic, or the kind of hysteria often to be found in the mass media.

- A return to the aetiology (the study of causes) of crime, a topic neglected by both left idealism and the new administrative criminology of the Home Office. Explanations draw heavily on such frameworks as anomie and subcultural theory: 'Crime is one form of subcultural adaptation which occurs where material circumstances block cultural aspirations and where non-criminal alternatives are absent or less attractive' (Young 1997: 490). From the beginning, substantial use has been made of the concept of relative deprivation (where people feel themselves to be deprived in relation to others with whom they compare themselves), which is said to be applicable to crime throughout the social structure, not only to economic crime, and does not make the error of assuming that deprivation *per se* will lead to crime. Explanations of victimization and the state's reaction to crime are also required.

- As part of its mission to convey the impact of crime, realism stresses the need to base this on people's experiences. Thus there is a need for research to provide 'an accurate victimology' (Young 1986: 23), which will tell us who is vulnerable to crime, and the effects on their lives. Left realists have therefore been involved in a number of local crime surveys, which attempt to chart these and related matters, such as the Islington Crime Surveys (Jones *et al*, 1986; Crawford *et al*; 1990), and those in Merseyside (Kinsey 1984) and Edinburgh (Anderson *et al*, 1990). Such surveys are said to need complementing with smaller-scale qualitative studies. It has thus attempted to take seriously victims and fear of crime, concerns said to be lacking in left idealism.

- A willingness to contribute to policy debates of the immediate, as well as the long-term variety. As an example, a case was made for increased democratic accountability of the police to improve relations between communities and the police, which, it was argued, would lead to increased flows of information and improved detection rates for crime (Lea and Young 1984). Left realism is anxious to avoid the 'impossibilism' of left idealism, said to be dismissive of piecemeal reform and only interested in fundamental social and political change. Realism has stressed the need for a multi-agency approach and intervention at all levels, although priority is given to intervention at the level of the social causes of crime (Young 1997: 492).

The impact of left realism has been great, including offshoots in other countries such as Canada (e.g. MacLean 1992). Walklate (1998: 70) concludes that it has 'certainly shifted the academic agenda and contributed to the policy one both locally and nationally' but that it remains to be seen if it has added to our understanding of crime. She makes the point that the reliance on relative deprivation as a key concept does not provide a broader picture of the political economy of crime, in the way that Currie's (1985) version of realism (in the USA) does. The most recent works of Young (1997, 1999), however, attempt to cover this ground in some depth. Left realism has been criticised for its uncritical and conventional definition of crime, which is said merely to reflect media, political and public concepts, and leads to a focus on street crime. Pearce and Tombs (1992: 96) argued that the still 'individual-centred nature of much left realist writing' is a handicap in the study of corporate crime, where, for example, the individual offender–individual victim scenario does not typically apply.

The reliance on victim surveys as a method of research has also been questioned. To what extent can these imperfect instruments, with their focus on the attitudes and experiences of *individuals*, be used as a basis to reflect 'reality', with its complex web of wider *relationships*, such as those involving power? How can a policy agenda be compiled from these responses, even after the required debate between the public and the expert? Doesn't this leave a lot of questions unanswered about how the policy-making process can be managed (Walklate 1998: 62)?

Some have complained that the policy recommendations of the left realists do not challenge existing power relations and are 'politically conservative in [their] conclusions about what can be done about the state' (Sim *et al*, 1987: 59), and that they often do not differ much from the more liberal ones of the Home Office (Downes and Rock 1998: 300). Although left realism has stressed the importance of class, gender, race and age, feminists in particular have argued that it has not examined their interrelationships, with an overemphasis on the first (Edwards 1989) and inadequacy on the second (Cain 1986: 261). To these points, it might be added that left realism has chosen to ally itself with a political party (Labour). It is not difficult to imagine that this may create its own problems and constraints. For Brown and Hogg (1992: 145), for example, this is one reason why left realism might be using an uncritical (conventional) concept of crime – 'as an ideological unifier: a mode for expressing the "real" and common interests of working-class people', as a way of connecting with the public, gaining votes and support for party policies.

Like almost all criminology to date, left realism is committed to what has been called *the modernist project*: the quest for knowledge of a privileged kind, a belief in progress and the solution of problems through the application of science and reason. Left realism and criminology in general have experienced the challenge of postmodernism, as have other social sciences. Postmodernism challenges the nature of criminology as a discipline. It questions our ability to grasp and represent some 'social reality' out there. It challenges the use of terms like 'crime', 'victim' as if they refer to some unified body of items with some essential nature in common. It challenges the ability of any criminology to make claims to 'truth' or objective knowledge, including those about the causes of crime. For postmodernism, left realism is hopelessly stuck in the past, unable to respond to these challenges, with its emphasis on representing the 'reality' of crime, and the 'lived realities' of victims, its quest for causes, and its search for knowledge that will assist in formulating those policies that will advance human progress. In the postmodern view, left realism, and most criminology, appears to be a hopeless case. It is time to look at the themes of postmodernism in more detail.

Postmodernity, postmodernism and the modernist project

Postmodernism, despite the label, is not a uniform and consistent body of ideas. It is more a collection of themes, which have their origins in the work of a number of thinkers, who would not necessarily want to be grouped under the title, and would not agree with each other on every detail, or even on certain major ideas. If this is not confusing enough, the language in which the material is expressed is frequently a barrier to communication, and there are at least two rather different sets of themes that are often discussed under the heading.

The first concerns the nature of the society in which we live, or are currently moving towards. Are the structural characteristics which we associate with 'modern' society, such as the class structure, industrialism and the nation state being replaced by new forms of relationships and organisation that are sufficiently different from the 'modern' to be called 'postmodern'? Are consumerism and global information and communication technologies producing very different forms of culture and social organisation, including our sense of time and space (Lyon 1999: 3)?

These are huge questions which cannot be answered here, but it is worth noting that the influential work of Giddens (1990, 1991) argues that despite important social changes, modernity is still with us: the concept of late modernity is currently more appropriate than that of postmodernity. It is important that the implications of such changes for crime and crime control are explored by criminologists (see, for example, Bottoms and Wiles, 1997: 349–354; Lea 1998). Another reason why those who are happy to investigate such changes, however, may not be so happy to accept the label of 'postmodernist' is the presence of a second set of themes that are often grouped under the heading, themes that concern the nature and status of knowledge – epistemology: ' "Post-modernism" in the hands of some writers has had methodological links with epistemological relativism, an intellectual position we reject, and so we would prefer "late modernity" in order to focus on the empirical transformations presently taking place' (Bottoms and Wiles 1997: 349). To put it crudely, 'epistemological relativism' is seen as getting in the way of describing what is going on.

Perhaps the most frequently quoted statement used to identify the first key idea in this respect is: 'Simplifying to the extreme, I define postmodern as incredulity towards metanarratives' (Lyotard 1984: xxiv). Since the European Enlightenment of the eighteenth century, reason and science in particular (a main metanarrative), have been seen as the provider of knowledge that will bring emancipation. Any overarching system of thought that claims to tell us what is 'really' going on the world and how to solve our problems can be regarded as a metanarrative, such as Marxism, feminism and criminology itself. Postmodernism is thus incredulous towards such ambitious claims to knowledge, truth and emancipation, seeing these activities as networks of 'language games'.

A second key idea is 'deconstruction' – that accounts, texts, discourses are never settled or stable and can be broken down to show how they have been constructed and what themes have been accentuated or repressed in the process. Such 'knowledges' are thus intimately connected with the operation of power, in their origins and their effects. We have seen earlier how some have argued for the need to deconstruct concepts such as crime, victim, women, men, masculinity, and so on to reveal the diversity and differences hidden by such unifying terms, as well as whole bodies of knowledge, such as mainstream criminology, to reveal 'repressed' or hidden subjects, such as women and gender. The implication that all knowledge is relative, never objective, certain or absolute, is what is meant by the 'epistemological relativism' referred to above.

According to some, something similar to deconstruction has been going on for some time, but without the title. For example, the labelling perspective made the concepts of crime and deviance problematic in a similar way, as we saw in an earlier section. The main problem with pure deconstruction, according to Lea (1998) is that of 'infinite regress': that any deconstruction that takes place can itself be deconstructed. With postmodernism, any stopping point appears to be arbitrary. In addition, while the approach can point to the origins and effects of 'knowledges' in terms of power, it has no developed account of power, so that its contribution to our understanding is limited. Similarly, the rejection of metanarratives appears to distance the postmodernist from any overall concept of justice or rationality and how we might strive to achieve them. Bearing these points in mind, it is hardly surprising that postmodernism is often accused of producing practical and political inertia.

Some do not despair, seeing a way out of this dark forest, arguing that although pure deconstruction may be appropriate in the realms where it originated, such as the analysis of literary texts, it is hardly enough in the 'real' world with which criminology connects, a world of human suffering where immediate measures and a longer-term strategy are required. For Stan Cohen(1998), a kind of double life is called for: '[s]urely it is possible to be sceptical and ironical at the level of theory – yet at the level of policy and politics to be firmly committed' – not expecting the kind of integration between theory and practice advocated by Marxists and left realists. The pragmatic position offered by Cohen seems to rather different from that of those who deconstruct (or 'demystify', or 'debunk') one account of 'reality', 'surface appearances' or 'common sense' and produce a different account produced in accordance with some master narrative, an activity that many sociologists, Marxists and others have been attempting for years. Lea (1998: 172) suggests that this is in a way what Carol Smart (1990) does in giving privileged status to the accounts provided by certain subjects, such as lesbians, gays, black people, Asians and feminists.

Most remarkable is the 'postmodernist constitutive' theory of crime developed by Henry and Milovanovic (1996). They contrast those who practise deconstruction alone (sceptical postmodernists) with those like themselves (affirmative postmodernists), who 'retain revised elements of modernism, particularly the idea that deconstruction also implies reconstruction, and who use deconstructionist epistemology as the basis towards reconstructing a replacement text/discourse that goes beyond the nihilistic limits of the sceptical position ...' (Henry and Milovanovic 1996: 5). What follows is their own account of human nature, society and social order, the role of law, definition of crime, crime causation, and justice policy and practices. In a sense, therefore, they too are replacing one 'metanarrative' with another. This shows how difficult it can be to follow the postmodern deconstructionist approach through to its conclusion, for most criminologists are reluctant to abandon entirely the project which gave their discipline its reason for existence – the modernist project. Although the foregoing discussion may seem very abstract and academic, it raises a key issue for criminology and criminologists – how to manage the relationship between theory and practice, between intellectual detachment and political commitment, between doubt and action. In the case of postmodernist ideas, this dilemma is raised in a particularly stark form, but is there for all criminologies.

Conclusion

This chapter has attempted to give an overview of a range of sociological and other broadly based perspectives in criminology. In doing so, a number of themes have emerged. First, that these perspectives relate questions about crime to aspects of the wider society, in their different ways, from the Chicago School with its focus on the city, to feminism with its focus on gender and power relations. Second, we have seen that the earlier approaches took as their major task to identify the (social) causes of crime. Gradually, different perspectives began to emerge which saw the concept of crime as problematic, an issue we also discussed in the first chapter of this book. In these perspectives, the focus shifted from the study of causes of crime to the study of how certain acts and persons came to be defined as criminal; in other words, the focus was on criminalization and the notion that crime was a social construct.

For some (e.g. Taylor *et al*, 1973), the study of criminalization was a neglected but complementary (to the study of the origins of deviant action) field of study for any comprehensive criminology For others, the question of the 'causes of crime' was no longer a question worth asking:

> If it is the case that 'crime' is a status accorded to some acts and not others at some times and not others and in some places and not others, and that those acts are engaged in to some degree by most people at least some of the time, then it is highly questionable whether there is anything special that needs to be explained about criminal acts.
>
> (Hester and Eglin 1992: 269)

The above statement is worth careful study; it is one version of a view that has been advanced since the 1960s. Although it is true that the quest for the causes of crime went into some decline in the 1970s, there has been a revival of interest in the topic in recent years, including from the left realists, who see crime as a problem that needs to be taken seriously in terms of explanation and the need to do something about it on a social level. As in the past, the understanding of causes is often taken to assist in the development of crime control policies.

Although Henry and Milovanovic (1996: 152) suggest that sceptical postmodernist thought denies the possibility of causal statements, they find this 'too extreme' and their own 'affirmative postmodernism' develops its own approach to causality. We find, therefore, a diverse and rather confusing picture among these broader perspectives in criminology; for example, if the prime focus of criminology is the study of crime, there is no clear agreement about the appropriate questions to ask about it. This diversity and dissensus is one thing that makes criminology such a challenging subject. This chapter has attempted to provide a guide to some of the major differences and disagreements.

Chapter 4

Thinking seriously about serial killers

This chapter is concerned with a topic of apparently great fascination. Serial killers seem to be all around us – judging from films, books and magazines of the 'true crime' genre. And yet, thankfully, they are a relatively thin on the ground in the 'real world', despite the attempts of some to 'talk up' the problem. Although your chances of coming across an active serial killer in one week's TV viewing are quite high, you are unlikely to meet one as you go about your everyday activities. Why the fascination with the topic? Does it connect with deep-seated anxieties and fears, providing an ambivalent mix of repulsion and excitement, giving us the ability to feel a rush of adrenaline from the safety of our armchairs? Are there vested interests at work, realising that careers and fortunes can be made riding on the back of the topic, if packaged in a particular way?

It may be that some will scoff at our inclusion of this topic, suggesting that it is sensationalist, attempting to pull in readers in any way that we can. At the same time, looking at serial killers can tell us something about criminology's attempt to grapple with the understanding of crime. What steps are usually taken in this quest? What problems arise? What perspectives are commonly employed? The chapter will begin by asking 'what is serial murder?' Then we shall look at estimates of its extent and trends over time, before moving on to the attempt to divide it into a number of different types. We shall then examine what progress has been made in trying to understand such murders and the people who carry them out, looking in particular at the contributions of biology, psychology and sociology. Finally, we shall attempt to place the 'serial murder problem' in a broader context. What does it tell us about ourselves, our society and our culture? The topic thus provides an illustration of a number of different approaches to the study of crime, many of which have been introduced in earlier chapters.

Murder most horrid: defining serial murder

Criminologists often begin by defining key terms to be used in their enquiries. This is a wise move, for failure to do so can lead to confusion. Although Holmes and Holmes (1998:9) begin their well known book on serial murder by saying that 'for the purposes of this book, homicide and murder are used interchangeably', the term homicide can be used very broadly to refer to any killing of a human being. This may therefore cover a wide variety of circumstances, including where a sentence of death is carried out after a trial, or in armed combat when countries are at war. We might say that criminologists are concerned with unlawful homicides, although this does not put an end to the matter to everyone's satisfaction. Legal codes, whether within one state territory or international ones, saying what is lawful and unlawful, are not necessarily uncontested or unchanging. Consider the execution of King Charles I of England, who lost his head in 1649. By the 1660s, following the restoration of the monarchy, the dominant definition of the event had become murder, and those found to be primarily responsible were savagely punished. All of this underscores the point made earlier in this book that power and political authority are important elements in defining crimes.

In England and Wales, there are three major types of homicide which are violations of criminal law: murder; manslaughter; and infanticide. Murder is the unlawful killing of another with 'malice afore-thought', whereas manslaughter in unlawful killing without malice expressed or implied. Infanticide is an offence created by the Infanticide Act 1922 (amended 1938) to cover cases where a woman causes the death of her child (under 12 months in age) while the balance of her mind is affected by the experience of giving birth or its after-effects. A number of other related offences are classified separately in *Criminal Statistics England and Wales* (Home Office 1998), such as causing death by dangerous or careless driving.

Many murders involve only one event and one victim. Where there are a number of murders committed by the same individual or group, this is referred to as *multiple murder*. Holmes and Holmes (1998) have suggested three types of this: mass murder; spree murder; and serial murder. *Mass murder*, according to them, involves three or more victims, in a single episode, although there may be short interruptions (to look for further victims, for example), and takes place in the same general geographical area. An example is the case of Thomas Hamilton, who in 1996 went into a school in Dunblane, Scotland and opened fire, killing sixteen children, a teacher, and himself. *Spree murder* is also said to involve at least three victims, but the killings occur within a thirty-day time period and take place in more than one location. To these three items, Holmes and Holmes add a fourth to their definition: that the spree is also accompanied by another felony (i.e. another criminal offence). This would be better left out of the definition; they admit that we do not have the information on how many spree murders are connected to other offences, which suggests that this should not be considered a defining characteristic in the present state of knowledge.

The suggested dividing line between mass and spree murder is by no means clear cut. Consider the case of Michael Ryan, who shot and killed one victim, drove to a petrol station and shot at the attendant, and then drove to the town of Hungerford, where he killed fifteen people before shooting himself. Is this a mass or spree murder? Some feel that the concept of spree murder should be omitted altogether as an unnecessary complication (Hickey, 1997). Holmes and Holmes (1998) also suggest that both spree and mass murder, unlike *serial murders*, have no 'emotional cooling off period' between killings. Again, it may be unwise to imply that such a cooling off cannot happen within an arbitrarily chosen thirty-day period, and will always happen in any longer period. We must remember that such definitions and distinctions are produced by the commentator and are not 'natural' categories; as such, they are more or less useful depending on how helpful they in achieving what their purpose, such as staking out a field of study in a clear and helpful way.

According to Holmes and Holmes (1998) the third type of multiple murder, *serial murder*, involves three or more victims, who are killed over a time period of more than thirty days, with a 'significant cooling-off period' between the killings. Examples from England that fit this definition spring readily to mind: Peter Sutcliffe, the 'Yorkshire Ripper', known to have killed thirteen women before capture in 1980; Dennis Nilsen, who is believed to have killed up to sixteen people in the early 1980s; Fred West, who was accused of twelve murders before committing suicide in prison before he could be brought to trial, and his wife Rosemary, who was convicted in 1995 of murdering ten women and girls; Harold Shipman, the family doctor, who in January 2000 was convicted of the murder of fifteen mostly elderly patients and, according to the Manchester coroner, may have been responsible for many more. In the light of this brief list of some of the best known cases, consider the extensive definition offered by Egger (1990: 4):

A serial murder occurs when one or more individuals (males, in most known cases) commit a second and/or subsequent murder; is relationshipless (no prior relationship between the victim and attacker); is at a different time and has no apparent connection to the initial murder; and is usually committed in a different geographical location. Further, the motive is not for material gain and is believed to be for the murderer's desire to have power over his victims. Victims may have symbolic value and are perceived to be prestigeless and in most instances are unable to defend themselves or alert others to their plight, or are perceived as powerless given their situation in time, place or status within their immediate surroundings (such as vagrants, prostitutes, migrant workers, homosexuals, missing children, and single and often elderly women).

This passage is giving us a lot of useful information about what may indeed be common or typical characteristics of serial murder, the circumstances under which it is committed, the motivation behind it and the attributes of victims. This is, however, not the same thing as a definition, which attempts to identify what all instances share in common. In addition, certain apparently required elements in the above can be questioned. It is unwise to stipulate that there is always no prior relationship between the victim and attacker (in many of the cases involving the Wests and Shipman, there were clearly such relationships), and that material gain never enters into the situation (see Hickey 1990 on these points).

Eagle-eyed readers might also have noticed that Egger's definition merely requires a minimum of two murders to be included, whereas Holmes and Holmes require at least three. Other writers seem to be operating with a minimum figure of four killings (Levin and Fox 1985). Such matters may seem unimportant, but can lead to confusion, such as when attempts are made to assess the extent of serial murder. If people are using different figures as part of the definition, they will come up with different estimates (see below).

It is crucial to keep in mind the purpose for which definitions are to be employed. In the early stages of investigation, it is best to have something as brief as possible which seems to encapsulate some basic necessary characteristics such as in the following definition:

Serial homicide involves the murder of separate victims with time breaks between victims, as minimal as two days to weeks or months. These time breaks are referred to as a 'cooling off period'.
(Ressler, Burgess, D'Agostino and Douglas 1984, in Egger 1990: 5)

Such a definition has the advantage of not building in too many assumptions at an early stage.

We have already made the point that Egger's (1990) attempt at a definition is nevertheless useful in identifying some common characteristics which have emerged from research on serial murder. It is important to identify these, for they can have major implications. For example, if serial murders tend to be ones in which there is no prior relationship between offender and victim, this contrasts with much 'ordinary murder'.

In the majority of cases of murder, there is a pre-existing relationship between the killer and the victim. In 1997, 54 per cent of male victims and 79 per cent of female victims in England and Wales knew the main or only suspect before the murder (Home Office 1998: 70). This feature has the consequence that such crimes are often relatively easy to solve. This, together with the fact that greater resources are devoted to such crimes for obvious reasons, means that they have a very high clear-up rate (in 1997, the clear-up rate for homicide was 90 per cent). If, by contrast, serial murders are typically ones in which there is no prior relationship of the usual kind, these offences will be correspondingly difficult to clear up. In such instances, it is easy to see the attractions of investing in such techniques as offender profiling, which attempts to make judgements about the characteristics of the perpetrator from the way in which the attack was carried out, and the scene of the crime.

How many serial murders, murderers and victims?

> Without accurate quantitative assessments of the extent of serial murder, we will be unable to develop informed typologies, theories, and policy decisions. Indeed, we run the risk of creating a social problem, the magnitude of which may be grossly exaggerated.
>
> (Kiger 1990: 36)

Once criminologists have looked at the definition of what they are studying, the next step is often to assess the extent of it. Assessing the extent of crime, offenders and victims is a notoriously difficult problem for criminology, which has been described as having been haunted by the 'dark figure' of hidden (unrecorded) crime throughout much of its history (Coleman and Moynihan 1996). The problems are particularly difficult in the area of serial murder, as we shall see. There are no routinely collected statistics that provide us with figures for this category of murder, although there are such statistics for the broad categories of homicide referred to earlier (murder, manslaughter and infanticide). Other ways of collecting numerical information about crime commonly used by criminologists do not help much. Victims of serial murder find it understandably impossible to take part in victimisation surveys, and offenders of this type may be reluctant to confess such acts in a self-report study!

The absence of any ready-made figures on serial murder has not stopped people making estimates. For example, Holmes and DeBurger (1988) suggested that a 'reliable' estimate for the number of victims each year in the USA ranges from 3,500 to 5,000. They calculate this on the following basis:

- there are about 5,000 murder victims where the offender is unknown in the USA each year;

- between a quarter and two-thirds of these, they suggest, are victims of serial killers;

- there are a number of undetected victims, especially among those children who go missing every year.

They suggest that the typical number of victims for each killer is 10–12. Dividing their estimated figure for total victims of serial murder by this number for each killer (uncharacteristically using the lower estimates this time!), 3,500 divided by 10, gives them a figure of 350 serial killers at large in the USA at any one time – an alarming prospect indeed.

The assumptions on which these estimates are based have been subject to considerable scepticism, especially the notion that such a large proportion of murders where the offender is unknown and many recorded cases of missing children are necessarily attributable to serial killings (Kiger 1998). Fox (1990) has described these estimates as 'preposterous' and probably ten times too large. At least the basis for the estimates are made clear and open to some inspection. Norris (1988: 19) says that the FBI's estimate of active serial killers 'at large and unidentified' is 500, but the basis for this figure is not revealed. More sober estimates have been given for the number of active offenders at any one time, such as 35 by Levin and Fox (1985), while Ressler *et al* (1988) estimate the number of *multiple* murderers (a broader category) to lie between the low 30s to over 100.

Gresswell and Hollin(1994: 6) attempt a similar exercise for England and Wales:

> Such figures are difficult to generalise from outside the United States. If the more conservative figures are applied to England and Wales and equated with the smaller population, then one might expect there to be between six and twenty killers active. However, if the general murder rate for England and Wales (six times less than in the United States) is taken into account, but assuming that detection rates are similar in both countries, an estimate of up to four active killers may be more realistic.

As they imply, however, the actual figure will be affected by such matters as police efficiency, the amount of time taken to detect the offenders and the balance between the different types of multiple murderer (mass and spree murderers are typically at large for short periods, compared with serial murderers).

It is hard to disagree with Kiger's (1999: 37) conclusion that 'there is no doubt that the nature of this phenomenon makes estimation difficult and any absolute numbers representing a reliable reflection of the scope of the problem, impossible'. However, the range of the estimates is great enough to be interesting in itself, and some of the reasons for this are clear, such as the data sources used, the assumptions made, and the definition of serial murder being used (for example, the number of victims being used as a defining criterion can have a considerable impact upon such estimates). Later in the chapter, we explore the possibility that it is also tempting for some vested interests to maximize the scale and impact of a problem with which they are concerned.

A growing menace?

Criminologists are not only interested in the extent of crime, but also in changes in that extent over time (trends). There seems be a prevailing idea that serial murders have been on the increase in the USA in recent decades. Using a combination of the existing literature and press reports, Leyton (1989) constructs a table to convey the recorded instances of multiple murderers in the USA, between 1920 and 1984, and summarises the main trends in the following way:

> There was essentially no change in the production of multiple murderers until the 1960s, for the decades between the 1920s and the 1950s produced only one or two apiece. In the 1960s, this jumped to six cases during the decade, for an average of one new killer every twenty months. By the 1970s, this had jumped to seventeen new cases, for an average of one new killer appearing every seven months. During the first four years of the 1980s, the total had leapt to twenty-five, for an average rate of production of one new killer every 1.8 months.
>
> (Leyton 1989: 365–66)

Leyton, who is aware of some of the problems of such calculations, makes parallel estimates of trends in the number of victims, concluding that the frequency in the first four years of the 1980s was one hundred times that of the 1950s (Leyton 1989: 367). His reservations about the figures seem to centre upon the likelihood that they are an underestimate, but attempting to track trends over time is an even more difficult exercise than estimating contemporary figures. The use of press reports is particularly risky, for what is undeniable is the growing media interest in this type of murder, both in fiction and non-fiction publications, which has been sensitised to look for and interpret killings within this kind of framework. Leyton's view would presumably be that such pronounced trends in his figures are unlikely to be fully accounted for by such possible sources of bias. Other commentators come to similar conclusions about trends for serial murder in the United States, in recent times at least: see, for example, Lowenstein (1989); the subtitle of one book on the topic published in the late 1980s was *The Growing Menace* (Norris 1988).

Can we in England and Wales (to which Home Office crime statistics relate) sleep more soundly in our beds? Jenkins (1988) attempted to track the incidence of serial murder (defined in this instance by four or more victims) in the period 1940–1985; he estimated that serial killers were responsible for 1.7 per cent of murders over this period, but for as many as 3.2 per cent in the 1973–83 period. Gresswell and Hollin (1994) take Jenkins' data, combine them with additional data for the 1980s from the Home Office, and present figures for each decade 1940–1989. This gives the following numbers of serial killers, with number of victims in brackets:

1940–9: 3 (18); 1950–9: 1 (7); 1960–9: 3 (13); 1970–9: 5 (60); 1980–9: 2 (11) (Gresswell and Hollin 1994: 7).

They conclude that,

> there is little empirical support for the idea of a dramatic increase in serial killers since the war. Although the decade 1970–9 produced a large number of killers and victims, 39 of the victims were killed by just two men: Peter Dinsdale (26 victims) and Peter Sutcliffe (13 victims).
>
> (Gresswell and Hollin 1994: 6)

The authors warn us that such figures are likely to underestimate the extent of serial murder. The Home Office figures only include those cases where victims have been clearly identified and attributed to a particular offender. A less restrictive definition of a serial murderer (such as one involving three victims) would also give a less rosy picture on numbers. However, such data, despite their limitations, do give us some indication of broad trends over time, and hardly suggest that there has been a recent epidemic of serial murder in England and Wales.

Types of serial murderer

Once criminologists have charted as well as they can the extent of the phenomenon they are studying, they commonly then attempt to develop their understanding of it. They attempt to describe the common characteristics, making generalisations about it. When this is being done, it may be found that instances cluster into certain key groupings or types. When a systematic classification of cases into a number of types is presented, this is often referred to as a typology. Despite the relatively small numbers of serial murderers, some writers have seen important differences between them and have thought it worthwhile to subdivide the category into such types. It is possible to develop typologies of murders, murderers, or victims. Most commonly, typologies have been developed for serial killers.

Ressler *et al* (1988), for example, used information from the analysis of murders, their crime scenes and interviews with offenders to construct profiles of murderers as either 'organised' or 'disorganised'. An 'organised' murderer would normally be profiled as, for example, someone with good intelligence and social skills, likely to plan murders, target strangers, demand submissiveness from victims and use a vehicle in the commission of the crime. By contrast, the 'disorganised' murderer is profiled as having only average intelligence, being socially immature, likely to live or work nearby and may know the victim, who is likely to be killed spontaneously and suddenly, leaving an untidy crime scene with no attempt to conceal the body. Those characteristics listed here are only some of those in each profile. Since the originators of the framework were working under the aegis of the US Federal Bureau of Investigation, it should be no surprise that the primary purpose of it is to aid the investigation of such crimes.

A rather different classification has been suggested by Hickey (1991, 1997: 26), who delineates three groups: first, travelling serial killers, who may cover many miles in the course of a year, leaving victims dispersed in different places; second, local serial killers, 'who never leave the state in which they start killing in order to find additional victims'; and third, 'place-specific killers', 'who never leave their homes or places of employment, whose victims already reside in the same physical structure or are lured each time to the same location' and who include people such as nurses, housewives and the self-employed. Although it is clear that serial killers can be classified according to their degree of geographical mobility, it is unclear what the wider purpose of the typology might be. Does it, for example, help us in understanding the motives of such offenders, or the meanings which their actions have for them?

Perhaps the most widely known typology is that developed by Holmes and DeBurger (1988) and Holmes and Holmes (1998), who have developed separate typologies for male and female serial killers. For males there are four types.

Visionary
These killers are said to be responding to inner voices or hallucinations. The break with reality is such that these individuals are often said to be 'psychotic'. Key features are said to typify their murders, such as the victims being randomly selected strangers, the murder spontaneous and disorganised, and the location concentrated in certain areas.

Missionary
This type has decided to rid the locality or the world of particular groups he deems undesirable, such as drug dealers, drug users, prostitutes or homosexuals. Although such individuals may be seen as being characterised by a fixation, they are not normally considered psychotic. Their victims are randomly selected strangers from specific types of person, the act planned and organised in concentrated locations.

Hedonistic
This is a mixed group with three sub-types. *Lust murderers* are those for whom violence and sex are intimately linked, and sexual practices and mutilations may follow after the death of the victim. *Thrill killers* are similar, but the victim is kept alive as long as possible in order to relish their suffering. *Comfort killers* are those who kill for financial or other material gain.

Power/control type
This killer is motivated by the desire to have, quite literally, the power of life and death over the victim. Although sex may occur, this is not the primary motivation.

A separate typology has been developed for female serial killers (Holmes and Holmes 1998), although there is a considerable overlap with the typology for males. The *visionary* corresponds to the male type, and the *comfort murderess*, who kills for 'creature comfort' reasons, corresponds to the male hedonistic/comfort type. A frequently cited case of this type is that of Dorothea Puente, who was charged with nine murders in California in 1988. She kept a rooming-house and was charged with poisoning some of her guests in order to benefit from their social security cheques. The *hedonistic* type corresponds broadly with the other male hedonistic types, but sex is less likely to figure. The fourth type is the *power seeker*, for whom murder is 'a way to attain a sense of power' (Holmes and Holmes 1998: 45). Although this sounds very much like the male power/control type, in this case power and attention is sought not over the victim as such, but in relation to other people. An example is the mother who puts her child into life-threatening situations and eventually kills the child, thus gaining power over, and recognition from others. The fifth and final type also represents a departure from the male typology – the disciple murderer, who acts under the influence or orders of the leader of a group. Holmes and Holmes note that female serial killers are relatively uncommon, and that most of them will fall into the comfort type.

How do we judge such typologies? The first point to make is that they can only be judged in relation to some purpose or objective, which should be clearly specified before the typology is constructed. How good is the typology in achieving that objective? We have already made the point that the typology developed by Ressler *et al* (1988) was primarily to assist in the detection of offenders. As such, it should be judged in that light. Seltzer (1998: 131) comments,

> although the types of 'organised' and 'disorganised' killers are directly at odds, it has become routine to find apprehended killers designated as 'mixed' types. ...Despite the profilers' high profile in the media, however, there remains a basic disagreement about what contribution this technique has made.

By contrast, the primary objective of the Holmes and DeBurger (1988) and Holmes and Holmes (1998) typologies is to reveal the patterns of motivation of serial killers. These typologies are based on particular psychological ideas about the origins of this particular form of behaviour. If these ideas are accurate, they may contribute to a theory of serial murder that will help us to understand and explain it.

The second point is that typologies are intended to help us to make sense of a wealth of detailed information. They attempt to impose order, to allow us to see patterns rather than simply a wealth of individual detail. They are thus an attempt to go beyond the seemingly endless description of individual cases, to group instances together, to see common features between them. All typologies must strike some balance between simplicity and complexity. The simpler they are, the more readily understandable they usually are, but they may not do sufficient justice to the phenomena; they may impose over-simplistic patterns on complex reality. The more complex they are, the more they can deal with differences and variation in the social world, but the less clear and readily understandable they may be. The typology of Hickey (1986, 1997) is clearly one of the most simple typologies, whereas that of Holmes and Holmes (1998) is one of the most complex. Typologies will always have limitations, precisely because they must balance competing demands of simplicity/clarity on one hand and complexity/depth on the other. Wherever the balance is struck, something will be lost.

The third point to make is that typologies in criminology must decide on the primary focus in terms of, for example, the crime, the offender or perhaps the victim. Most of the typologies in the area of serial murder focus on the offender. That of Holmes and DeBurger (1988), for example, had this focus, and more precisely, looks for motivational patterns. Such motivational patterns of offenders do not provide a complete explanation of events. Other factors may be important in accounting for these. The behaviour of the victim and situational factors, for example, may be very important in explaining actual outcomes (for example, some victims selected may die, others not), a general point which has received much attention in criminology in recent years.

Such a typology also seems to suggest a consistent and enduring pattern of motivation on the part of the individual who is so labelled. A common observation is that those who are eventually apprehended as serial killers have often had the ability to 'blend in' and give no indication of their chilling activities, leading relatively 'normal' lives most of the time. This suggests that we need extra explanations to account for actual killing sequences, such as the notion of 'triggers' which may precipitate them.

Criminological typologies and explanations must avoid giving the impression that individuals have been simply programmed into serial killing, rather like the killing machine in the film *Terminator*, the cyborg with only one mission, with little need to shop or do the laundry. Serial killers may have different motives for different victims, and these motives may change over time. Gresswell and Hollin (1994) give an example from the account of the case of Dennis Nilsen (Masters 1985), who in the middle of a killing sequence is said to have murdered one victim not for the 'usual' reasons, but because he was annoying and in the way. The general point, then, is that typologies that focus on offenders and their motivation, will not necessarily give us a good account of events and may even mislead us into thinking that motives of any particular offender are always pretty much the same.

A final point concerns the scope and comprehensiveness of any typology – does it leave certain things out that should be considered? Holmes and DeBurger (1988), for example, leave out 'contract' or hired killers, arguing that their motivation is 'extrinsic' rather than 'intrinsic'. This seems odd, given that they include the hedonistic comfort type and comfort murderess type, both of whom may kill for largely 'extrinsic' motives, such as to benefit from others' insurance policies or social security cheques (this anomaly is rectified in later work: see Holmes and Holmes 1998). What is also striking about the literature on multiple murder and serial killings is the way in which some of the most dramatic and large scale examples are neglected or ignored. We are thinking of such things as war crimes, genocide and ethnic cleansing, which have disgraced human history up to the present. Gresswell and Hollin (1994: 1) do at least show an awareness of these and exclude them from consideration in the following way:

> There are many different forms of multiple homicide, ranging from the large scale, apparently politically motivated, killings of Joseph Stalin or Idi Amin, through the seemingly motiveless killings of Peter Sutcliffe and Michael Ryan. In this paper, we will focus on the phenomenon of non-politically motivated homicide in England and Wales, particularly the type of perpetrator that clinicians and criminologists are likely to encounter through the criminal justice or secure hospital systems.

It is quite legitimate to limit one's attention to particular parts of a topic, perhaps feeling that to include all instances would make the project too diverse and unwieldy. In this instance, there seems to be an assumption that there are 'politically motivated' murders, in which the analysis will be very different and can therefore be separated off from the analysis of 'non-politically motivated' multiple murder. This may prove to be the case, although there may still be similarities worthy of study, such as a tendency to see victims as unimportant or less than human.

What is more significant here is the conventional concentration of criminology upon the problem as defined by criminal law of the nation state and its criminal justice system. Instances that are seen as somehow 'political' can be seen as not being part of its central focus, perhaps to be studied by other disciplines, such as political science. On the other hand, there are those who recognise that the subject matter of criminology is inherently political, and that simply to study crimes against the state is a political decision when crime by or on behalf of some states is equally deserving of our attention. Those taking this view urge the study of such topics as the crimes of the state (Cohen 1993) and the criminology of war (Jamieson 1998). In addition, a focus on those normally processed by the conventional criminal justice system and secure hospitals tends to result in a concentration upon individual offenders and their clinical and psychological backgrounds, rather than those responsible for multiple murders which occur in settings with a wider political context.

Understanding serial murder

Definitions, measuring the extent of serial murder, and typologies of it, help the criminologist to map out a field of study. When criminologists try to understand something like serial murder, the next step is often to look for theories that might help us. One view of the nature of criminological enquiry is that theories are systematic sets of statements that provide possible explanations for phenomena that we find puzzling – and serial murders certainly come into that category. This view suggests that theories contain hypotheses that can be tested by research (the collection and analysis of data relevant to the validity or invalidity of hypotheses). Until this happens, the hypotheses remain hypothetical. If the data seems to contradict the hypothesis, it needs to be rejected or reformulated, unless the data can be rejected as not being an adequate test of the hypothesis. Even if the hypothesis survives unscathed from the encounter with research data, the statements in the theory remain provisional – subject to further testing, reformulation, and possible rejection in favour of a more satisfactory theory in the future. We have seen in the last chapter that contributions to theories of crime have been made by various disciplines.

The most common contributors to theories of crime in general, and to serial murder in particular, have been biology, psychology and sociology. Each will be considered in turn.

Biology: natural born killers?

The biological approach concentrates on characteristics and processes in the human body and their possible role in the causation of crime. We have examined something of the history of this in chapter 2. A number of biological factors have been put forward as possible contributors to serial murder. The first example to mention will be familiar – the idea that heredity and genetics 'have a role to play' (Holmes and Holmes 1998:49).

Genetic factors

The suggestion has been made that the possession of an extra male (Y) chromosome in the genetic make-up of some individuals (what is called the *XYY syndrome*) may predispose them to violence, or even to serial murder. Clear evidence for a causal link between the XYY pattern and criminal behaviour has always been lacking (Mednick and Volavka 1980) and the suggested link with serial murder seems to have been based on one or two examples of serial killers who have had, or are thought to have had, this genetic abnormality. Arthur Shawcross, who was arrested in New York State in 1990 and confessed to the murder of eleven women, having already served a prison sentence for one of two earlier killings, is reported to have had this extra chromosome (Hickey 1997: 48). Just as one swallow does not make a summer, one case does not make a generalisation.

Head trauma

The case of Shawcross brings to our attention a second possible biological factor: head trauma. Shawcross had suffered head injuries as a child and as an adult. 'Considering that abuse is a common theme in the childhoods of serial killers, we must also be concerned with those who received head trauma. While head trauma may not directly cause violent behaviour, the persistent correlation must not be ignored' (Hickey 1997: 46). Again, there are general lessons for the criminologist. It must first be demonstrated that serial killers are more likely to have suffered head trauma than other people who are in other ways like the killer group (a 'matched' comparison). Even then, a correlation does not necessarily amount to causation. For instance, alternative explanations for the correlation need to be discounted, e.g. that the association is produced by a third factor, such as cold, uncaring parenting leading to both physical abuse of a child and a psychological make-up conducive to victimising others. As we saw in chapter 2, establishing causal generalisations is more difficult than we might think.

Abnormal brain activity

A third possibility is a link between abnormal brain activity and violent behaviour. Holmes and Holmes (1998: 47) cite the work of Burgess *et al* (1986), who found that EEG (electroencephalogram – a device for measuring brain activity) abnormalities tended to disappear in people in their thirties. As serial killers tend to cluster in the 25–35 age range, could it be that these are often individuals whose brains have yet fully to develop, leading to immature, childish behaviour, such as fits of rage? Do we detect much speculation here, built on rather slim foundations, in a way that is rather typical of much of this literature?

Other biological factors

Other authors mention other possible biological factors. Holmes and Holmes (1998: 48) cite the work of Norris and Birnes (1988) who favour biological explanations. Apart from the mention of head trauma, they claim that almost all serial killers suffer from psychomotor epilepsy or serious hormonal imbalance, which may result from a malfunctioning limbic system (the so-called 'animal' or emotional brain). Holmes and Holmes (1998: 48) point out that no sources or evidence are presented to support these claims, although, in a manner reminiscent of Lombroso, descriptions of the heads of some serial killers are provided. In a more cautious vein, Hickey (1997) suggests a number of other biological factors which, if subject to more research, may be useful in helping to understand violent crime, such as:

- hypoglycaemia (a condition of low blood-sugar, which affects brain function);

- levels of serotonin, a substance which seems to have a calming effect, low levels of which may result in poor impulse control;

- differences in the characteristics of the nervous system, which make it more difficult for some individuals to be socialised into conforming conduct, as suggested by Eysenck (1977).

Having surveyed these views on the role of biology, it is hard to come to any positive conclusions. It appears that very little systematic research has been conducted into the role of such factors in serial murder. This is hardly surprising, given the difficulties of conducting such research. As Holmes and Holmes (1998: 49) say, until a proper sample of serial killers has been put together and tested systematically for such factors, there is 'no scientific statement that can be made' of the kind that seems to be the objective of many of these writers. David Canter (1994: 209) gives this verdict on the biological approach:

There is, of course, likely to be some biological basis to psychological differences between people. This could contribute to their general characteristics in such a way that under certain circumstances they might be more prone to commit a crime than a person who had less of that particular aspect of their biological make-up. But this chain of influences is so long and marginal that for most practical purposes it is irrelevant.

Psychology: inside the mind of the serial killer?

Psychology is the systematic study of human behaviour and mental processes, often with a particular focus upon particular characteristics and processes which distinguish individuals from each other (see our discussion of psychological approaches in Chapter 2). One common stereotype of the psychologist is that of the expert with a mid-European accent who spends hours and hours with one individual, attempting to bring to the surface deep-seated conflicts which are beyond the subject's everyday consciousness. The stereotype is loosely derived from that branch of psychology called *psychoanalysis*, which is by no means the only variety of the discipline and has actually been rejected by many academic psychologists because of what they see as its 'unscientific' nature.

Psychoanalysis traces its ancestry to the pioneering work of Sigmund Freud, even though more recent work has often departed from his original ideas. Key elements include a stress on the importance of the early years of life, especially parent–child relationships, in the psychological development of the individual, which can be seen as being divided into a number of stages. Problems can arise when conflicts cannot be dealt with at the time and are repressed into the unconscious mind, to have an influence on the later behaviour and well-being of the individual.

A relevant example is the work of Abrahamsen (1973), who stresses that traumas in childhood often have a sexual basis; if the child is unable to deal with these at the time, they may be repressed into the unconscious mind, but may surface later in the form of murder with strong sexual components. The sexual components involve inflicting pain and suffering on the victim as a way of gaining a sense of power and control which was clearly lacking in the childhood experiences of the killer. Such murders thus reflect such early experiences and attempt to compensate for them. Although many psychologists distance themselves from the ideas and approach of psychoanalysis, it is interesting how often the literature on serial murder comes up with ideas and findings that are consistent with it.

It might seem reasonable to suggest that people who kill repetitively are suffering from some form of mental disorder which would go a long way to explaining such behaviour. The field of mental disorder is a complex and still developing one, and we can only give a brief overview of possibilities here.

Psychosis
The first possibility to consider is that serial killers are suffering from a form of psychosis, the symptoms of which are said to be one or more of the following: 'delusions, hallucinations, disorganized speech, or grossly disorganized or catatonic behaviour' (Hickey 1997: 53). It is all too easy to point to examples that seem to fit this category. Joseph Kallinger claimed to be haunted by a large floating, tentacled head called Charlie, telling him to kill people and mutilate their genitals. The obedient Kallinger duly obliged, murdering his own son and others in the local community. Psychotic episodes or states are said to be brought on by 'physiological malfunctioning, environmental stressors, or substance use' (Hickey 1997: 53). Although fitting well into the type of 'visionary' killers outlined earlier, it seems that 'serial killers are rarely found to be suffering from psychotic states' (Hickey 1997: 54), according to one author who has been working in the field for a number of years.

Dissociative disorders
The second possibility to consider is the dissociative disorders. Dissociation refers to:

> a normal psychological process which provides the opportunity for a person to avoid, to one degree or another, the presence of memories and feelings which are too painful to tolerate. Dissociation is a continuum of experiences ranging from the process of blocking out events going on around us (such as when watching a movie) to Multiple Personality Disorder (MPD) where personalities are separate compartmentalized entities.
>
> (Carlisle 1998: 88)

Dissociation therefore ranges from something that is very common to something that is extreme. *Multiple personality disorder* makes for good stories and film scripts from Jekyll and Hyde onwards, but does not seem to figure much in the world of serial murder. Kenneth Bianchi is thought to have faked the disorder in order to support his plea of insanity, and Hickey (1997: 55) concludes that 'there do not appear to be any well documented cases of MPD in serial killing'. The disorder is sometimes referred to as the 'UFO of psychiatry' because some doubt its very existence as a clinical entity.

Less extreme is Carlisle's (1998) account of the role of dissociation in the development of what some killers have referred to as 'the shadow', 'the beast' or 'the entity'. Traumatic memories and feelings may be buried (by 'splitting off' or 'blocking out'), while a rich fantasy life is developed to provide a sense of relief and excitement which is increasingly turned to when the person experiences stress, depression or emptiness. The fantasies are focused upon the things which cannot, at first, be done in real life. At first, they may focus on being a hero, being the kind of person to be admired; as time goes by and these fantasies are not fulfilled, they may come to focus upon revenge, or sex coupled with violence. The person is leading a kind of double life; one real, one fantasy: a struggle between the parts is experienced. The individual may eventually find himself in a situation that corresponds to the fantasy and 'automatically carrying out an act he has practised so many, many times in his mind' (Carlisle 1998: 93). He may initially dissociate the crime, and vow that it will never happen again. But the wish to feel such power and control becomes so strong that eventually another murder is committed. The individual has become what he has always feared; a fundamental shift of identity has occurred. Guilt is compartmentalised so that it is not consciously experienced. His secret, 'dark side' is experienced as having gained the upper hand over his very being. In order to neutralise the strong self-hate that may be engendered, he may even begin to idealise what he has become. Carlisle (1998: 99) claims that while this model may not fit every serial killer, it will fit most cases. Holmes and Holmes (1998: 72) suggest it is a theory of 'at least the sexually motivated and power-motivated serialists'. Although it leaves a number of questions un-answered, it does point to some important themes we shall encounter elsewhere.

Psychopathy

Perhaps the concept most tempting to apply to the serial killer is that of *psychopathy*. Henderson (1939: 19) described it as 'a true illness for which we have no specific explanation'. Cleckley (1976) listed sixteen characteristics of psychopaths, and building on this, Hare (1991) has developed a psychopathy checklist which includes such items as:

- glibness/superficial charm;
- conning, manipulative behaviour;
- lack of remorse or guilt;
- callousness/lack of empathy.

Hickey (1997: 65) states that although most psychopaths are not violent, a common feature is their 'constant need to be in control of their social and physical environment. When this control is challenged, the psychopath can be moved to violent behaviour'. He also notes that the attraction of the term lies in the 'catch-all' nature of the label, apparently able to accommodate even killers who had seemed to be Mr Nice Guy on first impressions. But one drawback is that 'researchers and clinicians alike have yet to arrive at a consensus as to the proper definition of the term' (Hickey 1997: 66). We might add that, even if it may be a useful descriptive term, this does not necessarily constitute an explanation: we still do not know how these individuals came to have these characteristics, although there have, for example, been attempts to discover a genetic or biological basis for it (Schulsinger 1977). Perhaps not surprisingly, many psychiatrists prefer to view particular violent offenders as suffering from *anti-social personality disorder*, with its roots in childhood or adolescence (Hickey 1997: 61).

Multiple-factor explanations
Perhaps the most illuminating avenue at present is provided by those who try to take an overview of the main research findings, constructing a model which is divided into a series of stages. It is clear that the explanation of serial murder is very complex, and not to be achieved by a focus on one concept or factor. Instead, any theory of such a rare phenomenon is likely to include a wide range of elements, which on their own or even in combination with some of the others, are likely to have been experienced by a large number of persons without them becoming serial murderers. In addition, the research evidence is not substantial in any case, because of the rarity of serial murder and the various difficulties involved in conducting research on it. As such, theoretical models or frameworks must be regarded as highly provisional. Gresswell and Hollin (1994) provide one such model summarising the research on multiple murder, and divided into three main stages: predisposing factors; maintaining factors; situational factors and triggers. It provides a good illustration of how psychological criminologists might approach the explanation of such a crime.

- *Predisposing factors* include a childhood in which attachment and empathic bonding between the child and carer fails to develop. As such, the child may become cold and aloof towards others (Burgess *et al* 1986). The child is not helped to deal with traumatic experiences, but aspects of them (such as sadistic violence, sexual abuse) are incorporated into a fantasy life. These fantasies are a source of pleasure and a feeling of power and control which are lacking in 'real' life. As such they are 'reinforced' (rewarded) and he is more likely to become dependent upon them. The child misses chances to acquire pro-social skills and values and develops a distorted picture of himself and social relationships.

- *Maintaining factors* are divided into three types. *Cognitive inhibitory processes* are involved in overriding, or the prevention of the learning of, inhibitions to aggression. For example, people who have experienced the kind of background described in the previous paragraph may end up feeling isolated and alienated, and are therefore relatively immune from feedback in respect of inappropriate violence. Such children may also lack the capacity to relate with empathy towards others, who can therefore be more easily victimised (Burgess *et al* 1986). Victims may be literally depersonalised, and acts of childhood delinquency can escalate to more serious acts in later life. *Cognitive facilitating processes* refer to the role of fantasy, originally developed as a form of escape, as a precursor to multiple murder. For example, Prentky *et al* (1989) found that 86 per cent of their sample of serial sexual murderers admitted violent fantasies, while only 23 per cent of their single sexual murderers did so. *Operant processes* are those in which both positive and negative reinforcement affect the likelihood of repetition. Thus fantasy, rehearsal/ trial runs and murder itself are positively reinforced by feelings of power and control, and negatively reinforced in so far as they provide an escape from the negative experiences of 'normal' life. Prentky *et al* (1989) suggest that serial killers are involved in a quest to match fantasy with reality, an attempt which is only likely to be partly successful and therefore likely to be repeated.

- *Situational factors and triggers* are often identified by criminologists to take the explanation a little further: to explain why a crime happens where and when it does. So, for example, Ressler *et al* (1988) found that all of their sample of 36 convicted sexual murderers had experienced various sorts of problems (concerning jobs, money matters, legal matters and relationships) before the murder. A third said they had been experiencing emotional states that made them 'open for opportunities'. Gresswell and Hollin (1994: 11) suggest that individuals with well rehearsed murder fantasies are more likely to act these out (rather than engage in some other deviant act) when faced with a disintegration in their psychological equilibrium and familiar social world. Again, the various factors need to be taken in conjunction to provide a more complete explanation.

The trauma-control model

Another model, the trauma-control model, has been provided by Hickey (1997). Although he accepts that there may be predispositional factors, such as biological ones, destabilising traumatizations in the formative years of life hold a key place in the model. Most commonly, these are said to take the form of an unstable, abusive and rejecting home life. Some may respond to these experiences in a destructive way. Such experiences foster feelings of low self-esteem which encourage the development of fantasies. A process of dissociation (the memory of painful experiences or the feelings they created are suppressed) may occur; a facade of self-confidence and control is presented to the outside world (as in the concept of the psychopath). The individual may begin to use facilitators, such as alcohol and other drugs, pornography, or books on the occult; these are not suggested as causal factors as such, but can lower inhibitions and feed fantasies, which are said to be a 'critical component in the psychological development of the serial killer' and 'likely to be found in the minds of most, if not all...' (Hickey 1997: 91).

The fantasies increasingly involve violence, often sexual, and control over the victim, and eventually the individual attempts to replicate them. This is never fully achievable, but each attack may provide material for new fantasies. Elements of the original childhood trauma may surface in the ordeal to which the victim is subject. When a sense of control has been reached, the victim may be slaughtered, and the individual feels a temporary sense of equilibrium that has been missing in his life. If the quest for fantasy fulfilment has become all-consuming, or the feelings of low self-esteem and rejection are precipitated by events (trauma reinforcement), the process may begin again.

Such models, which provide a kind of moving picture of a typical case, appear to help us to understand to some extent the enigma of serial murder. We must remember, however, the rather flimsy basis on which such models are constructed: interviews with small, probably unrepresentative samples of some of the most devious research subjects, and case studies. To what extent is the model applicable to all the types of serial killer or to only some of them? Are all the factors to be found in every case, or are different combinations possible? Are there important factors which have been omitted? To what extent are offenders driven by forces beyond their own consciousness and/or control? These are the sorts of questions that criminologists might ask about such a model, but even if defective in certain respects, it is still useful in attempting to summarise what is thought to be the case in the present state of knowledge, and provides something that can be tested out by researchers in the future. Although caution is recommended, it seems a little too pessimistic to say that 'those who commit fatal violence are compelled by forces beyond our understanding' (Holmes and Holmes 1998: 59).

Sociology: outside the mind of the serial killer?

Sociologists are not primarily interested in individual differences in behaviour, mental processes and personality in the way that psychology is. They are more concerned with aspects of society and broad social groupings within it (such as class, race and gender) and their impact on behaviour. We have seen how psychological approaches to serial murder tend to look for the causes of it within the characteristics and personal experiences of the individual. We might expect this to be the best place to look with such an unusual and apparently esoteric crime, with the emphasis on individual pathology (i.e. what went wrong with the individual) fully justified. Sociologists, however, may argue that such a focus upon individual pathology neglects the social and cultural context within which these crimes are located. The famous sociologist Emile Durkheim (1952, originally published in 1897) conducted a study of suicide to demonstrate the helpfulness of a sociological perspective with a similarly highly individual phenomenon. Corresponding to their rather different focus, sociologists tend to ask rather different sorts of questions. In the case of serial murder, the following might be three examples.

- Why do there seem to be more serial killers in one society than in another?

- If the incidence of serial murder seems to be changing over time, why is this?

- Why do particular societies, at particular times, focus on particular problems (such as serial murder), and see those problems in particular ways?

We look initially at the first two questions. Then we move on to look at the third.

The thoroughly modern multiple murderer

Despite the inherent difficulties of the enterprise, Elliott Leyton's (1989) *Hunting Humans: the rise of the modern multiple murderer* is an example of a traditional sociological approach to the topic. His key question is, 'why does modern America produce proportionately so many more of these 'freaks' than any other industrial nation?' (Leyton 1989: 11). The answer comes in several stages. Leyton's view is that multiple murderers are not random 'freaks', but products of their historical time – thrown up by specific stresses and changes in society. Multiple-stranger murders are said to be rare in pre-industrial societies, but the economic and social upheaval of the industrial revolution eventually produced new kinds of murderer. In particular, there were 'middle class functionaries – doctors, teachers, professors, civil servants, who belonged to the class created to serve the new triumphant bourgeoisie – [and who] preyed on members of the lower orders, especially prostitutes and housemaids' (Leyton 1989: 350). But why? Leyton seems to believe the answer lies in 'a defensive status hysteria – which manifests itself as a kind of extreme personal insecurity – that is found so often among those who have risen or fallen dramatically in the social hierarchy'. Multiple murder seems to be seen as one way of 'disciplining the social inferiors who threatened [a murderer's] position' (Leyton 1989: 356, 358).

But Leyton's principal concern lies in more recent decades, where, as we have previously seen, he presents some data to show that multiple murder has dramatically increased since the 1950s. Since the late 1960s, it is suggested that the American economy has increasingly ceased to provide middle-class positions for 'socially ambitious, but untalented (or unconnected) young men' (Leyton 1989: 363–4) from the working- and lower middle-class. Some of these begin to fantasise about revenge, and a 'tiny, but ever-increasing, percentage of them began to react to the frustration of their blocked social mobility by transforming their fantasies into a vengeful reality' (Leyton 1989: 364).

Sociologists would recognise this as a *strain theory* of deviant behaviour: society creates a frustration or problem of adjustment, to which deviance is seen as a response (see chapter 3). But strain theory alone cannot necessarily account for the nature of this deviant response: why turn to violence rather than, say, alcohol or depression? To do so, Leyton points to the cultural context of American society, a culture which glorifies violence 'as an appropriate and manly response to frustration' (Leyton 1989: 364), and which stresses individualism and the freedom to explore one's self and its impulses.

To strain and this cultural context is added a third ingredient to complete the explosive cocktail: personal and spiritual insecurity on the part of certain individuals. Leyton examines the backgrounds of 23 multiple murderers from the USA, to show how frequently they come from that part of the population (which he estimates as 12–20 per cent in a modern nation state) with one of four characteristics: adopted, illegitimate, institutionalised as a child or adolescent, or their mother married three times or more. Such a family background, he suggests, will often leave these individuals feeling socially excluded or marginal. This insecurity is said to be the breeding ground for the modern multiple murderer.

This is an interesting thesis, with strengths and weaknesses. It is helpful to draw attention to the cultural context, so often lacking in psychological and biological approaches. As a social anthropologist, Leyton is aware of the differences between cultures in respect of violence and the significant consequences these have for patterns of behaviour. But the psychological perspectives we have examined seem more adept at linking childhood experiences with the development of violent fantasy and later serial murder. Furthermore, the kind of background he describes for the offender is actually the lot of many individuals in the USA, so why so *few* serial murderers, not why so many? There are so many loose connections in this circuit, that it is hardly surprising that the lights rarely come on. It is major enterprise to forge links from the economy right through to such a relatively unusual event as serial murder: a great deal more research needs to be done in order to do so.

Putting gender on the agenda

Another way in which we can place serial murder into a wider social and cultural context is to consider issues of gender. Gender as an issue was once very much neglected in criminology and in the social sciences more generally. Major contributions have been made to rectify this in recent years, especially by those working from a broadly feminist perspective (see chapter 3). However, these developments do not seem to have had much influence in much of the literature on serial murder. This is surprising, for one 'fact' upon which most researchers seem to be agreed is that the majority of serial killers are men, and many of their victims, but by no means all of them, are women. For example, in a list of 43 serial killers given by Holmes and DeBurger (1988: 22–23), only three were women. One rather cursory attempt to say why this should be seems to rely on either biological factors, especially the influence of hormones, or 'social learning' – that 'there are many ways in which children are taught that aggression is more appropriate for men than for women' (Hale and Bolin 1998: 34). The relative contribution and interaction of biological and socio-cultural factors (the 'nature – nurture debate') is a key but very difficult issue, which is avoided by these authors.

David Canter (1994) takes as central that most serial killers and violent criminals are men. His explanation for this is very much socio-cultural, suggesting that the 'inner narratives' or stories that we construct and through which we live our lives are taken from the wider society and culture. Although much of his account is psychological, concentrating on the characteristics and backgrounds of individuals of the sort described in the section on psychology, his view is that 'criminal narratives' are on the whole 'drawn from those which our society provides for men' (Canter 1994: 239). By contrast, 'the typical representation of women as victims rather than protagonists is reflected in the fact that it is relatively rare for women to write themselves into actively violent scenarios (except as victims)' (Canter 1994 : 232). The fact that there are relatively few female equivalents of Rambo may help us to understand not only why most serial killers are likely to be men, but also that the victims are often women. Canter (1994: 239) also suggests that 'out of a self-perception of loneliness and the distorted search for intimacy, there grow feelings of impotence and isolation, embedded in anger towards others who are seen as crucial in defining the criminal's identity, typically women'.

A further 'fact' that is often put forward by writers in this field is that whereas 'lust' or sex is often identified as a feature of serial killing by men, 'lust is simply not a strong motive for murder among female serial killers' (Hale and Bolin 1998: 46). If serial murder simply has its origins in childhood trauma, especially sexual abuse, we might expect more women to be involved, and for their murders to involve sexual sadism more frequently than seems to be the case, for there is no evidence that girls are largely exempt from child abuse. Clearly, more than this is required to account for gender differences in serial killing. Cameron and Frazer (1987), in their discussion of sexual murder (by men) from a feminist perspective, see 'transcendence' – the wish to attain some kind of immortality by an extra-ordinary action – as a reason for male predominance in this crime. Such men are extreme products of an exaggerated culture of masculinity, for whom aggression and male sexuality have become inextricably linked. Such men cannot be understood apart from that wider culture which, in one way or another, affects all our lives. Jane Caputi (1987) goes further, suggesting that the twentieth century is characterised by a new form of genocide – sexual murder as the ultimate expression of sexuality as a form of (male) power. It is certainly undeniable that masculinity – or at least certain forms of it – may be partly responsible for some very undesirable outcomes.

The social construction of a problem

Another perspective to which we wish to draw attention asks rather different questions. The social constructionist approach questions the very foundations of what is 'known' about a problem and what should be done about it. How are problems identified in the first place? Why are some issues rather than others singled out for special attention? Are they interpreted in particular ways? If so, why? Are particular interests in-volved in this process? Are some interests more successful than others in making their claims/interpretations count? As a result, is the concern and reaction to some problems out of all proportion to the threat that they constitute? Can we speak of there being a 'moral panic' about some issues? These are the sorts of questions that have been asked about serial murder by some sociologists (Soothill 1993, Jenkins 1994).

The suggestion is that there are vested interests involved in creating and maintaining a focus upon serial murder as a problem. Although multiple murderers have existed for many years, the term serial murder is a relatively recent invention, and the 'framing' of it as a problem has much about it that is new. Much is to be gained by certain agencies if the problem is seen to be a growing menace. First, there are what are often called the social control agencies. According to Jenkins (1994: 213), a new problem of serial murder was established 'as a problem of law enforcement and federal power rather than one of mental health or social dysfunction'. The agencies largely responsible for this were the US Justice Department and the FBI's Behavioural Sciences Unit (BSU) at Quantico, a new unit keen to expand its resources and activities in such areas as offender profiling and crime scene analysis. With its direct access to such offenders and its national jurisdiction, such an agency was able to establish itself as the authority on serial offending. It shared with certain other groups 'a common vested interest in emphasising certain aspects of the murder problem, above all its very large scale' (Jenkins 1994 : 216):

black groups who viewed it as part of systematic racial exploitation; feminists who saw the offense as serial femicide, a component of the larger problem of violence against women; children's rights activists concerned with missing and exploited children; as well as religious and other advocates of a ritual murder threat.

(Jenkins 1994: 212)

In his view, the BSU personnel knew how to work an audience and to cultivate the media, with the master-stroke of allowing the filming of *The Silence of the Lambs* to take place at Quantico.

The mass media are the second major agency with vested interests in the serial murder issue. It has become all too clear that the issue sells newspapers, books and magazines, raises TV ratings and fills cinema seats. According to Jenkins (1994: 221), 'serial murder represents for the media the perfect social problem', fulfilling as it does the criteria for a newsworthy story: it invokes an emotional response; there is drama in the battle between good and evil; it involves a real harm and a potential threat for readers and viewers, from the 'quiet, apparently harmless person down the street' (as killers are often subsequently described by neighbours); excitement often accompanies the hunt for the offender; shock value will be contained in the unusual violent or sexual activity; offenders often acquire a celebrity status so that coverage can be personalised; it often comes with ready-made attention-grabbing features and powerful visual images. Fiction and non-fiction alike (the distinction between the two is by no means clear cut according to this analysis) contribute to forming the prevailing images and 'monster' stereotypes, with a heavy reliance on the material provided by the accredited agencies, such as the BSU.

Killers themselves often play an important role in this process, and have an intricate relationship with the media. Serial murderers often appear to be avid consumers of media accounts of earlier cases, from daily newspapers through to academic psychological discussions. It seems highly likely that they will be influenced in some way by these sources, 'which may go far in explaining why killers in different eras tend to reproduce explanations of their offense that closely mimic the prevailing ideological perspective of their day or even of the particular investigator to whom they are confessing' (Jenkins 1994: 224).

What killers say about their deeds may also be affected by the kind of outcome they may be seeking, such as an insanity defence, or to appear in the *Guinness Book of Records*: for example, some offenders have confessed to murders they could not have committed. If the psychopathic personality type is frequently to be found amongst such offenders, we should remember their propensity to manipulate and to say whatever might please the listener, whether investigator or researcher. For all these reasons, we should be treating what killers say with an enormous pinch of salt; this is worrying when such accounts are often used as the main basis for explanations and claims by interest groups. In fact, Jenkins suggests that the various 'confessions' made over the years by any offender may contain enough different threads and contradictions to allow a claims-maker to choose the one that seems most convenient to whatever they are trying to argue.

A similar analysis has been provided by Soothill (1993), who focuses more on the developing panic in Britain, a panic all the more remarkable in view of the very limited extent of the problem compared with the USA. Soothill also stresses the benefits for social control agencies, especially the police, and for media interests. To these he adds business interests, which may benefit as law enforcement seeks the expensive advanced technology seen to be necessary to grapple with the problem. He cites the introduction of HOLMES – a computerised system to process large quantities of information in connection with major enquiries – in the wake of the case of the 'Yorkshire Ripper'. Such a system, it was argued, would help to avoid 'linkage blindness' – a failure to see connections in large quantities of information collected, a feature that had characterised the Ripper investigation. Finally, he notes the vested interests of a new breed of experts, with careers and reputations to advance. The best known figures in the field of psychological profiling Britain are David Canter and Paul Britton. An impression of the kinds of things at stake is provided by Britton (1997: 142–158), who includes some rather uncomplimentary remarks about the work of Canter. There can be research funds and reputations to be gained if experts can impress government of profiling's potential and their own superior expertise in the field.

It can be seen how the social constructionist account urges us to take a sceptical look at what is 'known' about serial killers and to ask different sorts of questions. As we have seen, it asks about the fascination that seems to exist with such offenders in the wider society. Seltzer (1998: 109) suggests that this is one manifestation of the 'wound culture' that characterises the USA: 'the public fascination with torn and opened private bodies and torn and opened psyches, a public gathering around the wound and the trauma'. The popularity of such TV programmes as Jerry Springer, Oprah, Ricki Lake, and ER are other elements in a culture in which serial killing appears as a 'career option', a way of claiming an identity, a role for which popular psychology has already provided scripts (profiles).

A similar question is asked by Duclos (1998) who answers that

Anglo-American culture is attracted to uncommon killers because they reflect its own image as an uncommon society. They are a reminder of its legendary tales, which transmit deep-seated values and in which violence has always had a central role as something which is at once desired and feared.

(Duclos 1998: 7–8).

His attempt to trace some of the elements of this culture to Germanic and Norse myths is one highly individual (and sometimes strained) example of the focus upon *representations* of violence and murder. Cultural representations may not only have an influence on the nature and extent of serial murder, but they may help to structure the data collected by researchers (such as the way in which killers attempt to represent their actions in interviews) in a very significant way. However, such an approach still leaves us with the question of why particular individuals find themselves taking on the role of serial killer. Giving an answer to this question is rather more difficult than we might have thought.

Post-mortem

Much of the research on serial murder follows a particular pattern that is common in criminology. Much of it has been concerned with definitions, estimations of its extent and trends, and the development of typologies. A great deal of work has been involved in gathering information on such matters as the methods used, the locations for killings, and the characteristics of victims. One major impetus for this has been to gather knowledge that might help in the investigation of crime and the formulation of policy. More important from a theoretical point of view has been the attempt to identify biological, psychological and sociological factors which might help us to make sense of this kind of murder. As in criminology in general, the quest has been to develop a theory that might help us to explain why these crimes occur. Such theories are ideally tested by empirical research, in order to see how valid they are. Even by its own standards of good procedure, such empirical work on serial murder has been based on shaky foundations. Most samples are confined to apprehended offenders who may not be typical or reliable; secondary sources, such as newspapers, have often been used, rather than primary sources; sample sizes have often been very small; and there has been no agreed definition of the use of the term (Kiger 1990: 37); for various other reasons too that we have discussed, such offenders are some of the most difficult to research by conventional techniques.

An alternative strategy is to work from the 'bottom up' – to accept the difficulty of the task and to concentrate on a particular case study at a time. To build understanding by attempting to grasp the totality of one case, rather than jumping to the development of a general theory, which may in any case be a false quest. Such understanding should be theoretically informed, however, drawing on principles and findings of academic study in a wider context. Otherwise it can be nothing more than journalism. As an example, Jefferson (1997: 546) praises two works on Peter Sutcliffe, the 'Yorkshire Ripper', which he claims 'render life comprehensible, at least after a fashion'. Both (Smith 1989; Ward Jouve 1988) draw on the ideas of psychoanalysis and masculinity to argue that his background and events in his development, 'repeatedly demonstrating his failure to live up to the social expectations of manliness, led him first to blame the feminine in himself, to hate part of himself, and then externalize that hatred and destroy women' (Jefferson 1997: 545). Those who might object that there must be more to it than that are, of course, quite right. The devil is, almost literally, in the detail and we cannot do justice to it here:

> It was a grisly resolution. It was not inevitable. It was in some sense chosen. But it is a resolution and a choice that displays a logic only within the detail of a life observed through a lens of masculinity which is simultaneously social and psychic, alert to the multiple contradictions within and between these dimensions, the anxieties and ambivalences these set up, and the compounding influence of contingencies.
>
> (Jefferson 1997: 545–6)

The two broad approaches outlined here are not necessarily contradictory or mutually exclusive. Much of the literature on serial murder attempts some combination of them. However, some would argue that, with serial murder, and perhaps with certain other kinds of crime, the second broad approach is currently more likely to add to our understanding than the first.

Finally, we have encountered another perspective on serial murder, which does not take its primary task as attempting to understand why a given type of crime occurs. Instead, it looks at the way in which a particular problem or crime has been socially constructed, and the various sources of that particular construction. The focus here is on representations of serial murder, and the notion that such representations can be deconstructed to reveal the processes and interests that contributed to them. This illustrates perspectives that have been introduced earlier in this book; the implication is that we should not simply accept the way in which a problem has been defined and the seemingly authoritative 'knowledge' presented to us, but to examine them in a questioning frame of mind. This can tell us something about our society, its culture and the way in which it defines and reponds to crime and the offender.

Chapter 5

Policing and the police: key issues in criminal justice

Introduction

The police are by far the most visible institution of the criminal justice system. While most people will have had little or no contact with prisons, probation or the courts, there must be few who by the age of majority have not come into personal contact of one kind or another with the police. Indeed, for the most part, the police want to be seen. Their distinctive uniforms with helmets fashioned to elevate their stature, and their clearly marked patrol cars equipped with sirens and flashing blue lights are clearly designed to draw attention to themselves. This is, of course, no accident; the police are the visible presence of the state in civil society.

From the establishment in London of the New Police in 1829 by Sir Robert Peel, visibility was the order of the day. There were originally to be no detectives who could move freely among the citizenry in plain clothes, for this would resemble a continental model of policing which, as one parliamentary committee of the time declared, 'would be odious and repulsive' to the British idea of liberty. Nor were the police to be attired in the fashion of the military, for one of the prime justifications for the setting up of the New Police was the failure of the army to maintain order without recourse to gross and excessive force. This had occurred with some frequency in the preceding fifty years and most tragically at Peterloo, when in 1819 a demonstration was set upon by the army and hundreds were injured and eleven people killed.

When, therefore, on 29 September 1829 the citizens of London beheld the spectacle of groups men being marched to their beats dressed in 'blue-tail coat, blue trousers ... and a glazed black top-hat strengthened with a thick leather crown' (Critchley 1978: 51), they were witnessing the birth of a new institution. It was an institution that was symbolically differentiated from both the military and continental models of policing through its distinctive uniform (modelled on civilian business dress of the day), and effectively differentiated by its mandate, which was first and foremost preventative. This was to be achieved by providing a visible deterrent to acts of crime and disorder. As the new Commissioners wrote in their first force instruction: 'It should be understood that at the outset the principal object to be obtained is the prevention of crime.'

The public visibility of the police can be contrasted with the relatively low visibility of the police in the criminological endeavour. Traditional criminology largely ignored the police: Ferri's book on *The Positive School of Criminology*, published in 1906, hardly mentions them; sixty years later Mannheim's (1965) major 800-page, two-volume work *Comparative Criminology* had no discussion of the police institution. Even as late as 1979, Holdaway (1979: 1) could write: 'the relative dearth of research into the British police has achieved the status of a cliché amongst sociologists. The British police have remained largely hidden from sociological gaze.'

Criminological theory was essentially concerned with why people broke the law and neither an analysis of law nor its enforcement seemed relevant to this discussion. It was assumed that the relationship between police and the law was straightforward: the police simply enforced the law. Criminology paid little attention to how and why criminal sanctions came to be invoked by the police against certain types of behaviours and not others. Nor did it ask whether sanctions were applied equally to all individuals engaged in similar types of infraction. In fact, even when this problem was raised by authors such as Merton (1938) or Morris (1957), it was asserted that police records and statistics based on them, despite their limitations, did adequately represent the distribution of crime – in particular, that crime was concentrated among the lower classes. Attention was not, therefore, focused upon police organisation or the practice of enforcement.

In the formative and middle years of the development of criminology, the police institution was thus either ignored or seen as non-problematic. However, all this was to change with the publication of Howard Becker's *Outsiders: Studies in the Sociology of Deviance* (1963), which was to become a key text in the emergent interactionist and labelling approaches to the study of crime and deviancy. Becker's simple and even trite assertion that deviant behaviour is that which is so labelled (see chapter 3) heralded a decisive shift in the criminological agenda, both in scope and method.

The crucial role of the police in identifying and labelling persons and actions as deviant was increasingly recognised by criminologists. What had previously been taken for granted was now up for debate and examination. In particular, Becker and others expanded the criminological gaze to include in its focus not just law-breakers, but law-makers and law enforcers as well. The process of law creation was important to Becker and the interactionist school because it raised questions about why only some deviant acts were criminalized. This, in turn, raised questions about how some social groups were able to assert their power to make criminal the activities of others. The processes of enforcement were seen as important because Becker and others did not assume a simple translation of the 'law in the books' into the 'law in action'. The rate of criminal behaviour in a society was to be understood from the interactionist perspective as the product of actions of persons within the criminal justice system who defined, classified and recorded those behaviours as criminal – and these activities were themselves worth of study.

For the interactionists, it was not the quality of the act that was important to understanding deviancy, but the label applied to the act. This means that they were not interested, as traditional criminology had been, in the constitutional, psychological or physiological characteristics of offenders, but in the processes leading to a person being officially defined and labelled as deviant. The focus of criminological interest was thus shifting away from offenders and deviants *per se* towards the criminal justice system itself, its component parts and its processes. Given that the police are the most important gatekeepers of the criminal justice system and therefore highly influential in determining who is officially labelled as criminal, criminological research on the police and policing assumed a new importance. And for the interactionists, this required a different methodology – not studies of crime rates and aggregate statistics but, ideally, detailed and in-depth observational studies of the actual practice of policing.

In the 1960s and 1970s then, there was a gradual opening up of the police institution to criminological and sociological scrutiny, often informed by the concerns of labelling theorists and interactionists. As Reiner has noted,

> The most characteristic type of work was close participant observation of police patrol work, primarily concerned with laying bare the occupational culture of operational policing...in order to describe and account for the rules and meanings that constitute it
>
> (Reiner 1992b: 441)

However, once Pandora's box was opened, these early concerns gave way to new issues. The police became interesting in their own right, and in the 1980s in Britain the issues of public order (signalled largely by widespread riots in inner city areas), police efficiency and effectiveness (given prominence by the Conservative government's concern with 'value for money' and limiting overall public expenditure) and miscarriages of justice (many of which were shown, in part at least, to have emanated from poor or corrupt policing methods), all gave rise to the police institution being subject to an intense criminological gaze.

In the rest of this chapter we propose to outline what we regard as some of the key issues which have preoccupied criminologists in studying the police over the past four decades:

- Definitions and delivery: what do we mean by 'the police' and 'policing'? What do the police do? Is their primary role the control of crime?

- Discretion and discrimination: how does police discretion operate? Does it discriminate against certain groups in the population? In this context, we discuss the concept of police culture, which has frequently been used to explain the way in which police discretion is exercised.

- Due process and deviancy: to what extent does police practice conform to a 'due process' model? How does police malpractice in violation of due process come about?

Definitions and delivery

The word 'police' is derived from the Greek word 'polis', meaning city. As Johnston (1992: 4) notes, before the eighteenth century, in English the word 'police' was used to refer to the general governance and administrative regulation of the city. Thus the activity of policing embraced the whole range of functions necessary for the maintenance of civic society, and if this broader definition were still in currency today, it would include the activities of tax inspectors, environmental health officers and school-crossing patrols. Indeed, until the 1970s, the police in most parts of England and Wales retained responsibility for such matters as taxi-licensing, dog-licensing, diseases of animals and animal movement orders and abattoir inspections. However, as Johnston (1992: 4) argues:

> It was only in the mid-eighteenth century that the word 'police' began to be used, in its continental sense, to refer to the specific functions of crime prevention and order maintenance. From then, it was but a short step to defining 'police' in terms of specific personnel.

What this means is that when we use the terms 'to police' or 'policing' we tend to equate them with what the police currently do, rather than with their broader historical meaning. Indeed the most contemporary definition of 'police' in the Oxford English Dictionary reflects this shift, since both the personnel and function are conflated in the same definition:

> The civil force which is entrusted with the duty of maintaining public order, enforcing regulations for the punishment or prevention of breaches of the law and detecting crime. (*OED*)

The importance of this is that as criminologists we need to be careful about simply equating policing with the police. Other agencies (such as Customs and Excise and the Factories Inspectorate) perform policing functions, and Shearing and Stenning (1987) and Johnston (1992) have argued that the neglected but important growth of the private security sector also requires criminological attention. This is of particular significance, given that in 1994 it was estimated that the private security industry had a turnover of nearly three billion pounds and employed in excess of 164,000 personnel; it is therefore starting to rival the police in terms of expenditure and has already overtaken them in terms of manpower (Morgan and Newburn, 1997).

Moreover, private companies are encroaching on duties that have been the traditional preserve of the public police. Court security and the associated prisoner escort is an obvious example. In Doncaster in 1996 Household Security, a private company, employed eleven staff to provide car and foot patrols to residents at a cost of one pound a week to each subscribing household (Sharp and Wilson, 2000). Thus the increasing importance of the private security industry and the blurring of the boundaries between public and private police reminds us that merely to equate the activity of policing with the police misses a vast amount of activity which should come under the banner of policing.

So far we have stressed the inappropriateness of conflating policing with the police but this does little to tell us how to define what the public police do. The most common way of dealing with this problem is to define the police by their functions. As we have already seen the original instructions to the New Police issued by the first Commissioners stressed that:

> the principal object to be obtained is the prevention of crime ... to this great end every effort of the police is to be directed. The security of person and property, the preservation of the public tranquillity, and all other objects of a police establishment will thus be better effected than by the detection and punishment of the offender after he has succeeded in committing the crime.
>
> (quoted in Critchley, 1978: 52;
> see also Morgan and Newburn, 1997: 76)

In the early 1960s the Royal Commission on the Police reviewed these aims for the first time in 130 years and although they extended the roles somewhat to take into account the modern circumstances of the police, the prime responsibilities of the police were still defined as being:

- to maintain law and order and to protect persons and property.

- to prevent crime.

- to be responsible for the detection of criminals.

Some thirty years later a joint sub-committee of the Association of Chief Police Officers (ACPO), the Superintendents' Association and the Police Federation also presented a definition of the police in terms of their core functions. In their *Statement of Common Purpose and Values* they state:

> The purpose of the police service is to uphold the law fairly and firmly; to prevent crime; to pursue and bring to justice those who break the law; to keep the Queen's Peace; to protect, help and reassure the community; and to be seen to do all this with integrity, common sense and sound judgement.
>
> (quoted in Morgan and Newburn 1997: 77)

We can see that over the course of over 170 years there is a clear continuity in these functionally based definitions of the police: the prevention or crime, the detection of crime, the enforcement of law, and the maintenance of order remain at their heart. For some this represents the genius of the original formulation. However, there has been a growing dissatisfaction amongst criminologists with defining the police by a set of idealised roles which, some argue, are largely unattainable. To examine the source of this dissatisfaction, we intend to examine the extent to which the police are able to fulfil these functions

Enforcement, prevention and detection: the police role examined

Ironically, the majority of police work is not related to law enforcement. For instance, Punch's study of calls for police assistance in three East Anglian towns revealed that between half and three-quarters of all re-quests for assistance were for 'service', such as dispute settlement and attending at road accidents, rather than law enforcement functions (Punch and Naylor 1973). Ekblom and Heal's (1982) study of incoming calls to a subdivisional control room confirmed Punch's earlier findings. Only 18 per cent of calls required the preparation of a fresh crime report and calls relating to service functions made up by far the greatest proportion of demand. In Punch's terms, the police represent a 'secret social service'. It is secret because of the lack of recognition of the wide range of such tasks routinely performed by officers. These early findings have been confirmed by more recent studies: Morgan's (1990) study and Waddington's (1993) study found that, respectively, only around 35 per cent and 25 per cent of calls to police were crime related. Shapland and Vagg (1988: 39) argue that the attempt to categorise calls into simple categories like 'crime' and 'service' at the outset is fraught with difficulties; their study categorised calls for service according to whether they *might* involve crime. On this basis over half of calls (53 per cent) were categorised as 'potential crime'.

If a different measurement device is used, that of task analysis of how patrol officers spend their time, then even smaller proportions of police activity are shown to be directly related to law enforcement. A study by Comrie and Kings (1974) showed that, in both rural and urban settings, only about 6 per cent of a patrol officer's time was spent on incidents that are finally defined as criminal. This figure is broadly supported by the findings of the 1988 British Crime Survey which estimated that only 18 per cent of contacts between police and public were crime related (Skogan 1990), although the Islington Crime survey, based on a Inner City London borough, found that 51 per cent of contacts concerned crime (Jones *et al* 1986).

The accumulated evidence from various ethnographic studies also confirms, and gives colour to, the broad range of non-crime related activities that the police are called to deal with (Banton 1964; Cain 1973; Holdaway 1983; Policy Studies Institute (PSI) 1983: Vol. 4; Norris 1989). From our own experience of the reality of routine patrol the following tasks would not be untypical of the tasks falling to uniformed patrol officers:

- looking after a lost child

- dealing with sudden and unexplained deaths

- attending the scene of a road traffic accident

- securing entry for a resident to check on the safety of an elderly neighbour whom she has not seen for two days

- moving on some youths who are playing football in a private residential street

- taking a report of a burglary that happened while the residents were at work

- settling a dispute between two neighbours about the ownership of a parking space

- moving on a drunk who has collapsed in a doorway

- informing a local resident that their father died earlier that morning and asking them to make contact with their family

- attending the scene of a noisy party and asking the occupants to turn the volume down

- warning a group of youths not to play on a building site as it was potentially very dangerous

- helping a bus driver evict a passenger who had sworn at him and refused to leave the bus.

The list could go on. Name any source of human conflict or emergency situation and the police have undoubtedly been called to deal with it. In the light of this, Egon Bittner (1974) suggests that the key function of the police is to deal with 'something-that-ought-not-to-be-happening-and-about-which-something-ought-to-be-done-now'. What is important is that it is largely the public, not the police, who define which situations require police intervention.

Although much police work is not directly related to law enforcement and crime control, it is often argued that the presence of patrols on the street has a deterrent and preventative function. A study conducted some years ago found that some 55 per cent of patrol officers' time was spent on random and uncommitted patrol (Comrie and Kings, 1974). Studies of both car and foot patrols tended to question the deterrent effect of patrolling. Both British and American data indicated that, although some patrol presence is necessary to deter potential offenders, the precise number of foot or car patrols made very little difference; it is only when patrols were removed completely that reported crime increases (Bright 1969; Kelling *et al* 1974).

This was hardly surprising, since foot patrol officers are only as effective as far as their eyes can see and ears can hear and, for that matter, so are car patrol officers. As Clarke and Hough (1984: 7) pointed out in their review on the literature on police effectiveness:

> given present burglary rates and an evenly distributed patrol coverage, a patrolling policeman in London could expect to pass within a hundred yards of a burglary in progress once every eight years and even then not realise that the crime was taking place.

To become a real deterrent, the level of patrolling would have to be increased to a point where the chance of discovery and detection of crime was a high probability, which is not an economically feasible proposition. Furthermore, burglars are well aware that the likelihood of being caught is low; therefore, any realistic increase in the level of foot patrol would be liable to have little effect. These findings were endorsed by the Audit Commission's (1993) evaluation of police patrolling strategies which concluded that they were grossly inefficient as a means of controlling crime. In recent years, police strategies have therefore attempted to shift towards a more proactive and intelligence-driven approach.

In the past, it was commonly thought that a system of reactive policing, with the primary aim of a swifter response to calls for assistance and complaints, was the strategy to replace traditional patrolling (e.g. Home Office 1967). Unfortunately, the theory behind rapid response generally failed to take into account the length of time that callers take to contact the police after they have discovered an offence. Ekblom and Heal's (1982) study found that over 60 per cent of callers had delayed at least five minutes before calling the police; Beick and Kessler's (1977) study in the USA found that over 50 per cent of people took between twenty and forty minutes before calling the police, with victims often discussing with relatives and friends what action they should take before calling. Quite clearly, rapid response is severely limited in its effectiveness by the delay between incident and reporting.

Contrary to the popular mythology surrounding police investigations which portrays them as involving painstaking detective work, piecing together disparate clues to put a name to an unsolved crime, the police are highly dependent on victims and witnesses for the identification of offenders. Burrows and Tarling's (1982) study of records drawn from three metropolitan police forces illustrates that the police are responsible for detecting either directly or indirectly only about 15 per cent of recorded crime. There now seems to be a general consensus of research findings that the public is primarily responsible for the detection of between 83 and 85 per cent of cleared-up offences (Steer, 1980; Mawby, 1979; Bottomley and Coleman, 1981).

In a recent review of detective effectiveness, Bayley concluded that detectives:

> know if perpetrators cannot be identified by people on the scene, the police are not likely to find the criminals on their own. Nor is physical evidence especially important in determining whether a case is pursued, it is used as confirmation – to support testimony that identifies suspects ... in short criminal investigators begin with identification, then collect evidence: they rarely collect evidence and then make an identification. If a crime can not be solved on the spot, the case will probably be closed and the detectives will move on to more promising cases.
>
> (Bayley 1996: 35–36)

These generalisations are not necessarily true for serious crime, but with most other offences, if the offender is apprehended, it is usually because they are caught red-handed or because a victim or witness can give specific information on the person who committed the offence. When the police do not have such information, the probability of detecting offenders is very low (Loveday 1996). Perhaps this is best illustrated by the case of the Yorkshire Ripper manhunt which, by July 1979, months before he was caught, had involved 500 police officers, 250,000 officer hours and had cost over three million pounds (Nicholson 1979). More recently, there has been a massive police effort in trying to establish the identity of the killer of Jill Dando, the presenter of BBC's *Crimewatch* programme, who was gunned down in the street by an unknown attacker in 1999. Forensic evidence, and such techniques as criminal profiling, have an obvious appeal in such cases, in which the investigation is pursued well beyond that in many other crimes.

In summary, then, it can be argued that the police have little effect on the prevention of crime, spend relatively little of their time dealing with it and do little to detect it. This should not be read as a criticism of the police, but merely a description of the reality of police work. It is however, for Bayley, a criticism of those who peddle definitions which seek to equate police work with a set of functions that they cannot fulfil. For him this is surely a recipe for disaster in three ways. First, more and more money is pumped into the police institution on the basis of a false understanding of what the police can achieve. Second, it leads to an undermining of public confidence in the police, as they are seen to fail. Third, it does nothing to address the problem of crime. Instead of a focus on crime, what is needed is a definition of policing which encapsulates the range of functions into some form of thematic unity. With this in mind, we now want to focus on the work of three criminologists, one British, Paul Rock, one American, Egon Bittner, and one Canadian, Richard Ericson, each of whom has tried to formulate a thematic definition of policing.

Paul Rock

Rock (1973) argues that there is indeed a functional unity to all the various police activities in that they are related to the primary role of being 'responsible for the boundary patrolling tasks of a system of social control. They control those deviancies which are proscribed both by external law-giving institutions and by their own law-interpreting behaviour' (Rock 1973: 174).

To perform this primary role, there are subsidiary functions which facilitate its implementation and these are what Rock (1973: 183) terms 'the incidental and unintended consequences of police work'. Thus, the range of non-crime-related tasks that the police find themselves involved in are a necessary price to pay for the police 'to continue to function as effective agents of control' (Rock 1973: 184). The involvement in these subsidiary tasks is a mechanism which enables the police to perform their primary control function without undue recourse to coercive measures, by cloaking the office in a shroud of legitimacy. Further, such interventions enable informal contacts with the community, resulting in an increased information flow about other, more serious matters. Thus, the 'coercive role style is tempered by a benign complexion' (Rock 1973: 184); coercive power is transposed into legitimate authority by the diversity of tasks that the police are prepared to engage in.

Although he regards non-crime tasks as subsidiary, merely involved in generating legitimacy to facilitate other primary tasks, Rock does alert us to the danger of seeing the police solely in terms of the enforcement, detection and prevention of crime. If other activities are seen as peripheral, they are in danger of being hived off to other institutions, such as private security guards, city wardens, social workers, and the like, so that the police can get on with their 'primary role'.

These ideas gained strong currency during the 1990s, especially in the Home Office. The Conservative Government White Paper on police reform (Home Office 1993) was clear in its view that the 'main job of the police is to catch criminals' (para 2.3). The view that there are 'ancillary' tasks that might be relinquished, leaving the (expensive) police free to concentrate on their 'core' task of controlling crime, was the impetus behind the Posen Inquiry (Home Office 1995), whose deliberations met with considerable resistance from police staff associations and in the end was hardly radical in its recommendations. The police role received yet more attention in the form of an independent inquiry set up by the Police Foundation and the Policy Studies Institute (1996). The report endorsed the police service's definition contained in the Statement of Common Purpose and drew upon research studies to conclude that the police can only have a limited impact on crime.

As Loveday (1996) has pointed out, the experience of Los Angeles, which in the early 1990s prioritised crime control above service and low-level order maintenance, does not support the idea of police concentration on crime. In LA, general patrol police officers were replaced by specialist units concerned with a narrow focus on crime control and, as a result, officers were not available to respond to the more mundane calls for service. There were, ironically, two consequences of this strategy: crime rates remained the same and Los Angles experienced the worst rioting in the USA for thirty years, after the police were filmed brutally beating a black suspect, Rodney King (see Loveday 1996: 96). In a special report commissioned by the Los Angeles police into the causes of the riots, it was argued that the development of specialist squads and a narrow focus on crime control had led to a situation where citizens only came into adversarial contact with the police. The report concluded that:

> The public, therefore, only saw the police pulling people over, standing over prone suspects and in other tense confrontational situations. It is not surprising that members of the community viewed the LAPD with fear and a degree of hostility.
>
> (quoted in Loveday, 1996: 97)

By making legitimacy the concept that unifies the diverse police functions with the core mandate, Rock has identified an important element of British and American police traditions. However, he still sees policing as being defined primarily by its law enforcement functions and this, as we have argued, is inappropriate. Egon Bittner in his book *The Functions of the Police*

(1975) sought a different solution to the problem of definition, by concentrating on the *means* rather than the *ends* of policing. He argued that the key to identifying the distinctive element of policing was in its use of force.

Egon Bittner

Bittner recognised that while other public and private officials had the right to use force to achieve their ends, these were strictly limited to their specific spheres of competence. Prison officers could only use force inside a prison, mental health officials on those in their care, parents on their own children, and so on. The police, on the other hand, have the right to use force against any person across the whole domain of a domestic territory and for a whole range of purposes. Thus he wrote: 'the role of the police is best understood as a mechanism for the distribution of non-negotiable coercive force, employed in accordance with the dictates of an intuitive grasp of situational exigencies' (Bittner 1978: 33).

At first reading, this seems a remarkably obscure way of defining the police: it certainly does not trip off the tongue, but that is because it is trying to move beyond the specific to find a level of generality that would make it universally applicable. If you read it again slowly, you will see that there are three principal elements to the definition.

First, the police are *a mechanism for the distribution of non-negotiable coercive force*; by saying this Bittner is drawing attention to the fact that modern states have attempted to limit the use of coercive force by private citizens, and have delegated this function to the police. The police thereby become the mechanism for its distribution by deciding when, where and against whom it is used.

Second, the police use *non-negotiable coercive force*. By *non-negotiable* Bittner means that if a police officer decides to use force in a situation it is difficult for anyone to legitimately challenge him or her; true the officer might face a complaint or criminal prosecution later on, but at the time they do not have to brook arguments or opposition – in that sense it is non-negotiable.

Third, this force is *employed in accordance with the dictates of an intuitive grasp of situational exigencies.* By this Bittner is noting that the justification for the use of force, as such, cannot be entirely derived from any external prescription. True, the law specifies the legitimate police use of force (in England and Wales s.3 of the Criminal Justice Act 1967 prescribes the circumstances and degree of force which can lawfully be used), but it cannot say exactly when and where it may be used: that can only be decided in the light of a police officer's particular reading of a particular situation at a particular time.

As Bittner notes, the utility of this definition is that it lends 'homogeneity to such diverse procedures as catching a criminal, driving the mayor to the airport, evicting a drunken person from a bar, directing traffic, crowd control, taking care of lost children, administering first aid and separating fighting relatives' (Bittner 1978: 38).

What has coercive force got to do with taking care of lost children? Bittner has the answer: if a lost seven-year-old is taken to the police station, the sergeant will probably try to keep him happy with sweets and fizzy drinks; if the child tries to leave before his parents arrive the sergeant will undoubtedly prevent him, if necessary by putting him in a room and locking the door.

Bittner's definition has been highly influential in providing a basis for analysing patrol work. However, there has been one notable criticism of Bittner. By making power and force equivalents, Bittner has made the other resources at a police officer's disposal subsidiary. As the PSI report notes (1983: Vol. 4: 173), 'the great majority of police officers habitually try to avoid using more force than is necessary'. Even in adversarial situations, the police rarely resort to coercion to secure compliance (Southgate and Ekblom 1986). Nor is this only true of British policing: in Reiss's (1980) study in the USA, over 90 per cent of arrests were managed without recourse to gross force, i.e. physical coercion, threat or handcuffs. The definition therefore obscures the diversity of strategies used to achieve compliance (Muir 1977; Bittner and Bayley 1983; Fielding 1984). In our view this is not a fatal criticism, but one that requires addressing.

Richard Ericson

Ericson attempts address this criticism by proposing a definition which specifies the function of policing. As we have seen, most incidents that the police involve themselves in do not end up with a crime report being filed, nor do the police have much effect on either the prevention or detection of crime. In the light of this, Ericson proposes that:

> The mandate of police patrol officers is to employ a system of rules and authoritative commands to transpose troublesome, fragile situations back into a normal or efficient state, whereby the ranks of society are preserved ... . Therefore the patrol police are essentially a vehicle in the reproduction of order.
>
> (Ericson 1982: 7)

The importance of this is that it allows thematic unity, as does Bittner's definition, but without prejudging the resources that are used to reconstitute order. It locates the police firmly as the guardians of the status quo. However, by focusing on reproduction, the question of order is made problematic; it is not merely transmitted but 'continually worked at through the process of conflict, negotiation and subjection' (Ericson 1982: 7).

Unity is derived at the level of function rather than of technique; the police are seen as restitutive in the variety of situations that they encounter. But the definition is not imperialistic in specifying 'whose' order. As Sykes and Brent (1983: 28) note, the police are often called into situations not as 'enforcers' of a public legal conception of order, but as 'reinforcers' of localised private normative conceptions of order. This results because people confuse their 'private informal order with the formal legal order'. In this situation, legal sanction is often inappropriate. Donald Black (1980), in his chapter on dispute settlement, makes the point that people call the police because the resources they possess for the resolution of conflict are insufficient. In the majority of these incidents, police officers are called to act as conciliators to try to reconcile conflicting parties. As Ericson notes, the resources that officers bring to bear cover a wide range, including the:

> general authority of his office; his procedural legal powers to detain, search, and use of physical force; his substantive legal powers to charge; and various manipulative strategies that form part of the recipe knowledge of his craft. In short, he 'negotiates order' variously employing strategies of coercion, manipulation and negotiation.
>
> (Ericson 1982: 9)

Ericson was primarily concerned with the work of patrol police in generating his definition. For completeness, Bayley also includes the work of detectives in specifying the functions of the police. Drawing on the work of Ericson, he conceptualises the modern police as performing two major functions: authoritative intervention and symbolic justice. Authoritative intervention is what most uniformed officers are responsible for and this is:

> almost wholly reactive, rarely anticipatory. Crime is involved only occasionally or ambiguously. The purpose of authoritative intervention is to restore order. Almost no attempt is made to correct the underlying conditions that have led to the need for police intervention.
>
> (Bayley, 1996: 34)

Symbolic justice, on the other hand:

> is the realm of detectives and traffic officers: also largely reactive, it is achieved through law enforcement. Its purpose is demonstrative, to show offenders and the public that a regime of law exists … . The success of the police in rendering symbolic justice is almost entirely dependent on information supplied by the public.
>
> (Bayley, 1996: 34)

Although we would argue that the distinction between uniformed and detective officers is somewhat overdrawn (for instance, in the UK uniformed officers make the majority of crime arrests – see Chatterton 1976), the overall point is correct. Public policing is largely concerned with achieving authoritative intervention to reproduce order, and imposing symbolic justice through the pursuit and arrest of offenders. Finally, there is also clearly a great deal more that could be said about the changing forms and functions of policing in late modern societies, including, as we have already suggested, the way in which 'public policing' is only one form of policing alongside others (see Johnston 2000).

Discretion and discrimination

As Waddington (1999: 31) has rightly observed: 'Prior to the revisionism of the 1960s, the prevailing assumption was that policing was little more than the application of law'. As we have seen, much criminological attention has been aimed at challenging this assertion. But what in practice does it mean 'to uphold' or to apply the law? Does it mean that whenever a law is broken the police must enforce it? If this were true, the police would merely be puppets of the legal system, blindly enforcing the law regardless of context or consequence. What we know from detailed studies of police work in Britain (Banton 1964; Cain 1973; Holdaway 1983; Waddington 1993), America (Black 1980; Rubinstein 1973; Van Maanen 1978; Bayley 1994) and Canada (Ericson 1982) is that this could not be further from the truth. The police use law, among a number of other resources, in order to restore order and impose symbolic justice. They are not slaves to law but law is their servant. This realisation is of profound importance because it signals the centrality of discretion to understanding police work. In this next section we want to examine the nature, consequences and importance of discretion.

Discretion

What is police discretion? Drawing on Davis's (1969) seminal, but general definition of discretion, Klockars proposed the following:

> A police officer or police agency may be said to exercise discretion whenever effective limits on his, her or its power leave them free to make a choice amongst possible courses of action or inaction.
>
> (Klockars 1985: 93)

We can note three salient points about this definition. First, Klockars does not use the word 'law', but the words 'effective limits'; this is because even where the law may insist on a course of action (in America there are 'full enforcement' statutes), if there is no mechanism for ensuring that officers comply, they are 'effectively' able to choose. In the context of police this is very important, since one of the most striking aspects of the police organisation is that the degree of discretion is greatest at the lowest level of the hierarchy, partly because much police work outside the station is of such low visibility to managerial oversight (Goldstein 1960).

Secondly, discretion is not just a property of individual police decisions in dealing with particular incidents, but of departmental policies, structures and organisation which frame those individual decisions. For instance, the setting up of a local robbery squad to tackle a recent rise in street crime is a discretionary decision, albeit one taken at a managerial or organisational level. Discretion at this level has been reduced in England and Wales since the Police and Magistrates Courts Act 1994. This enables the Home Secretary to set national policing objectives, and police authorities must produce annual local policing plans and set performance targets to measure the achievement of objectives.

Thirdly, the exercise of discretion can involve doing something or not doing something. This is important because the term 'discretion' has sometimes been equated with a questionable decision not to arrest someone where there were legal grounds for doing so. The important thing to note is that, in English law at least, the decision to arrest is itself discretionary.

Let us take a simple example to illustrate this point. Imagine that a police officer is called to the scene of two men fighting on a street corner. They are still fighting when the police arrive. The officer could:

- break it up with an informal warning to both participants and take no other action

- break it up, inquiring into the cause and attempting to conciliate and mediate between the two parties

- formally caution one or both parties

- attempt to find the cause of the fight and arrest the person they believe to be the most blameworthy

- arrest both parties on any appropriate public order or assault charges.

(Lustgarten 1986: 10)

As Lustgarten has rightly argued, 'all the suggested options are within the range of a constable's legal powers. To say therefore that he must uphold the law, or is responsible to the law, is in practical terms meaningless' (Lustgarten 1996: 11).

If discretion is so subversive to our notion of the rule of law, why do the police have it? In general there have been four major justifications for the existence of police discretion:

- the finite resources available to perform police work

- the need for interpretational latitude in applying law

- the need to preserve legitimacy

- the need for efficiency.

We will examine each in more detail below.

Resources
Given that the police have finite resources, they have to make choices about how to deploy them and this inevitably means prioritising some activities over others. Moreover, if the police were rigorously to enforce some high volume offences like speeding, the capacity of others within the criminal justice system to process them, such as the Crown Prosecution Service and the courts, would soon be exceeded. As already noted, however, the scope for discretion in setting priorities has been lessened by the Police and Magistrates Courts Act 1994.

Interpretational latitude
The law as it is written in the books purports to be clear and unambiguous, but the messy reality of life rarely falls easily into the neat categories of the law. All criminal statutes in England and Wales say that 'a police constable may arrest...'. Police officers have to interpret what they find to find a fit between the events and the law, and they need to temper the law with notions such as justice/fairness and appropriateness. As Klockars (1985: 98) notes, the law 'overreaches' itself and criminalizes more than it intends. For instance, would the interests of justice be served by prosecuting a surgeon for travelling at ten miles an hour over the speed limit, on her way to perform life saving surgery, or the driver of a vehicle which due to his own carelessness had swerved off the road resulting in the death of his wife and daughter? Probably not.

Legitimacy
Full enforcement would lead to an undermining of the basis for police legitimacy. One of the advantages of under-enforcement is that the police can build up credit with a citizenry who, in acknowledgement that they have been dealt with more favourably in the past, are more likely to cooperate with police requests for help in the future. 'Policing by consent' is a key concept in this context. At the extreme, some have argued that full enforcement would completely undermine the social fabric: 'Any society that committed the energy, resources and personnel to root out and punish all wrongdoers would set off enough mass paranoia, violent conflict and savage repression to become a charnel house, and pass into oblivion' (Blumberg, 1970, cited in Rock, 1973: 179).

Efficiency

A policy of full enforcement would not allow the police to differentiate between important and trivial crimes, and between cases where some productive outcome can be achieved and those where this is unlikely. Where resources are finite (see above), decisions need to be made about the most efficient or effective use of them. Full enforcement would also make it impossible for the police to 'trade' the threat of sanction for information. One of the key investigative strategies, especially in 'victimless' crimes, of letting the little fish go, in exchange for information so that bigger fish can be caught, would be unworkable (see Dunnighan and Norris 1999).

Criminologists have, then, recognised the inevitability of discretion, that police work is only partially concerned with law enforcement, and even when there are clear infractions of law, there is no guarantee that arrest and prosecution will follow. This realisation has had two major implications for criminology.

First, that recorded crime statistics cannot be treated as an accurate or reliable measure of the nature, distribution and extent of criminality. As Kituse and Cicourel noted, crime rates should be 'viewed as indices of organisational processes rather than as indices of the incidence of certain forms of behaviour' (Kitsuse and Cicourel 1963: 135). This insight led to a number of important studies documenting how crime statistics were a social construction (Bottomley and Coleman 1981; McCabe and Sutcliffe 1978; Young 1991), and the development of alternative measures of crime and victimisation which are not reliant on police processing, such as self-report studies and victimisation surveys (see Coleman and Moynihan 1996 for a review).

Second, if the law does not provide the full answer as to what police officers should do in a situation, attention shifts to what else influences their decisions. As Klockars points out, this issue strikes at the heart of democratic governance, with its emphasis on 'the rule of law'. As he writes:

> Under a government of laws police should not be allowed to make what amounts to their own laws, amend laws that have already been made, or decide that some people should have certain laws enforced on them while allowing others to violate the same laws with impunity. The whole idea of the police enjoying some broad discretionary power seems to open the door to arbitrariness, favouritism and discrimination.
>
> (Klockars 1985: 95)

For this reason, much criminological attention has been focused on what, given such discretion, shapes police decision-making and the extent to which this leads to policing which is *discriminatory*, in the sense that the law is unevenly applied in relation to different social groups in a way that is 'unjustified by legally relevant factors' (Reiner 1992a: 162).

Discrimination

There is little doubt about the existence of what Reiner calls differentiation – that the exercise of police powers falls disproportionately upon some groups rather than others. Police enforcement activity largely falls upon the young rather than the old, the poor rather than the affluent, men rather than women, the urban rather than the rural, public rather than the private domains, and so on. Whether and to what extent differentiation involves discrimination are more difficult questions to answer. For illustrative purposes, we will briefly concentrate on two areas: the 'over-policing' of black people and the 'under-policing' of incidents of domestic violence.

The 'over-policing' of black people

The 'over-policing' of black people has been consistently documented by a range of studies at the level of stops, arrests and post-arrest decisions:

Stops: studies have consistently found that black people are more likely to be stopped than whites, with estimates ranging from between two and four times what one would expect on the basis of their presence in the population. Not only is the rate of stops greater, but a black person is more likely to be repeatedly stopped during the course of a year (Willis 1983, PSI 1983, Skogan 1994, Norris *et al* 1992, Macpherson 1999).

Arrests: studies by Stevens and Willis (1979), PSI (1983), Walker *et al* (1990) and Phillips and Brown (1998) have all found evidence of a higher black arrest rate than one would expect from their presence in the population. For instance, one of the most recent surveys, Phillips and Brown (1998), found that in eight out of the ten police stations they studied, black people were between two and eight times more likely to be arrested than whites.

Post-arrest decisions: studies have also revealed how other areas of police discretionary decision-making also seem to disadvantage black people, such as in the choice of charge (Blom-Cooper and Drabble 1982), the decision to caution rather than commence formal proceedings (Landau and Nathan 1983, Jefferson and Walker 1992, Phillips and Brown 1998) and the decision to recommend bail (see FitzGerald 1993 for a review).

Of course, one possible explanation for these differences is that black people actually do commit certain types of crime more than whites and are therefore are more likely to be targets of police action. In this case, it could be argued that the differentiation is justified on the basis of differential offending profiles of the black and white communities. Despite this issue being hotly debated amongst criminologists (see Reiner 1992a, Lea and Young 1993), there is no easy resolution to it. For example, we do not in this instance have enough satisfactory studies of relative crime rates that are independent of police practice. There have been few self-report studies of offending behaviour that have looked at ethnic differences, although one of the few to have been conducted in this country (Bowling *et al* 1994, Graham and Bowling 1996) found no significant differences between black and white self-reported offending. However, this study has been criticised on methodological grounds (Coleman and Moynihan 1996). As FitzGerald (1993: 4) wrote in her report to the Royal Commission on Criminal Justice, 'it is impossible to know the precise extent of ethnic differences in offending rates once all other relevant factors are taken into account [such as age, employment status, area of residence, etc.]; and this makes for uncertainty in interpreting ethnic differences at the point of entry'. The broad consensus amongst many criminologists is that while differences in offending behaviour may explain some of the over-representation of black people in the criminal justice system, they only explain *some* of it (Lea and Young, 1993; Smith, 1997).

For some commentators (see particularly Gilroy, 1982; Bridges 1983), the over-enforcement of law against black people can be explained by the informal norms, values, attitudes and beliefs which they see as comprising the occupational police sub-culture. In particular they draw on the findings of a raft of ethnographic studies, which document the use and prevalence of racist language by the police and a range of negative attitudes towards black people in general. From this it is argued that it is easy to see how police discretion produces over-enforcement: it is the result of officers' prejudice and discriminatory behaviour.

However, following Reiner (1992a), we would argue that the pattern of differentiation cannot be seen as simply a product of higher rates of offending or as simply arising from attitudes found in the police sub-culture; the process is far more complex and multi-layered than this. Taking the evidence from various observation studies (including James 1979; Holdaway 1983 and PSI 1983: Vol. 4), Reiner (1992a: 157) argues that categorical discrimination (i.e. action against members of a particular group only on the basis that they are members of that group) is probably the least important form of discrimination that may be operating. If discrimination does occur, it is more likely to be operative because of other practices which are outside of the purview of the individual police officer, or not related to his or her attitudinal values. These additional forms of discrimination Reiner terms transmitted, interactional, institutionalised and statistical discrimination (Reiner, 1992a: ch 4).

- *Transmitted discrimination* operates because the police are heavily dependent on calls from the public and, thus, differential enforcement rates may result. If the public are more likely to call the police to incidents involving members of ethnic groups, then it is discrimination by sections of the public rather than the police that is operative. Furthermore, in their role as dispute settlers, the police are often dependent on the preference of the complainant as to what action to take and a higher arrest rate for ethnic groups may be the result of public prejudice.

- *Interactional discrimination* results from the officer using discretion, not on the basis of legally relevant criteria, but on aspects of the interaction between the suspect and the officer, such as the level of respect accorded by the suspect to the officer. The greater the disrespect shown, the more likely that an arrest will follow. Given relationships between some young black people and the police, such groups may thus be more likely to have formal action taken against them. As Reiner (1992a: 167) notes, while 'contempt of cop' is not a valid reason for arrest, it may provide a possible basis for a valid booking of a suspect who would otherwise have been let off.

- *Institutionalised discrimination* can arise, for example, from the more intensive policing of particular areas with high rates of crime and deprivation (which may also be areas of greater black residence). Thus, particular sections of the community living in those areas are dis-proportionately stopped, searched and arrested. Thus police policies and procedures at an organisational level 'may work out in practice as discriminatory because of the structural bias of an unequal society' (Reiner 1992a: 158).

- *Statistical discrimination* can be a predominant factor in proactive polic-ing, especially in stop and search operations. If the lifestyle of a group is thought to involve a legally proscribed activity, such as New Age travellers or Rastafarians using marijuana, those identified as a member of that group can become a target for police attention. An attempt has been made to rule out stop and search on the basis of such things as appearance and apparent lifestyle by the Police and Criminal Evidence Act 1984. However, such practices may perhaps be one reason why black people are more likely to be arrested as a result of proactive policing strategies (see Phillips and Brown 1998: 38–9). Even so, it should be remembered, as Reiner points out, that the basis for such actions is a misguided concern with effectiveness – by targeting those thought to be the most 'likely' suspects. The Stephen Lawrence Inquiry

(Macpherson 1999) concluded that 'institutional racism' was apparent in a number of areas; in its view, despite the complexities involved in the interpretation of the evidence, there remained 'a clear core of racist stereotyping' (para 6.45) in stop and search.

The 'under-policing' of incidents of domestic violence

If the police appear to over-enforce the law in relation to black people, then conversely it has been shown that in relation to domestic violence, the law is under-enforced. Detailed empirical studies, mainly carried out in the 1970s and 1980s, have shown how the police were reluctant either to arrest or prosecute perpetrators of domestic violence, even when there was clear evidence of an offence having been committed (Pahl 1982, Edwards 1989). Moreover, even when the police did arrest, it was often for an offence of less seriousness than the evidence would warrant, such as for 'breach of the peace' rather than 'assault occasioning actual bodily harm'. As Kemp, Norris and Fielding (1992: 119) concluded:

> Our research indicates that police officers as a matter of course tend to decriminalise domestic disputes where there is evidence of a criminal infraction. Even when there is a *prima facie* case for arrest and charge ... they under-utilise their legal powers in order to achieve an informal resolution, recommend civil proceedings or make an arrest on resource [usually lesser] charges.

In a similar way to that in which the over-policing of black people has been attributed to the values and beliefs of officers transmitted through the occupational culture, so too has the under-enforcement of laws relating to domestic violence. Again some commentators note the prevalence of sexist language, stereotypical attitudes towards women in general, the marginalisation and harassment of women police officers, and a general-ised belief in the inappropriateness of police intervention in domestic affairs, consigning it to the status of 'rubbish' work. From this it is argued that it is easy to see how police discretion produces a pattern of under-enforcement; again it is seen as a result of prejudiced attitudes and values contained within the occupational culture (Edwards 1989, Stanko 1985). There have been concerted attempts to change police policy and attitudes in this area in the last decade or so since these studies were conducted.

There are, however, problems with academic accounts and policy initiatives which see a simple translation of attitudes into behaviour. For instance, Hoyle's (1998) study of the policing of domestic violence found that a general open-ended question to police officers about domestic disputes elicited a whole range of negative responses, but these generalised attitudes were often belied by how they said they handled specific disputes. As she reported:

The initial comments were indicators of how domestic disputes are still, to some extent, trivialised by officers within a canteen culture discourse, whilst the response to questions about what officers actually did in practice indicate the divide between certain negative cultural attitudes and behaviour.

(Hoyle 1998: 76)

This gap between attitudes and behaviour was similar to that reported in relation to 'race' some years ago by the PSI study *Police and People in London* (1983):

Our first impression ... was that racialist language and racial prejudice were prominent and pervasive and that many individual officers and also whole groups were preoccupied with ethnic differences. At the same time, on accompanying these officers as they went about their work, we found that their relations with black and brown people were often relaxed and friendly ... we are fairly confident that there is no widespread tendency for black or Asian people to be given greatly inferior treatment by the police.

(PSI, 1983: 109 and 128)

This possibility of a gap between what officers say and what they do undermines the simplistic use of a concept of occupational culture (usually based on what officers say) as guide to, and explanation for, actual police behaviour (usually that considered undesirable)

A number of criminologists (Holdaway 1983; Norris 1989; Hoyle 1998; Manning 1977; Waddington 1999) have adopted a more complex view of police culture, which recognises that while police culture may have negative and undesirable traits, in itself that culture has to be understood as embracing far more than just negative attitudes. Police culture may still be used to help explain the difference between law in action and the law in the books, but that culture is seen as arising from the common problems that officers face in the course of their work. It not only contains attitudes and beliefs, but a stock of recipe knowledge on how to achieve the policing task: a set of working rules for managing the vicissitudes of the job (Manning 1982). And here it should be remembered that the job is not primarily about the prevention of crime or the enforcement of laws but about reproducing order by providing authoritative intervention and symbolic justice. As Chatterton (1983: 208) has argued:

The decisions and actions taken at incidents reflect the concern to control relationships between themselves and the various publics on a division, to maintain their capacity to intervene authoritatively in any incident and to preserve their own and others' beliefs that they were 'on top of the area'.

Moreover, officers are also concerned with satisfying organisational demands that incidents are satisfactorily terminated: for example, that once a police officer has dealt with an incident they are not called out again, for this would suggest that the officer failed to negotiate or enforce an effective closure to the incident in the first place, raising questions about his or her competence (see Chatterton 1983: 201).

It should be stressed that such issues as over- and under-enforcement and discrimination and differentiation cannot be understood in terms of the police culture alone, but have to be seen in terms of the complex inter-relationships between the individual officer, suspects, the public, the occupational culture, the police organisation, the law, and the police role.

Thus the ideal of law is of even and equal enforcement and therefore that similar offences should be treated in similar ways. The patrol officer, on the other hand, is not primarily concerned with such abstract notions in individual encounters, but with authoritatively intervening to reproduce order. Meanwhile, the occupational culture provides a set of 'recipe rules' for determining how this should be achieved, such as that disrespectful and uncooperative suspects deserve to be arrested, and about the extent to which victims' preferences should be taken into account (Waddington, 1999; Hoyle, 1998). Simultaneously, the police organisation, as represented by the shift sergeant and inspector, is less concerned with the specific outcome of any individual incident than with its speedy termination on the ground and bureaucratic resolution at the station. Dealing with incidents quickly and effectively and 'clearing the message pad' so that an officer is free to deal with the next potential emergency becomes a primary goal in reactive policing (Fielding *et al* 1989). In this context arrest, which will take an officer away from routine policing, may be seen as an undesirable outcome; on the other hand, targets in policing plans may encourage arrests to be made, so a balance has to be struck. Finally, we should add that the officer also brings to any incident their own individual norms and values, which make the individual officer the 'final arbiter and mediator' of the legal, organisational and cultural influences (Fielding, 1988: 60). In this context, the concept of police culture can only be one possible contributor to our understanding of police discretion.

Due process and deviancy

Not only is there law which defines the range and nature of criminal offences (such as murder or theft) – substantive criminal law – but there is also law which attempts to regulate the treatment of those suspected of crime – the law of criminal procedure. There are legal rules which govern such procedures as stop and search, search of premises, arrest, and the detention and questioning of suspects. For example, the Police and Criminal Evidence Act 1984 and its associated Codes of Practice were a major attempt to provide for police and suspects a set of procedures in these areas that would be clear, workable, fair, open and accountable. There are also a whole host of subsidiary rules governing police practice set down in non-statutory guidelines and force standing orders. Such rules, it is often asserted, ensure that police powers are not exercised arbitrarily, but constrained by the 'due process of law'. As Sir Robert Mark, the former commissioner of the Metropolitan Police, expressed it, 'The fact the British Police are answerable to law, that we act on behalf of the community and not under the mantle of government, makes us the least powerful, the most accountable and therefore the most acceptable police in the world' (Mark 1977: 56).

One of the most enduring yardsticks for evaluating the operation of legal rules and the criminal justice system has been the model developed by Herbert Packer (1968; see also King 1981) in the late 1960s. Packer argued that systems of criminal justice can be usefully examined to see what extent they correspond with two theoretical models: due process and crime control. The models are 'ideal' types, each at either end of a continuum; we would be unlikely to find a pure due process or crime control model in reality. Let us briefly examine each in turn.

Due process

For Packer, a due process model emphasises the following.

- Rules protecting the suspect or defendant from error: for instance, as identification evidence is notoriously unreliable, it is essential that when the police carry out identity parades they are conducted in accordance with strict protocol and procedures.

- The presumption of innocence: the police are not the arbiters of guilt and innocence; this is the proper function of the courts. The role of the police is to lay before the courts all the available evidence so the court may judge. The police should therefore be under a duty to disclose evidence which is helpful to the prosecution case but also to the defendant. Nor is it the role of the accused to incriminate themselves and thus they have a right to silence.

- Effective restraints on the use of arbitrary power: for instance, the police may only arrest and detain on the basis of evidence, rather than on personal whim or prejudice, and there must be effective means of reviewing these decisions

- An equality between the parties: suspects and defendants should be able to draw on similar resources to the police in order to defend themselves against charges brought against them. For instance, the right of legal advice at the police station is a due process requirement which seeks to balance the power of the police with the rights of the suspect.

In the context of policing, the due process model sees the inviolability of legal rules governing police powers as essential. The rules are there to protect suspects against arbitrary power and when the rules are broken cases should be dismissed, since otherwise this might lead to error and the chance of a wrongful conviction.

Packer likened the due process model to an obstacle course which guarantees that only those most likely to have committed a crime will proceed to the next stage. Any weakness or impropriety at an earlier stage will ensure that a case is discontinued. If it is not, there is a chance that the innocent will be found guilty and, above all, the due process model seeks to protect against this eventuality.

Crime control

In the crime control model, the following are examples of features that would be emphasised:

- Disregard of legal controls: departure from legal propriety is seen as inevitable. Formal legal rules get in the way of convicting the guilty and therefore police malpractice is tolerated and even condoned.

- Implicit presumption of guilt: the police are seen as acting in good faith, so that when they arrest and charge someone it is because they are guilty. In this case there is little necessity for the courts to thoroughly review cases before them; their job is merely to rubber stamp the decision.

- High conviction rate: under a crime control system a high conviction rate is necessary because if the courts were to acquit too many people this would undermine the deterrent effect of the criminal law, and the faith in police efficiency at bringing the right people to justice.

Whereas the primary function of the due process model is the acquittal of the innocent, the crime control model prioritises the punishment of the guilty.

The enduring significance of the two models has been in the realisation that while policing is presented as being in line with due process values, this rhetoric is undermined by the operational reality of police practice.

This was particularly highlighted by the spate of miscarriages of justices which led to the setting up of the Royal Commission on Criminal Justice in 1991. A recurring feature in many of the cases was the role of the police in fabricating evidence, the use or threat of violence or other non-legal sanctions to obtain confessions, and the failure to disclose information relevant to the defence (see Rozenberg 1992 for a review of these earlier cases).

This should come as no surprise to criminologists, who have frequently discovered the predominance of crime control practice rather than due process values to be at the heart of police work. To take three examples:

The right to legal advice

Even though access to legal advice is a fundamental due process right which tries to ensure fairness and equality between the suspect and their interrogators, Sanders *et al*'s (1989) study on the provision of legal advice at the police station found that a variety of police practices had the effect of discouraging suspects from seeking such advice.

The supremacy of the courts

Dunnighan and Norris (1996, 1999) have argued that the fundamental due process principle of English law that the police must never mislead a court has been routinely undermined in the police use of informers. They found, from a sample of 31 police prosecution case files which had involved official payment to informers, that in not a single case was the role of the informer disclosed to the Crown Prosecution Service. Furthermore, one-third of officers said they would be prepared to lie in court to protect an informer.

Fabrication of evidence

The findings of the Independent Inquiry into the working practices of the West Midlands Serious Crime Squad (Kaye 1991) revealed that in every one of the 67 cases reviewed it had been alleged that officers fabricated incriminating evidence. In 23 of these cases charges were dropped, the judge directed acquittal, the jury found the defendants innocent or the conviction was quashed on appeal (Kaye 1991: 72–73).

How can we explain this subversion of due process values? One answer to the question is that such acts are the result of the aberrant behaviour of individual officers who had gone off the rails. From this 'rotten apple', perspective it is argued that any organisation employing tens of thousands of people is bound to contain the occasional maverick. However good the recruitment, training, and supervisory systems, occasionally someone will slip through the net. There are two fundamental problems with such a position.

First, unlike with most deviant or criminal acts, the malpractice exposed in these cases does not, in any direct sense, result in personal gain. 'Rotten apple' theories may have utility in explaining some instances of police corruption where the motivation is straightforwardly financial. In cases where the deviant police behaviour is to ensure the judicial punishment of the accused, there is, however, no direct personal gain. It is therefore necessary to explain what motivated the individuals concerned to commit such acts (so-called 'noble cause' corruption).

Second, in the light of evidence from the major miscarriages of justice, it is not feasible to consider them as resulting from the actions of the isolated deviant. In the Birmingham Six and Guildford Four cases, for instance, the malpractice required the active cooperation and connivance of colleagues and supervisory officers. These were thoroughly group affairs. Senior and supervisory officers condoned the denying of suspects their legal rights and participated in the physical abuse of suspects, and officers of all ranks perjured themselves in the witness-box to support their colleagues' malfeasance. Even those who were not actively involved were implicated by their willingness to remain silent.

In the Birmingham Six case, it was precisely the fact that so many would have been implicated in having participated or acquiesced in a cover-up that was used to undermine the defendants' case at trial and subsequent appeal. According to the trial judge, if the Six were telling the truth the police 'had been involved in a conspiracy unprecedented in the annals of British criminal history' (Mullin 1987: 201).

The issue of police malpractice, then, cannot be understood in isolation from the organisation in which it occurs and the role that the organisation has in suppressing or facilitating deviant behaviour.

As Sir John Woodcock, Her Majesty's Chief Inspector of Constabulary at the time of the Royal Commission on Criminal Justice observed:

> For many, many years, in truth and in anecdote, the judicial system was complicit in police wrongdoing, wrongdoing that the police were allowed to believe, firstly, was only part of a game and, secondly was necessary to shore up the eccentricities of the judicial system. Police malpractice of this kind is primarily the fault and responsibility of police leadership. However, such malpractice could not long exist save in an atmosphere which tolerated it, even, might I say, required it, and to that extent other parts of the criminal justice system have been complicit in police misbehaviour.
>
> (Woodcock 1992: 5; see Rose 1996: 38–41 for further such comments.)

But this perhaps does not go far enough, for it is not just individual police officers and the police organisation which can subvert due process, but the law itself.

As McBarnet (1979, 1981) has argued, in practice the law often favours crime control rather than due process. Thus, while many police researchers have described the rule-breaking and illegality of the rank and file practices, McBarnet carefully illustrates how crime control practices were enshrined in the law, particularly *ad hoc* case law, in Scotland of the 1970s (McBarnet 1981: ch 3). The consequence was that:

> the police are in a sense the 'fall guys' of the criminal justice system, taking the blame for any injustices in the operation of law, both in theory (in the assumption ... that they break the rules) and indeed, in the law. ... The law on criminal procedure in its current form does not so much set a standard of legality from which the police deviate as provide a license to ignore it.
>
> (McBarnet, 1979: 39)

Her work has a wider significance in pointing to the possibility of 'a clear gap between the rhetoric of legality and the actuality of law in both the procedures laid down and the reasoning behind them' (McBarnet 1979: 39). In our concentration on 'police deviance' we must not neglect the law itself, assuming by default that it is the embodiment of the rhetoric of legality. In England and Wales, for example, a great deal of effort has been expended on the law of criminal procedure. As we have suggested, the Police and Criminal Evidence Act 1984 and its associated Codes of Practice were a major attempt to provide a set of clear, workable, fair, open and accountable procedures for the treatment of those suspected of crime. Opinions differ on this legislation and its impact (see, for example, Dixon 1992, 1999 on the debate about this).

McBarnet (1981) makes a further telling point: where the police operate within what is called an adversarial system of justice (as opposed to an inquisitorial one), this leads to a 'winner takes all' attitude, which effectively militates against the police engaging in a dispassionate search for the truth. An adversarial system, such as the one we have in England and Wales, is one where the judge in a court of law leaves the presentation of the evidence to two sides: defence and prosecution. This can 'turn a search for the truth into a contest played between opposing lawyers according to a set of rules which the jury does not necessarily accept or even understand' (Royal Commission on Criminal Justice 1993: 3). In this system, the police are encouraged to identify with one 'side', and direct their energies towards its support. Again, this point alerts us to the need to be aware of the wider context within which policing takes place when we consider issues of due process and police deviance. It is insufficient to point simply to 'rotten apples' or to 'police culture' as explanations.

Conclusions

- The police should not be equated with policing, an activity that can be performed by a number of agencies. The role of the police is better thought of as the reproduction of order by authoritative intervention and symbolic justice, rather than in terms of crime control.
- Given the constraints, police discretion is inevitable and even desirable. Police powers fall disproportionately on certain groups in the population. Although the situation is complex, it appears that some part of this is discriminatory. It is misleading simply to attribute such discrimination to individual attitudes or 'police culture'.

- While criminal justice processes are usually presented in terms of 'due process' values, certain police practices have been shown to violate such values, and to be more consistent with a 'crime control model'. Rather than being understood in terms of 'rotten apples', examples of police malpractice in violation of due process values seem to be related to the organisational context in which they occur, and to the wider legal framework and the adversarial system within which they are located.

Chapter 6

CCTV and crime prevention: questions for criminology

In this chapter we want to explore how criminologists have responded to the dramatic rise of CCTV (closed circuit television) as a crime prevention strategy. First, we want to briefly examine the concept of crime prevention and locate CCTV as a particular type of crime prevention activity within a broader social and political context. Second, we want to highlight what has often been seen as one of the core concerns of criminology: the evaluation of criminal justice policy initiatives to provide evidence as to 'what works'. Finally, we want to consider the broader questions raised by CCTV, particularly those addressed by criminologists operating from a more radical or critical perspective.

Crime prevention

There are many ways to prevent crime and criminologists have sought to delineate and differentiate the main strategies involved in crime prevention. Although there is a variety of classifications (see Hughes 1998 and Pease 1997), for our purposes the typology developed by Weiss (1987) is most useful. Weiss identifies three main types of crime prevention activity: primary, secondary and tertiary; we will examine each in turn.

Primary crime prevention is focussed on the offence rather than the offender, and is often associated with situational crime prevention strategies which focus on the immediate and localised context of the offence. At its simplest, primary prevention may involve target hardening or removal. Target removal strategies can include such measures as the switch from public telephones that require coins to ones accepting only telephone cards. Hardening strategies might include fitting metal grilles to shop windows, steering locks to cars, and pavement bollards to prevent ram-raiding. Most significant for our discussion, they include enhanced levels of surveillance, such as by increasing the numbers of security guards, or through the use of CCTV cameras.

Secondary crime prevention is concerned with offenders rather than offences and seeks, by intervening in the lives of those who are most at risk of offending, to prevent them committing crimes in the future.

Tertiary crime prevention strategies focus on reducing or preventing the criminality of already known offenders, and this will typically involve forms of rehabilitation programmes with convicted criminals.

These three different types of crime prevention strategies prioritise different aspects of the relationship between the individual and society. Tertiary strategies have often been the province of the probation officer or prison psychologist who, by working with individuals or small groups in a therapeutic relationship, tries to 'treat' and therefore change the offender. This might take the form of programmes of 'anger management' for those convicted of domestic violence, or drug treatment programmes for those whose offending is driven by addiction. In the main such strategies are underpinned by a their concerns with the differences between offenders and non-offenders which we discussed in chapter 2.

Secondary crime prevention, on the other hand, aims to intervene before an offence has been committed, and divert potential offenders from embarking on a criminal career. For instance, it could involve taking 'at risk' teenagers on a visit to a local prison in an effort to deter them from starting a 'life of crime'. More broadly, it may involve creating leisure facilities for youth so as to reduce 'time for crime', or setting up a job creation programme, to counter the effects of youth unemployment, with the aim of reintegrating the most economically and socially marginal. These strategies tend to emphasise the social context of crime rather than individual differences, and tend to be theoretically located in the theories we discussed in chapter 3.

Primary crime prevention, however, is neither concerned with the wider social structural causes of crime nor interventions aimed at fundamentally altering the individual. In secondary and tertiary strategies, crime is conceptualised as being caused by a deficit, whether it be inadequate socialisation, lack of self-control, blocked opportunities, lack of jobs, or inadequate parenting skills. In primary crime prevention, particularly in its guise of situational crime prevention, crime is seen as normal. Drawing on rational choice theory, crime is seen as being committed by individuals who, having weighed up the cost of benefits of crime, choose crime. Central to this is an evaluation by the potential offender of two questions:

- will I succeed in carrying out the crime?

- if I do succeed, will I get caught?

If the answer to the first question is 'yes', and the second 'no', for those so motivated, crime is likely to occur. However, the aim of primary preventative strategies in any given local context is to alter the balance of probabilities so that the answer to the question, 'will I succeed?' is 'no' and 'will I be caught?' is 'yes'.

Primary preventative strategies do not therefore try to change the basic motivation of the offender but to increase the costs and risks associated with committing a particular crime at a particular time. It is therefore concerned with opportunity reduction, through target hardening and removal, and increased chance of detection though surveillance. Moreover, crime is not seen as 'determined' by individual traits or social pressures; offenders are not propelled into crime by forces outside of their own control, but choose to commit crime, and therefore can be held accountable for their actions. In short, situational crime prevention is grounded in the traditions of classicism rather than biological, psychological, or social positivism, and just as the history of criminology can be seen as a battle between these two competing visions, so too can the history of crime prevention (Roshier 1989).

As Jock Young has argued (1994), in the post-war period (1945–1972) the debate about crime and its control was largely dominated by what he calls social democratic positivism. In this model it was assumed that crime was a product of poverty and other forms of hardship and deprivation. With the coming of the welfare state with the provision of free universal health care and education, full employment polices, and a social security safety net, it was often assumed that the major causes of crime would be eradicated. Where crime still arose then rehabilitation programmes, aimed at correcting the faults of inadequate psyches or faulty socialisation, would mop up the residual problem cases. In this era, secondary and tertiary strategies were in the ascendency.

But, as many now argue, history did not validate the beliefs of the social democratic positivists. Throughout the 1950s and 1960s social conditions improved, incomes rose, full employment was the norm, but crime, rather than falling, continued to rise. It was not just faith in secondary crime prevention that was undermined, but the rehabilitative ideal, embodied in tertiary crime prevention strategies also came under attack. In the mid-1970s several influential reports were published which showed that rehabilitation programmes were largely ineffective (Martinson 1974; Brody 1976; Folkard 1976). This also chimed with the changing political climate; the New Right, championed by Margaret Thatcher in Britain and Ronald Reagan in the US, combined economic liberalism, reduced public expenditure and an emphasis on individual moral responsibility, with

populist law and order policies. In this context, rehabilitation could be seen as absolving criminals from moral responsibility, and pandering to the needs of offenders, while social intervention programmes, which located the causes of crime in wider structural terms, could be neither ideologically nor economically justified. Ideologically, individual moral weakness was blamed for criminality, while economically the need to reduce public expenditure would not permit such expensive rehabilitation programmes.

The appeal of primary crime prevention strategies comes, then, not just from their supposed efficacy, but also from their depoliticisation of the problem of crime. As Ron Clarke, one of the leading exponents of situational crime prevention has noted, it relies 'not on improving society or its institutions, but simply on reducing opportunities for crime' (Clarke 1992: 4).

Situational crime prevention techniques do not raise awkward questions about the relationship between wider social processes and crime, and exclude consideration of issues such as inequality, justice and fairness and how these may contribute to crime. Thus for the New Right, committed as it was to a fundamental restructuring of economic and social relations, which in the short term, at least, would inevitably result in mass unemployment and a massive increase in inequality, situational crime prevention could be seen as particularly attractive. Because of its emphasis on free will, blame for crime could be located squarely at the door of the individual 'rational' offender, rather than on structural forces. Moreover, primary prevention does not necessarily entail large-scale public expenditure programmes. Indeed, part of its great appeal is that the state can pass on the costs of crime prevention to businesses, consumers, and private citizens, who are urged to buy locks, bolts and alarms.

As we have seen, one of the core elements of situational crime prevention strategies is increased surveillance, coupled with target hardening and removal strategies. The introduction of CCTV seeks to influence the decison-making of the 'rational' offender who, on calculating the risks, will choose not to commit crime under the gaze of the cameras because there will be a strong possibility of being caught. It is therefore primarily a strategy based on deterrence, although, of course, even if it does not deter it should presumably increase the chances of an offender being caught. It is perhaps then the common sense simplicity of this logic, coupled with its underlying ideological and political appeal, that accounts for the dramatic rise in CCTV surveillance in Britain over the last decade.

The rise of CCTV

In Britain, at least in the 1990s, CCTV totally dominated the crime prevention programme of the Home Office. Bulos and Sarno (1994) found that there were only two local authority schemes in operation in 1987. By 1994 the Home Office indicated there were 79 town centre schemes (Home Office, 1994); by 1996 all the major cities with a population over 500,000 boasted city centre schemes, and there were in excess of 200 police and local authority schemes operating in high streets and smaller towns (Norris *et al* 1998: 255); by 1998 this had risen to at least 440 town centre schemes (Goodwin *et al* 1998).

In financial terms, between 1994 and 1997, central government made available £37 million to fund the introduction of CCTV schemes, but on the condition that local authorities and private business also contributed an equal amount. Indeed Goodwin *et al* calculated that some 78 per cent of the Home Office crime prevention budget was committed to CCTV during this time. Moreover, the trend does not appear to be slowing down, as in 1999 it was announced by central government that a further £170 million would be made available to fund the introduction of new CCTV schemes or to extend existing ones in town centres, car parks, residential communities and other crime 'hot spots' (Painter and Tilley 1999: 2).

It may be thought that the rush to install CCTV during the 1990s was based on a firm foundation of supporting research evidence to show that it was effective. This was not so. CCTV was introduced in town centres, and the government funded its expansion, *prior* to conducting any systematic evaluation of its effectiveness in reducing crime in such locations. What evidence did exist prior to 1994 came from small-scale evaluations on systems in car parks (Poyner 1992), buses (Poyner 1988), housing estates (Musheno *et al* 1978), football stadia (Hancox and Morgan 1975), and the London Underground (Burrows 1979). As Short and Ditton note, the results of these independent and competently conducted evaluations were 'fairly contradictory regarding the effectiveness of CCTV as a crime prevention method' (Short and Ditton 1995: 11), with some initiatives showing no effect (Musheno *et al* 1979), others suggesting high levels of displacement, rather than an overall reduction (Burrows 1979), and others showing clear reductions (Poyner 1988 and 1992).

However, between 1988 and 1992 the Conservative Government had witnessed an almost unprecedented growth in recorded crime from just under four million offences to just under six million; for the party of 'law and order', this represented a major policy failure and a potential electoral disaster. In early 1993 however, CCTV was thrust into the limelight by two events. First, there was the tragic killing of the two-year-old toddler, Jamie Bulger, as his abduction by two ten-year-olds was caught on camera. Second, the two men responsible for planting a bomb outside the Harrods department store in London were subsequently identfied from CCTV footage. In the glare of national publicity to which CCTV was subjected in the wake of the Bulger case, the few schemes that did exist boasted major benefits from its introduction. It is hardly suprising that the beleaguered

Home Secretary should jump at this 'silver bullet' which, through its very public introduction onto city streets, would visibly show the government was doing something to stem the inexorable rise in recorded crime. As he stated in May 1995:

> CCTV catches criminals. It spots crimes, identifies law-breakers and helps convict the guilty. The spread of this technology means that more town centres, shopping precincts, business centres and car parks around the country will become no-go areas for the criminal ... CCTV is a wonderful technological supplement to the police.

However, the evidence for the Home Secretary's belief in the 'wonderful' technology was not that of the professional and independent evaluator but from 'post hoc shoestring efforts by the untrained and self-interested practitioner' (Pawson and Tilley 1994). And as Pease has recently observed, 'for those exercising stewardship of public money, good evidence about effects should be necessary before public money is spent, although one is tempted to ask where rigorous standards went in the headlong rush to CCTV deployment' (Pease 1999: 53). Thus even though hundreds of millions of pounds have been spent on CCTV over the last decade, by business, local communities and central government, there are still major questions about its effectiveness.

Does CCTV reduce crime? Methodological concerns

At first sight this would appear to be a simple question to ask and many people probably think that they already know the answer. Indeed, representatives of the police, politicians of all persuasions, and members of the CCTV industry have consistently answered the question with a resounding 'yes', and this belief has been endorsed by largely uncritical and complacent media coverage (Norris and Armstrong 1999: chapter 4). However, one of the key remits of any academic discipline is to challenge taken-for-granted assumptions, and criminology has an obligation to subject crime and its control to critical scrutiny. The first task in the process is to analyse apparently simple questions and lay bare their underlying assumptions in the hope that we might be able to answer them more satisfactorily. To answer the question, 'does CCTV reduce crime?', it is necessary to consider three crucial elements contained within it:

- what is meant by CCTV?

- what is meant by crime and how can it be measured?

- what is meant by a reduction in crime and what would constitute satisfactory evidence of a reduction occurring?

151

We will address each of these questions in turn.

What is meant by CCTV?

The first problem we must confront is: what exactly is CCTV? As Graham (1998) has shown, CCTV is actually a very diverse phenomena, both technically, organisationally and contextually. Technically, at its simplest a CCTV system consists of a single static camera coupled directly to a monitor by coaxial cable; these were the earliest CCTV systems installed in many retail establishments from the 1960s onwards, and are still found today in many newsagents and corner shops. A slightly more sophisticated system might have a number of fixed cameras and be coupled to both a monitor and a video recorder, enabling images of past events to be scrutinised at a later date. This sort of system would be not untypical of many that are found in small towns and villages throughout the United Kingdom.

At a higher level of sophistication are systems that include pan, tilt and zoom cameras (PTZ), which can be controlled from a central point and used to track people and vehicles as they move through space, and zoom in to take close-up pictures for the purposes of identification. Such high level systems may link hundreds of cameras, both fixed and PTZ, allow for time-lapse recording of signals from multiple video inputs, and display the video images on a huge bank of monitors, which can be watched generally but 'pulled down' to the operative's dedicated monitor and recorded in real time, if there is something of interest (see Constant and Turnbull [1994] for a discussion of the technical aspects of CCTV).

It is not just in the level of technical sophistication that systems vary, but in their organisational implementation. Systems vary in their staffing, ownership, management and linkages. They may be staffed by police officers, employees of private security companies, police civilian employees, or local authority employees. In operational terms some systems are completely 'unmanned' and the tapes only reviewed after an incident comes to light, while others are 'manned' twenty-four hours a day. Systems also vary in their ownership and management; some are owned and fully controlled by the local police, while others are owned, run and housed by the local authority. In some systems the CCTV control room is fully integrated (and housed) within the police command, control and dispatch system, while others rely on technological linkages such as telephone and monitors to link them to a dispatch capability.

Finally, the range of contexts in which CCTV systems are deployed is enormous; city centres, urban high streets, market towns, and villages all now boast CCTV systems. While city centre systems watch over largely anonymous spaces inhabited mainly by busy commuters and pedestrians merely 'passing through', village systems monitor a more stable and intimate community with the watchers often knowing the personal identities of those under the camera's gaze. Moreover, CCTV has been deployed in a variety of institutional settings, from schools to hospitals, to football stadia and transport systems. In a recent initiative in Hull, CCTV cameras are to be deployed in the back of taxi-cabs, in order to deter loutish behaviour and fare evaders.

So, if we want to answer the question, 'does CCTV reduce crime?', we need to be clear about what CCTV is. Clearly there is a huge variation in technological and organisational arrangements between systems, and this has important consequences for our ability to generalise about the effectiveness of CCTV. This relates to what evaluators term the problem of external validity. In the main, when researchers carry out a study they aim to make claims that go beyond the single case of their experiment or study so as to be able to generalise their findings to a wider community. Even if researchers themselves are often wary about the applicability of their findings to different settings, others may be much less hesitant.

As Jupp notes researchers have distinguished two types of external validity, population validity and ecological validity. Population validity refers to the extent to which the findings can be generalised to the wider population, and ecological validity refers to the extent to which the findings can be generalised to other contexts and settings (Jupp 1989: 55). For instance, if a study showed that the introduction of CCTV reduced crime by 16 per cent, we cannot simply assume that a different CCTV system, deployed in a different place, targeting a different crime problem, with a system of different technological sophistication would have the same impact.

What is meant by crime and how can it be measured?

In asking the question 'does CCTV reduce crime?', we assume that there is something called crime, or more accurately a crime rate, which is susceptible to variation and that these variations can be accurately and reliably measured. Crime prevention evaluations in general and CCTV evaluations in particular have chosen to utilise 'notifiable offences recorded by the police' as their measure of the crime rate. However, the relationship between the crime rate, as represented by the crimes officially recorded by the police and the 'real' rate of criminal victimisation, is highly problematic (see Coleman and Moynihan [1996] for a review of this issue).

To count as a crime by this definition, crimes have first to be reported to the police by victims or witnesses; secondly, having been reported, they have to be officially recorded by the police. However, as the 1997 British Crime Survey (BCS) revealed, only half (44%) of offences on which it collects information from victims were reported to the police, and there was considerable variation in this figure between different offence types. Whereas 97% of thefts of vehicles were reported to the police, only 57% of robberies, 43% of thefts from vehicles and 35% of thefts from the person were reported (Mirrlees-Black *et al* 1998: 19). And we can see from Table 6.1 that not all of these were actually recorded by the police. Overall the BCS suggests that only about half (54%) of all such offences reported to the police are recorded, which means that the recorded crime figures only account for a quarter (24%) of the underlying crime rate, although this ranges from 84% in the case of motor vehicle theft to 10% for theft from the person.

This has some highly significant implications for measuring changes to the crime rate. This would be of little concern if there was an invariant relationship over time between reporting and recording rates but this is not the case. According to the BCS, between 1981 and 1997 the overall rate of reporting BCS offences to the police has fluctuated between 36% and 49%, and between the years 1991, 1993 and 1995 the rate of reporting for burglary from 73% to 68% to 66%. Similarly the rate of reporting theft of and from vehicles has consistently reduced from 56% to 53% to 51%. In Table 6.2 below we show the effect that changes in the public reporting rate and police recording rate between the years 1991 and 1995 would have on the trends in recorded crime.

In the context of CCTV, imagine a system being introduced to a mixed residential and shopping area in early 1992, where the evaluation took as its base-mark the recorded crime rate in 1991. These figures were then compared with the figures for 1993 and 1995. If the trends revealed in the British Crime Survey were replicated at the local level, regardless of the impact of the CCTV system, the official police recorded crime statistics would have shown a reduction in crime of 20%, merely because of changes in reporting and recording practices. For the offences of burglary, vehicle theft and bicycle theft reductions would have been 20%, 22% and 34% respectively. Unless the impact of these changes had been taken into account by the researchers, which they almost never are, the observed reductions would have been attributed to the CCTV system. In other words, the real rate of crime could have remained the same, CCTV having no impact, and yet the evaluators would have certainly claimed that CCTV was an unqualified success in reducing crime.

Table 6.1: Offences reported to and recorded by police in 1997

Offence	% reported to police	% of reported crime recorded by police	Overall % of crime recorded by police
All offences	44	54	24
Theft of vehicle	97	87	84
Robbery	57	30	17
Theft from vehicle	43	59	25
Theft from person	35	29	10

Source: Derived from Mirrlees-Black *et al* 1998: figures 4.2 and 4.3.

Table 6.2: *Percentage change in British Crime Survey offences reported to and recorded by the police 1991, 1993, 1995*

Offence	1991			1993			1995			% reduction 1991 to 1995
	% reported	*% reported recorded*	*% of total recorded*	*% reported*	*% reported recorded*	*% of total recorded*	*% reported*	*% reported recorded*	*% of total recorded*	
Burglary	73	62	45	68	60	41	66	55	36	20
All vehicle theft	56	65	36	53	60	32	51	55	28	22
Bicycle theft	69	59	41	72	48	35	63	44	27	34
All BCS offences	49	60	29	47	55	26	46	50	23	20

Source: Derived from Mirrlees-Black *et al* 1998: figures A4.1 and A4.4.

Ideally then, evaluators should utilise a measure of crime which is independent of the officially recorded police crime figures, preferably a local victimisation survey conducted before the CCTV system is introduced and then repeated twelve months and twenty-four months after installation. This would enable a more accurate assessment to be made of the impact on the real rate of criminal victimisation, and give an indication of whether changes were sustained over time. In reality this is rarely, if ever, done, since it would require that the plans for the evaluation were in place at least eighteen months before the scheme, and involve considerable expense in collecting the data. In the fast-moving, and financially constrained, world of local politics it is unlikely that system promoters would agreed to hold back the introduction of their system for at least a year, just for the sake of the evaluation, and agree to finance three costly surveys.

The concept of reduction and its measurement

The question 'does CCTV reduce crime?', implies that we expect a decrease; however, it is perfectly sensible to suggest that for certain offences, particularly those which rely on predominantly police-initiated activities, there may be an increase in recorded crime. If the cameras allow the police to see and find evidence of crimes which would have previously gone unreported, such as drug dealing, drunk driving and fights between young men, then rather than a reduction in such recorded crime, we will see an increase. This adds weight to our argument that, in order to interpet a change in the officially recorded crime statistics as indicative of a 'real' change in the incidence of crime, researchers need to be aware of any changes in police practices and public reporting behaviour. Moreover, this is compounded by four other possible threats to validity of the crime figures which would need to be addressed by evaluators who wanted to make claims about the effectiveness of CCTV on the basis of changes to the crime rate (however measured). These threats are:

- displacement

- changes to the area under surveillance

- reactivity

- other fluctuations and trends in crime rates unrelated to the influence of CCTV

We will discuss each in turn.

Displacement
One of the first problems in assessing any crime prevention initiative is that while it may appear that a number of crimes have been prevented, in

fact they may have merely been *displaced* to another area or committed at other times or in different ways. Criminologists have identified six types of displacement associated with crime prevention initiatives (Barr and Pease 1990; Gabor 1978).

- *temporal displacement* occurs where the offence is merely committed at a different time. For instance, CCTV may be effective at deterring crime during the day when visibility is good, but not at night when it is hindered by darkness and the generally low luminosity of street lighting. Temporal displacement would occur if perpetrators switched to committing their crimes at night when there was less chance of detection.

- *tactical displacement* occurs when the method of comitting the offence changes. For example, if cars are fitted with better security features and stronger locks offenders may no longer break into cars and 'hot wire' them, but wait until the driver has opened the door and grab their keys.

- *target displacement* occurs when the same crime is committed against different targets, such as if housebreakers refrain from burgling houses with visible alarms but continue to burgle houses without alarms in the the same area.

- *functional displacement* occurs where offenders may be deterred from committing one type of crime but merely switch to another type. For example, the presence of cameras may make street robbers switch from 'mugging' (which is a highly visible act) to 'pick-pocketing' which is less easy to detect.

- *geographical displacement* occurs where the same crimes are committed in a different geographical location. For example, the installation of a CCTV system covering town centre car parks may lead to car crime being displaced to residential side streets away from the cameras' gaze.

- *perpetrator displacement* occurs where the crime is displaced from one offender to another. This may occur with crimes such as drug dealing or prostitution, where if one offender is arrested another may be ready to take their place.

In the case of CCTV it is predominantly functional and geographical displacement that is most likely to occur and a number of studies have found strong evidence of displacement taking place. Skinns' evaluation of the Doncaster CCTV system, for example, found clear evidence of geographical displacement, for although there was a reduction in crime in the town centre streets of 16% this was offset by the increase in crime in the surrounding townships by 31%. When these were taken together the overall reduction in crime was only 6%. (Skinns 1998: 185). Similarly in Birmingham, the evaluation by Brown (1995) produced strong evidence for geographical displacement for two different offence types, 'street robbery and theft from the person' and 'theft from a motor vehicle'. In the case of the former, Brown concluded that:

> Since the installation of cameras, the incidence of these types of offences in areas surrounding zone A has increased sharply, and by the end of the study period, the number of offences per month is over three times as high as when the cameras were installed.
>
> (Brown, 1995: 35)

In Sutton the installation of the cameras led to a marked change in the pattern of thefts in the town centre, so that while thefts on streets declined by 7%, thefts inside commercial premises increased by 30% (Sarno, 1996). This would suggest that there is evidence for geographic, tactical and target displacement as it would appear that offenders switched locations, changed targets from pedestrians to in-store customers, and switched from purse-snatching to stealth thefts of handbags.

There are, however, serious methodological problems involved in measuring displacement. In particular, it is very difficult in practice to distinguish 'displacement' areas from 'control' areas. As Ditton (personal communication) has noted: 'The usual working distinction is superficially geographical: that is, the adjacent area is the displacement one, and one some way away is the control one.' The underlying assumption is that offenders are very geographically static, which in the age of the motor car and metro is not very convincing. Crime could easily be displaced to areas selected as 'control' ones, making invalid the usual assumption that such areas have been unaffected by the introduction of CCTV.

Changes to the area under surveillance

One of the key problems facing the evaluator is that in the real world, unlike the laboratory of the natural scientist, it is very difficult to hold other variables constant until the evaluation is complete. This is commonly refered by statisticians as the problem of history, which Smith defines as follows:

> Over the time span of data collection many events occur in addition to the study's independent variable. The history factor refers to the possibility that any one of the events rather than the hypothesised independent variable might have caused the observed changes in the dependent variable.
>
> (1981: 334)

In the real world then, it is likely that while the evaluation of CCTV is being undertaken, other changes are occurring to the town centre. For example, in Birmingham pedestrianisation was introduced to key areas of the city centre at the same time as the cameras were installed (Brown 1995: 37), perhaps attracting more people, but fewer cars, into the town centre, and this in turn may have had a completely independent impact on the crime rate. As Skinns notes in relation to Doncaster:

> In the real world it is not possible for evaluators to demand that nothing else changes in the experimental area. And indeed, in [Doncaster] there were changes in policing styles, particularly in the town centre and in the outlying areas; changes in parking arrangements in the town centre (restricting the number of cars parked on the street); and finally the growth of out-of-town commercial and entertainment centres.
>
> (1998: 185)

What impact these changes had is of course difficult to assess, but one might speculate that if more people are going out of town to shop and to be entertained, there might be fewer offences in the town centre.

Reactivity
A problem for all evaluators is the extent to which the very act of evaluation itself influences the results of the study. This is generally referred to as *reactivity* and can be defined as 'any time participants suspect or know they are being observed, experimented with, or tested there is a chance that their behaviour may be modified by the measuring instrument' (Smith 1981: 335). In the case of the newly installed scheme in Windsor and Eton it was revealed that officers would be redeployed from other areas to cope with the expected increase in workload that would arise from the introduction of CCTV in the town centres. The presence of the extra officers patrolling the town centre may well have had a significant deterrent effect on crime in its own right, thus making any claims about the success of the CCTV system impossible to disentangle from the effect of the increased police presence (Norris and Armstrong 1999).

Other fluctuations in the crime rate
Criminologists have for some time been aware that at the local level, say a police beat or a town centre, there are often large fluctuations in the levels of recorded crime, regardless of the influence of any specific crime prevention measure: Paul Ekblom has argued convincingly that any reductions at the local level have to be judged against these quasi-random fluctuations in crimes rates. Ekblom analysed recorded street crime in 19 police beats in the Metropolitan police area between January and June 1989 and the same period in 1990; many beats showed massive increases and decreases over

the previous year. For instance, beat 1 incurred more than a 50% reduction in recorded crime while beat 2 had an increase of over 70% and similarly beat 14 enjoyed a 60% reduction while beat 16 showed an increase of over 80%. There can also be fluctuations for total recorded crime within the same beat. For instance in one police beat in the West Midlands, Ekblom showed that recorded crime fluctuated over a three-year period from over 90 crimes per month to less than 20 (Ekblom 1992: 39).

These variations mean that if one had been measuring the impact of a new crime prevention measure introduced in June 1988 and compared the recorded crime figures for one year before and one year after implementation there would have been an impressive reduction by about one-third, regardless of the measure. On the other hand if the measure had been introduced in June 1989 there would have been a disappointing 25% increase in recorded crime (derived from Ekblom 1992: Figure 2). As Tilley has argued, 'these wide natural fluctuations in local rates, especially in a small area over a limited period ... make interpreting real effects as against pseudo-random short-term changes very difficult' (Tilley 1998: 142). Given such fluctuations, if in the years preceeding the introduction of CCTV crime had risen exceptionally in an area, one might naturally expect a fall. Interestingly, given that the rush to CCTV was funded by a competitive bidding process, it may well be that local partnerships only put forward areas with 'abnormally' high and rapidly increasing crime rates, ones which were likely eventually to show a decline, regardless of any crime prevention initiative (see Ditton and Short 1999: 216–7).

It is not just small-scale local random variations that evaluators have to contend with. There are also wider background changes to crime rates against which any changes have to be judged. For instance, if nationally crime trends are on a downward path then it is important isolate the impact of CCTV from the general trend. It is perhaps arguable that one reason for the widespread belief in the efficacy of CCTV was that the rapid growth of the number of CCTV systems (between 1993 and 1997) occurred at precisely the same time as the only sustained fall in recorded crime since the 1950s.

At the more local level, such changes are also important to take into account when judging the efficacy of CCTV: if crime falls faster in the areas not under the watchful eye of the cameras then surely one would need to be cautious about attributing the fall in the area under surveillance to the impact of CCTV. This point is almost entirely overlooked by politicians, the media, and local advocates of CCTV. For them a reduction is a reduction full-stop, and must be attributable to the effect of CCTV. If we take the example of Sutton, the evaluation conducted by researchers from the University of the South Bank showed a reduction in total recorded crime in the area covered by the cameras of 13%. However, in the police division as a whole it fell by 17% and across the borough it reduced by 30%

(Sarno 1996: 22). On the face of it, it would appear that rather than facilitating a reduction in crime, the introduction of CCTV hindered its reduction. However as Norris and Armstrong have argued, in the face of a reduction, few are prepared to accept that it may not be attributable to CCTV:

> The London *Evening Standard* argued in an editorial on the negative results of the Sutton evaluation that, since the findings did not accord with that 'older discipline called common sense' and 'crime professionals consider ... [cameras] ... critically important in identifying and deterring criminals', the authors must be wrong. Indeed the headline declared, in defiance of the study, 'Why cameras deter crime' (*Evening Standard*, 3 January 1996). This approach was echoed by a spokesman for the Association of Chief Police Officers (ACPO) who argued that 'it is impossible to prove one way or another whether the cameras work' but it was 'common sense' and 'patently obvious that if someone is going to put a brick through a window they won't do it in front of the cameras'.
>
> (Norris and Armstrong, 1999: 205)

What the above discussion has highlighted is that for the criminological evaluator, the simple statement that 'after CCTV was introduced crime reduced by 20%' cannot be treated at face value and needs to be interpreted in the light of the various *threats to validity* we have outlined above. The question of validity is absolutely central to the evaluator's effort, since validity refers to the 'degree to which the researcher has measured what he or she set out to measure' (Smith 1981: 333) and the extent to which the researchers are able to assert that the changes in the dependent variable (the crime rate) are caused by the introduction of the independent variable (CCTV) and not by other factors. This means that researchers must actively seek, through the design of their evaluations, to rule out alternative explanations.

Experimental design

The strongest form of research design to rule out alternative explanations is by evaluators mimicking the methodology of the natural scientist and utilising the experimental method. Classically this entails comparing two groups: an experimental group and a control group. Ideally, the units which comprise both groups should be chosen at random, since this eliminates systematic bias or error. Once the two groups are allocated, both groups are observed and measured before the experimental variable is introduced to the experimental group, while the control group is left untouched. Finally both groups are measured again and the results

Table 6.3: Classic experimental design

Time 1	Time 2	Time 3	Time 4
Group 1	pre-test (O1)	experimental treatment (X)	post-test (O2)
Group 2	pre-test (O3)	no treatment	post-test (O4)

compared. Any changes in the two groups are then compared and if the results are significantly different then it is legitimate to infer that it is the introduction of the experimental variable which caused the changes. The importance of the control group is that is allows us to see if any changes that did take place occurred 'naturally', that is not as a result of the introduction of the experimental variable. As Campbell and Stanley (1963: 13–16) have shown, if the procedures have been carried out correctly, the threats to internal validity discussed above may all be ruled out.

Of course, this strict control can only really be achieved under laboratory conditions; however, in the social sciences, there are many who advocate that researchers should at least strive towards the ideal of the classic experiment by approximating, as far as possible, experimental conditions in the field. These are generally referred to as quasi-experimental methods which, as Jupp notes, have a long pedigree in criminology and are often referred to as 'field experiments' or 'reforms as experiments' and have been used to evaluate a variety of new initiatives such as the most effective regimes for the control and treatment offenders (see Jupp 1989), neighbourhood watch (Bennett 1990) and police patrol strategies (Kelling 1974).

In the case of CCTV, one of the more imaginative quasi-experiments was conducted by Beck and Willis (1999), who wanted to examine the effect of introducing CCTV systems in the retail sector to prevent stock loss, mainly through shop-lifting. The study aimed to assess the impact of different types of CCTV systems on levels of stock loss in fifteen stores of a large national UK fashion retailer. The research used a before-and-after experimental design involving the following:

- a stock-take being carried out in each store before CCTV was installed.

- CCTV systems being introduced into each store. Three types of system were introduced to look at the differential impact (if any) of systems with varying levels of technical sophistication.

- a stock-take being carried out in each store after CCTV was installed to calculate the number of units stolen and their value. The stock-takes

Table 6.4: Quasi-experimental design as used by Beck and Willis (1999)

Time 1	Time 2	Time 3	Time 4	Time 5
Group 1	pre-test	experimental treatment	post-test 1	post-test 2
Group 2	pre-test	experimental treatment	post-test 1	post-test 2
Group 3	pre-test	experimental treatment	post-test 1	post-test 2

were carried out twice: 13 weeks after installation and then 28 weeks after. This enabled the researchers to assess the impact in both the short and the medium term.

There are a number of key features which distinguish this quasi-experimental design from the classic experimental method. Firstly, the three groups, which comprised in total 15 stores, were chosen from a total of 180 retail outlets of one fashion store chain. However, one of the first principles of experimental design has been sacrificed because they do not appear to have been chosen at random. This means that their selection may have been biased and in some way produced a set of stores that are atypical of the all the stores across the country, thus limiting the generalisability of the findings.

Second, there is no control group, i.e. a sample of stores not subject to experimental treatment. This is important because it is possible that there may have been a general reduction in shop-lifting nationally, perhaps caused by the courts getting particularly tough on shop-lifters at the same time and therefore providing a greater deterrent. Without a control group it is impossible to rule this out as an alternative explanation.

Third, and this is one of the study's great strengths, by including three types of CCTV system of different levels of technical sophistication the authors have implicitly recognised that CCTV is not a homogeneous phenomenon. Therefore the research design can inform us about whether different types of system have different impacts. In this way, the study mirrors the classic medical experiment where three groups of patients are given different dosages of the same drug to see which is the most effective dose. The patients are examined before the onset of the drug treatment and at three months and six months after the prescription, in order to examine the short- and medium-term impacts.

Fourth, and this is another strength of the study, it utilises both a short- and medium-term measure of stock loss, thus enabling comparisons between the two and giving a better indication of long-term trends.

What then did the study find? In the short term, based on the figures after 13 weeks, so far as the theft prevention possibilities of CCTV are concerned, the findings were impressive. Taking all the stores together, the average number of units lost per week fell from 72 to 52, a 28% reduction. In total, for the 15 stores in the study, if this trend continued there would have been savings of nearly £90,000 per year. Given that the total cost of introducing CCTV to these stores was £180,000, it would take two years for the savings made to pay for the capital costs of installation. In business terms, this can be seen as an adequate but not spectacular return on the investment but one that is probably worthwhile financially given that the savings might be expected to continue in the third and fourth years of operation.

But this projection is on the basis of figures collected after just three months of operation and criminologists are well aware that the effect of crime prevention measures often degrades over time. This frequently seems to be due to the fact that when new schemes are introduced, there is often an initial blaze of publicity which enhances any deterrent effects. Over time, as potential offenders either forget or become blasé about the new measures, they will no longer be deterred. Moreover, the professional or persistent offenders may gradually adapt their techniques to continue to avoid detection. For these reasons it is important that assessment about impacts be taken over longer rather than shorter time periods.

In this study, while the second stock-take only occurred after six months, it still allows some assessment of the medium-term effect and whether the impact has degraded. In the twelve stores that had a six-month stock-take, the average number of units lost per week before the introduction of the CCTV systems was 64; six months after installation the number had reduced, but only by one to 63. In financial terms, this represented an average reduction in weekly loss of merely £4 and on this basis it would take an average of 58 years to recoup the capital outlay.

Overall, and in the medium term, it would appear that CCTV is not a cost-effective measure of reducing stock loss and does little to prevent the crime of shop-lifting.

However, there is a final twist to this tale, arising from the fact that this rather negative finding is based on the aggregated results from different systems. The original experimental design, it will be recalled, included the introduction of three different systems of varying degrees of technical sophistication. At the lowest level this included a CCTV display monitor at the entrances to the store to alert people to CCTV, twelve dummy cameras, and no recording or monitoring facilities; the medium-level system had entrance display monitors, between six and twelve static colour cameras, the facility both to record and monitor the images from the cameras, but no provision for permanent monitoring; the high-level system had entrance display monitors, between two and four pan, tilt and zoom cameras, between eight and twelve static colour cameras, the facility to both record and monitor the images from the cameras, and the provision of permanent staff to continuously monitor the screens.

The aggregate results mask considerable variation in the impact of different systems since the high-level stores showed 'an impressive reduction of 26%, whilst there was an increase of 32% in medium-level stores and an increase of 9% in low-level stores' (Beck and Willis 1999: 260). In financial terms the results were as follows:

> For high-level systems with an average weekly reduction in loss of £178 set against a capital expenditure of £24,000, the pay-back period was now 2.6 years (135 weeks). For the medium- and low-level systems, however, the pay-back period was non-existent; it could not be calculated because the average weekly reduction in loss had disappeared altogether.
>
> (Beck and Willis, 1999: 261)

The strength of this study is that it allows us to give clear advice to the financially motivated retailer, concerned with the bottom line of profit-ability: 'If you are going to install a CCTV system, it needs to be a sophisticated one that is permanently monitored, otherwise your expenditure will be greater than your savings'. Even then, CCTV does not offer a magic bullet to the problems of stock loss and it will still take over two-and-a-half years to recover the investment. Moreover this does not include the costs of monitoring and running the high-level system, which on a conservative estimate would be in the region of £12,000 a year. If this is included, it would take nearly five years for the system to recover its costs and the hard-headed business person might decide that with such a slow rate of return, it might be more rational to just accept the losses!

Does CCTV reduce crime in town centres?
The evaluation evidence

To date there have been thirteen independently conducted 'quasi-experimental' evaluations which can be used to inform our judgement as to the effectiveness of CCTV in reducing town centre crime.[*] Collectively, these

*These studies have been conducted in Airdrie (Ditton and Short 1998; Short and Ditton 1996), Birmingham (Brown 1995), Brighton (Squires and Measor 1996, 1997), Burgess Hill (Squires 1998c), Burnley (Armitage, Smyth and Pease 1999), Crawley (Squires 1998b), Doncaster (Skinns 1998), East Grinstead (Squires 1998a) Glasgow (Ditton and Short 1999), Ilford (Squires 1998d), Kings Lynn (Brown 1995), Newcastle (Brown 1995), and Sutton (Sarno 1996).

studies represent the only reliable data on the effectiveness of CCTV in town centres, since their findings are based on a minimum level of methodological adequacy which rule out some of the major threats to internal validity.

- They all utilise before-and-after measures, based on an analysis of police recorded crime figures. In all cases this is not just by measuring two distinct points of time but by a form of trend analysis, either rolling averages or regression analysis. This enables the impact of both random fluctuations and wider long-term trends in crime rates to be addressed, both of which might spuriously influence the results.

- They all utilise some form of control group. This is rather different from the classic experimental control since none of the studies used another, similar town without CCTV as a comparison. However, by separating out the area under surveillance and comparing it to the immediate surrounding area and the wider area, this in effect creates a form of control because one can compare the changes in the rate between areas with CCTV and those without.

- They all recognised the issue of displacement and attempted to assess the extent to which crime was simply moved from areas with cameras to areas without cameras.

- None of the studies treat crime as merely an aggregate category, but examine changes in the recorded crime rate for different offence types.

Some of the threats still remain:

- The problem of reactivity is rarely addressed, although the main threat would be if the police changed their practices in a way that influenced the results of the study. In the absence of any data suggesting that they did, we will assume that reactivity is not a particular problem.

- The problem of changes to the area under surveillance occurring during the time of the evaluation, which may also have impacted on the crime rate, is only addressed by two of the studies. Again, in the absence of any data suggesting that there were such changes, we shall assume that this was not a particular problem.

- General changes to reporting and recording practices. Only one study explicitly mentions changes to recording practices that may have influenced the data. But, more importantly, only two of the studies utilise before-and-after victimisation surveys which would allow us to see if there had been a change in the 'real' rate of criminal victimisation, rather than just a change in police recorded crime data.

The findings

In Burnley, Armitage *et al* (1999) found a reduction of 25% sustained over two years. A decrease was found for every offence type measured by the study; importantly, the fact that the reductions were sustained over a period of two years indicated that they were not merely the result of quasi-random fluctuations in the crime rate. There was no evidence of displacement and some evidence of a diffusion of benefits. In crime prevention terms this is undoubtedy a success; however, as we shall see, no other study has found such consistent and positive results.

In Airdrie (Short and Ditton 1996) there was an overall reduction of crime of 21%, which the research demonstrated was greater than one would expect on the basis of the downward trends in the surrounding area. The reductions were sustained over a two-year period. However, unlike in Burnley, there were significant differences in changes to recorded crime levels for different offences. A number of offence categories showed increases, such as drug offences, low-level public order offences and minor traffic violations, while crimes of dishonesty, such as housebreaking and theft of and from motor vehicles showed a dramatic reduction of 48%. Since these crimes of dishonesty account for about 40% of overall recorded crime, reducing them by nearly half more than offsets the rise in other offence types. Moreover, as the authors state, increases in these offence categories 'are not necessarily indicative of the failure of CCTV... and increases in drug offences may reflect the surveillance ability of CCTV to detect crimes that might otherwise have gone unnoticed. The same could be said of "breach of the peace" offences, and minor traffic violations' (Ditton and Short 1999: 206). The researchers found no evidence of functional or geographical displacement and no evidence of a diffusion of benefits.

These success stories are paralleled by the findings from Newcastle and Kings Lynn (Brown 1995). In Newcastle, for example, although Brown does not provide figures for the decrease in recorded crime as a whole, he showed reductions in the major offence categories of burglary (–57%), criminal damage (–34%), theft of and from motor vehicles (–49%). The reductions were greater in the CCTV area than in the control areas. There was no evidence of displacement but some of diffusion of benefits, and there was some evidence that for motor vehicle crime the effects were fading over time.

However, these rather unequivocal success stories have to be measured against rather more mixed findings. Skinns' evaluation of Doncaster showed a 16% reduction which initially would seem to make the scheme an unequivocal success. However, this reduction was offset by a statistically significant increase for nearly all major offence categories in the outlying townships. There was also evidence, particularly for burglary, of a diffusion of benefits to the areas immediately surrounding the scheme. Overall, when both diffusion of benefits and displacement were taken into account the overall reduction was only 6%. Moreover, in the town centre, although there were reductions in recorded offences for burglary (–25%), criminal damage (–32%), and shoplifting (–11%), all these reductions are what would have been expected on the basis of pre-existing trends; the only reductions which remained significant were for theft of and from motor vehicles.

Similarly mixed evidence of displacement and/or increases in some categories of recorded crime has been found in Ilford (Squires 1998d) and Brighton (Squires and Measor 1996). Moreover, as Phillips points out, the evaluations carried out by Squires in the towns of East Grinstead, Crawley and Burgess Hill (Squires 1998a, b, c) 'reported reductions, over and above those in control areas, only for criminal damage' (Phillips 1999: 134).

Other town centre studies have found CCTV to have no overall impact. In Birmingham (Brown 1995: 46), there was a 'failure of the camera systems to reduce directly overall crime levels'. The only offence type that showed a sustained but small reduction was theft of motor vehicles. Robbery and assault with wounding increased marginally, while theft from motor vehicles increased dramatically. Moreover, there was strong evidence of both functional and geographical displacement.

These negative findings were repeated in Glasgow (Ditton *et al* 1999). When existing trends were taken into account total recorded crime actually rose by 9% after the cameras were installed. Again there was variation in offence type with increases for crimes of dishonesty (+23%) and indecency (+17%), whereas crimes involving serious violence (–22%), vandalism (–8%), and motoring offences (–12%) showed a decrease. A similar story is found in Sutton (Sarno 1996), where crimes fell further and faster in the areas surrounding the CCTV system and the division as a whole, and there was evidence of tactical displacement.

If we now return to our original question, 'does CCTV reduce crime?' we see that the criminological evidence is far from straightforward: the effects are neither universal or consistent. There is evidence for CCTV having a sustained and dramatic reductive effect in some areas, while having a negligible impact in others. When looking at individual offence types the picture is also unclear; for instance in Burnley and Ilford crimes of violence decreased while in Birmingham and Brighton they increased. Similarly in Airdrie, crimes of dishonesty decreased, while in Glasgow they increased. Evidence of displacement was found in Doncaster and Burgess Hill, but not in Burnley or Brighton

If we accept that the contradictory findings of these studies are not simply a result of methodological artifacts, and actually represent a 'real' measure of the incidence of criminal victimisation in the areas under study, then we can answer the question, 'does CCTV reduce crime?' with both a 'yes' and a 'no'. Of course for the local politician or police chief wanting to know whether CCTV will reduce crime in their area, this is hardly a useful reply. But it does invite us to ask rather different questions. If CCTV did reduce crime in Burnley, why did it not reduce crime in Glasgow? If we can answer this question, then we will be in better position to predict whether CCTV will work in a given locale and not in others. However, this requires a radically different methodological approach to the one typically adopted by evaluators of crime prevention measures; this approach, developed by Pawson and Tilley, is termed realistic evaluation and it is to a consideration of this that we now turn.

Realistic evaluation

The sort of mixed findings that we have described for CCTV evaluations should come as no surprise to crime prevention specialists. As Tilley (1998: 143) has noted, whenever the results of the evaluation studies are compared, the results are almost always inconsistent and contradictory. For Pawson and Tilley (1997), this considerably undermines the utility of evaluation studies for practitioners. This is because the focus of evaluations has been almost solely on outcomes (does the crime rate change?) rather than considering the processes, or 'mechanisms' which might account for the changes. The point has been forcefully reiterated by Gill and Turbin in the context of crime prevention in the business sector, which wishes to use the research as the basis for its security policy:

> There is no guarantee that the results of one study will have any relevance for a different location or context. The common sense observation that what has an impact in site A may not necessarily have an impact in site B has, to a large extent, been ignored by previous research that focuses largely on collecting figures to show whether the measure has worked at all. The main issue is not so much whether the measure worked but rather how it did so, conversely, why it failed to work when logic indicated that it should, or as Pawson and Tilley state, 'what works, for whom and in what circumstance'.
>
> (Gill and Turbin 1999: 181)

Ironically, it is the emphasis on the quasi-experimental design by social science evaluators which is partially to blame for this. The focus of these designs has generally been to determine whether a specific measure reduced crime in a specific context, and by utilising a properly constructed experimental design this question can be answered. But what it does not tell us is why the measure had the effect that it did. Realistic evaluation refocuses attention on the processes that produce the particular outcomes rather than just on the outcomes themselves. For Pawson and Tilley this requires evaluators to concern themselves with three issues: the context, mechanisms and outcomes.

Context

Context refers to the specific features of the the particular scheme being evaluated; this requires detailed description by evaluators and an analysis as to how these features may impact on the outcome of the study. For instance, consideration needs to be given to: the level of technological sophistication of the system; the organisation of the system and how it is integrated with deployment practice; the physical and social make-up of the area; the patterns of use of the area and the pattern and incidence of crime in an area.

By explicitly detailing the contexts, not only will this enable more systematic comparison between different evaluations but it will also facilitate an understanding of the particular mechanisms which are triggered by different contexts.

Mechanisms

In the context of CCTV, Pawson and Tilley (1994 and 1997) and Tilley (1998), have identified a range of potential mechanisms which may be triggered. These include:

- *Effective deployment* CCTV may enable more effective deployment of security guards/police thus deterring potential offenders by a more targeted patrol presence on the street.

- *Nosey parker* CCTV may increase 'natural surveillance' through increased usage of an area and thus increase the risk that offenders will be caught.

- *Active citizen* CCTV may increase confidence of members of the public to intervene, if they believe the situation is being observed and police back-up will follow.

- *You've been framed* CCTV may generally increase potential offenders' fears that they will be seen, caught and shamed or punished, or moved on for misbehaviour or unwanted behaviour.

- *Caught in the act* CCTV may help catch offenders, who may then be stopped, removed and punished, therefore both preventing the present offence and deterring the individual offender from committing future ones.

- *Appeal to the cautious* The presence of CCTV cameras and their associated publicity may remind potential victims to be more cautious in areas covered, thus lessening the opportunities for crime.

Clearly, in any context one or more of the mechanisms could be operating to reduce crime. But the chance that any mechanism will be triggered is largely determined by context. For instance, for the 'You've been framed' mechanism to deter potential offenders from committing crime requires them to be aware that the cameras are potentially watching them. In Glasgow, however, one year after the installation of the cameras, 'only between a quarter and a third of the ambulatory population were even aware of their existence' (Ditton and Short 1999: 216), whereas in Brighton 87% of those in the town centre were aware of the system (Squires and Measors 1996). Thus the difference in the effectiveness of the two systems may be related to the extent to which the specific context differentially triggered the deterrence mechanism: this can only be operative if people are aware of the system.

Outcomes

We can see that while standard evaluations have been concerned with a single outcome, the change to the recorded crime rate, realistic evaluation would be concerned with multiple outcomes. For example: what is the level of public awareness of the system? Has CCTV changed the pattern of usage of the city centre? Have deployments to incidents increased? Have more people been arrested? and so on. All of these are, in a sense, intermediate outcomes which will have an effect on the impact of CCTV. And it is only by measuring these that we can can start to unpack why CCTV has the effects that it does. For Pawson and Tilley, realistic evaluation requires that researchers explicitly hypothesize which mechanisms will be triggered in any given crime prevention context. These hypotheses should then 'frame the requisite data and research strategies, and thus call upon a range of evidence entirely different from the standard comparisons' (1997: 80).

It should be clear from the above discussion that the criminological evidence relating to the effectiveness of CCTV in reducing crime does not support the almost exponential increase in cameras on British streets as a crime prevention measure. But perhaps this is to miss the point: the introduction of CCTV was never dependent on it being effective. As Webster has argued, it was more about its symbolic potential to show that politicians at both national and local levels were responsive to citizens' concerns about crime, and were actively doing something about them (Webster 2000).

So far we have concentrated extensively on the methodological issues raised by criminologists' attempts to determine whether CCTV reduces crime. We would justify this selective attention by arguing that issues of effectiveness have largely dominated the the criminological and political agenda. However, as Hughes has argued, this focus, which is mirrored in the crime prevention literature as whole, is based in a tradition of administrative criminology which has been concerned with:

> the development of a body of technical and pragmatic knowledge aimed at helping those in power to put their ideas into practice through technical evaluation ... . This 'technicist' orientation thus sees crime as a technical and practical problem needing an administrative and apolitical 'solution'. This 'administrative' aim has been prioritised over the broader critical questioning of the main assumptions, principles and social consequences of the different approaches to crime prevention associated with the state and (increasingly) the private sector. As a consequence, there has been an absence of a critical body of work on the wider politics of the phenomenon.
>
> (Hughes 1998: 4)

CCTV, discrimination and social exclusion

In the portrayal of CCTV by the popular media and the rhetoric of politicians CCTV is 'the friendly eye in the sky', benignly and evenly watching over the citizenry who 'if they have nothing to hide, have nothing to fear'. However, in busy urban streets CCTV operators are, of course, presented with potentially thousands of different 'suspects' during the course of a day, and operators have to select for closer attention those incidents and persons which may be indicative of criminality. This issue informed the research by Norris and Armstrong, who set out to explore the processes by which the myriad of images entering a CCTV system are interpreted by CCTV operators to determine who should be targeted for extended and intensive surveillance. As they show, CCTV targeting is not an equal opportunity phenomenon. They conclude:

> The sum total of these individual discretionary judgements produces, as we have shown, a highly differentiated pattern of surveillance leading to a massively disproportionate targeting of young males, particularly if they are black or visibly identifiable as having subcultural affiliations. As this differentiation is not based on objective behavioural and individualised criteria, but merely on being categorised as part of a particular social group, such practices are discriminatory.
>
> (Norris and Armstrong 1999: 150)

This has some major criminological implications, since if one social group is being targeted disproportionately, then this will have the effect of increasing their criminalisation as more of their potential offences are revealed, while simultaneously lessening the criminalisation of other groups. This point is starkly reinforced by Ditton *et al* (1999) who report that, in one major city centre system, it was revealed that the technical capabilities of the systems enabled the camera to focus in on a car's tax disc from several hundred metres away. It could therefore determine whether the disc being displayed had expired. However, this was not seen as an appropriate use of the system (Ditton *et al* 1999: 47 fn 55). Thus the offences of the relatively affluent and older motorists are left unchecked while the scrutiny of poorer working-class and ethnic minority youth is intensified.

Moreover, for those who are constantly tracked by the cameras in city centre space, merely on the basis of their appearance and overt social characteristics, the CCTV gaze will not be seen as friendly and protecting but hostile and untrusting. How else should they react? They are being treated as a threat, as people who cannot be trusted, as persons who do not belong, as unwanted outsiders.

Unjustifiably selective targeting may have further consequences. Norris and Armstrong (1999) found women to be largely invisible to CCTV operators, with women accounting for only 7% of targeted surveillance, and they show how such targeting can be for voyeuristic rather than protectional purposes. Moreover, as Brown (1998) has shown, on the basis of extensive interviews in Middlesbrough regarding aspects of gender and community safety, CCTV is likely to be of marginal significance to women's perception of safety within town centres, and merely represent yet another, this time technologically mediated, male gaze.

> Being seen, for women, is a condition of everyday life: their feelings of extreme visibility in public are created by masculine regulation of the public domain. Their exaggerated visibility creates insecurity. More men, sitting in front of camera screens, adds visibility. It does not necessarily add security. The kinds of behaviour which CCTV can monitor and ostensibly provide a basis for action on are the rare and spectacular acts of physical assaults on women in the high street. It cannot monitor the alcohol-fuelled male gaze nor the alcohol-fuelled male display: indeed, in one sense it is part of the male gaze, and therefore part of the problem rather than the solution.
>
> (Brown 1998: 218)

Brown goes on to argue that the belief in technologically driven solutions to the problem of crime may divert attention, and funding, away from more imaginative and appropriate 'people-driven solutions': safer transport policies, the visible presence of capable guardians in the form of city centre wardens, or a more visible police presence, are three such strategies.

This echoes the concerns of Bannister *et al* (1998), who remind us that social order in public space is, by and large, maintained by the capable guardianship of the proprietors and users of the streets. It is highly localised, informal and personalised and as Jacobs argues:

> The first thing to understand is that public peace – the sidewalk and street peace – of cities ... is kept primarily by an intricate, almost unconscious, network of voluntary controls and standards among people themselves, and enforced by the people themselves.
> (Jacobs, 1961, quoted in Bannister *et al* 1998: 23)

There are two things to note about this. First, order is maintained not primarily through the intervention of police or security staff (indeed their intervention is often a sign of disorder) but by the ordinary mass of citizenry. Secondly, that order is localised and, as such, is capable of being sensitive to a diversity of community norms.

For Bannister *et al* (1998), cities are sites of difference: sites where those of different classes, races, cultures and backgrounds intermingle. And the encountering of difference brings with it not only excitement and stimulation but also fear. Fear is not necessarily something to be concerned about, indeed it is part of the the adventure of the city. However, while some 'visions' of the city celebrate and promote this aspect of metropolitan life, other, more powerful voices envisage the need to manage this fear and create homogeneous spaces through the exclusion of difference.

The exclusionary impulse is intimately bound up with the commercialisation of city centre space and in particular the threat posed to the commercial profitability of the town centre by out-of-town retail parks (such as the Metro Centre in Gateshead) where private finance has created sterile, orderly, but above all private areas for consumption. This leads to a fortress mentality where 'difference is not so much to be celebrated as segregated' (Bannister *et al* 1998–27). CCTV becomes part of the process whereby difference is excluded not by targeting the criminal, but by targeting the 'other': the homeless, the poor, the political activist, who do not contribute to the commercial success of the city. This exclusionary impulse is almost entirely overlooked by those who focus on the crime reduction potential of CCTV.

However, for a number of radical commentators, CCTV is part of the process whereby city centres are being transformed from democratic spaces to which all citizens have access and in which they can freely interact, whatever their race, class or status, to mere sites of consumerism. As the public realm becomes increasingly privatised, as housing, parks, leisure facilities, and shopping spaces are sold off to commercial developers, they become subject to private standards of justice and control. As France and Wiles warn:

There is a clear danger that as mass private property increases young people, or rather particular groups of young people, will be exluded from many of the locations ... . Even more worrrying is that most of the public law rights which were developed as part of the modernity project, and which protected young people from exclusion are now being evaded by the use of private law devices.

(France and Wiles 1998: 69)

These fears are well grounded: as McCahill (2000) has shown in his study of CCTV in shopping malls, the exclusion of 'flawed' consumers is actively promoted by the CCTV system, as it is used to systematically exclude youth and others deemed undesirable. Moreover, it leads to a form of private justice, where people are barred from certain spaces, on the authority of the security guards, who then use the cameras to collectively enforce such bans. This is achieved without any recourse to the formal criminal justice system and therefore bypasses legal safeguards embodied in the public justice of the courts.

This exclusionary impulse is starting to assert itself in what remains of the public sphere, as Reeve's study of town centre managers revealed. The managers wanted to discourage certain people and activities within the city centre which were seen as non-conducive to their consumer-led vision of the desirable. A quarter wanted to discourage political gatherings, a half to discourage youths from 'hanging out', and a half to prohibit begging in the streets (Reeve 1998: 78).

As Young has argued, this exclusionary impulse is not the outcome of over-zealous security guards inappropriately using the the system. It is embedded in structural changes in the nature of crime control in the transition from modernity to late modernity. While the modernist project had faith in the ability to intervene both structurally and individually, through secondary and tertiary crime prevention techniques, it was predominantly inclusionary; it sought to keep the deviant and potential deviant within the fold. In late modernity such hopes have largely been abandoned and instead society 'responds to deviance by exclusion and separation' (Young 1999: 26).

Chapter 7

Criminology: some concluding thoughts

This book began by inviting you to a party. Those who were seduced by this invitation and are still with us might be feeling rather disappointed by now. Perhaps anticipating party hats, games and laughter, readers have been taken aside by two rather serious academics who proceeded to ask a lot of rather difficult questions. Thankfully, parties don't often turn out like that. We hope that those who are still reading will agree that those questions, although difficult, are often important and interesting ones.

One major role for criminology is to subject 'obvious', 'common sense' knowledge – the sort of thing that often enters the conversation at parties – to critical scrutiny. As we have seen, although it may be thought obvious that more police patrolling the streets or the presence of CCTV cameras will inevitably reduce crime, things are more complicated than that. Criminology subjects such ideas to rigorous enquiry, which often includes systematic empirical research by a variety of methods. Whether or not this qualifies criminology as a science – another difficult question that has taken up a lot of energy over the years, often to little effect – is not an issue that we have discussed in this book. But the striving for knowledge that will somehow go beyond common sense, speculation, belief or assertion is certainly something that has characterised much work in criminology, a child of what has been called a modernist project.

In the first chapter, we began with some basic questions about crime and the criminal. We found that there are different views about the definition of these terms, which had some important consequences, including for the very scope and nature of the discipline. While many criminologists in the past did not spend too much time considering such definitional questions, we suggested that the terms should be regarded as problematic. According to this view, criminologists should consider the use of these terms when they appear. Even where the definitions of crime and the criminal are clear, there still remains the problem for criminologists of identifying crime and the criminal for research purposes. If a legalistic position is adopted, for example, can we use official data from the criminal justice system in order to assess the nature, extent and distribution of crime and offenders?

We then outlined in more detail what seems to be the subject matter of criminology, and its multi-disciplinary nature. Our position is that criminology is a broad-ranging subject, which benefits from the insights of a variety of disciplines and perspectives. There are, however, those working in these areas who do not consider their work to be criminology, and do not regard themselves as criminologists. Although the argument is still to be heard that criminology should be abolished and the study of crime and justice undertaken by other disciplines and perspectives, the future of criminology looks assured. It has become institutionalised, with apparently firm foundations in both academia and government, although the complexion it assumes often varies with the context and the sponsor. Finally, we tried to trace the history of criminology. Again, there were no easy answers here, with the discussion seeming to hinge on what is meant by 'criminology'. Nevertheless, such histories tell us a little more about the subject and where it (if, in view of the current fragmentation and diversification, we can speak of 'it') stands today.

No introduction to criminology would be complete without considering the attempt to develop theories of crime. We began our discussion of this in chapter 2 in looking at biological and psychological contributions to this enterprise. While early efforts involved crude attempts to spot biological or psychological differences between offenders and others, later research became increasingly sophisticated in this quest. First, it stressed the notion of a complex interaction between a range of different sorts of factors, whether biological, psychological, social or of some other sort. Second, it appeared to soften the deterministic tenor of some earlier pronouncements, by stressing that such factors operated in a probabilistic fashion – they were risk factors. Finally, it was often declared that attempting to develop a general theory of crime was a fruitless or unrewarding task. While some tried to refashion the subject matter as anti-social conduct or something similar, others suggested that we needed to be much more specific in what we are trying to explain – such as by focusing on aggression, or life-course persistent anti-social behaviour – in view of the heterogeneity of the offender population. We saw how what we called the new biology of crime was still engaged in the search for differences, often on this modified basis. By contrast, rational choice, routine activities and situational perspectives played down the idea of difference, partly because they were more interested in those aspects (usually in the immediate situation, rather than in the person) that could be more easily changed in order to reduce crime.

We continued our consideration of theories of crime in chapter 3, in which we looked at the way in which sociologists and others tried to develop an understanding of crime by reference to the social contexts and circumstances in which offenders were located. It was a version of spot the difference with a rather different focus. We saw how, over time, attention began to move away from looking for the 'causes of crime' (some thought that this was a question no longer worth asking) to the study of criminalization. This gave importance to a whole range of new topics for detailed study, including the police (see chapter 5). We have seen how criminology has experienced challenges from a variety of sources, such as interactionist and labelling perspectives, radical and Marxist approaches, feminist perspectives, and postmodernist influences. Partly as a result of these challenges, much of what is called criminology today is very different from 40 years ago.

Criminology has shown a remarkable capacity to assimilate ideas from such challenges (or to ignore them, for there are some areas of study that have changed relatively little). Perhaps the most enduring tension in the discipline is still that between those with an essentially applied, practical or policy focus, with their research often sponsored by the Home Office or other agencies, and those with a more 'academic' orientation, often critical of fundamental assumptions and ideas. Those working on studies of 'effective practice' with offenders, for example, do not seem to have much time for the idea that we should 'deconstruct crime'. We also saw, however, how even some of those who have been much influenced by the ideas of postmodernism have been unable to abandon entirely the idea that criminology, which came into being as part of the modernist project, should strive for knowledge that will help us not only to interpret the world but to change it, hopefully for the better.

We chose three examples of areas of criminological work in order to illustrate some of the themes and perspectives in contemporary criminology. First we looked at serial murder as an example of the attempt to study and understand a particular type of crime. We looked at the definition and measurement of the phenomenon, a common starting point in such studies. We then saw how the attempt to explain such a specific crime was by no means as straightforward as we might have thought. There appeared to be considerable heterogeneity among even this bunch of offenders. We were able show the scope and nature of contributions from three disciplines – biology, psychology and sociology – and assessed each in turn. We concluded by showing how what often passes as 'knowledge' in our society can be seen as socially constructed – that representations of the 'serial murder problem' and crime in general, in the mass media and elsewhere, can be regarded in a sceptical frame of mind, and the way in which they are presented subject to analysis to show the interests that they may serve.

Our chapter on the police and policing provides an introduction to the study of one institution of the criminal justice system. We began by questioning the common assumption that the core role of the police is, and should be, the control of crime. We then looked at the key issues of discretion and discrimination, suggesting that it is often a more complex matter than is commonly realised to show that discretion is being exercised in a discriminatory way, and that mere reference to the influence of individual prejudice or police culture as an explanation is not good enough. Issues of discretion and discrimination have a wider relevance throughout the criminal justice system. Finally, we considered due process and crime control models of the criminal justice process, and discussed them in the context of policing. We examined how so-called 'noble cause corruption' seems to occur, such as that which has contributed to some of the major miscarriages of justice of recent years. Our conclusion, that this is related to the organisational and wider contexts within which the police operate, has clear implications for the wider system of criminal justice.

Our final chapter introduced the area of crime prevention, before an examination of CCTV and whether it can be said to reduce crime. In spite of the enthusiasm with which this technology has been embraced, the evidence does not unequivocally justify that enthusiasm. In addition, while attention has been focused on the technical evaluation of whether it 'works', there are wider questions that criminology should consider. For example, it seems that CCTV can lead to discrimination and social exclusion for certain groups in the population. The chapter also served as an illustration of the procedures and problems involved in conducting empirical research in criminology. Here, as in policing and elsewhere in criminal justice research, there is clearly a place for detailed, observational studies to examine the actual operation of CCTV systems, policing, courts and prisons. These studies can be a valuable corrective to the managerialist perspectives that have become dominant in criminal justice in recent years, with their emphasis on technicist evaluation and the quantitative measurement of performance indicators, targets and the like. As always, a variety of methods, data, and perspectives will enrich our understanding of crime, criminal justice and related topics.

Bibliography

Abel, G., Becker, J. and Cunningham-Rather, J. (1984) 'Complications, consent and cognitions in sex between children and adults', *International Journal of Psychiatry and Law,* 7: 89–103.

Abrahamsen, D. (1973) *The Murdering Mind.* New York: Harper and Row.

Agnew, R. (1985) 'A revised strain theory of delinquency', *Social Forces,* 64: 151–67.

Agnew, R and White, H. (1992) 'An empirical test of general strain theory', *Criminology,* 32: 555–80.

Aichhorn, A. (1955, originally published 1925) *Wayward Youth.* New York: Meridian Books.

Akers, R. (1977) *Deviant Behaviour: A Social Learning Approach,* 2nd edn. Belmont, CA: Wadsworth.

Akers, R., Krohn, M., Lanza-Kaduce, L., and Radesovich, M. (1979) 'Social learning and deviant behaviour', *American Sociological Review,* 44: 635–55.

Alexander, F. and Healy, W. (1935) *Roots of Crime.* New York: Knopf.

Alexander, F. and Staub, H. (1931) *The Criminal, the Judge and the Public.* New York: Macmillan.

Anderson, S., Kinsey, R., Loader, I. and Smith, C. (1990) *The Edinburgh Crime Survey.* Edinburgh: Scottish Office.

Armitage, R., Smythe, G. and Pease, K. (1999) 'Burnley CCTV evaluation' in Painter, K. and Tilley, N. (eds) *Crime Prevention Studies,* Vol 10: 225–251. Special edition entitled 'Surveillance of Public Space: CCTV, Street Lighting and Crime Prevention'.

Atkinson, R. L., Atkinson, R. C., Smith, E. and Bem, D. (1993) *Introduction to Psychology,* 11th edn. Fort Worth, Tex: Harcourt Brace.

Audit Commission (1993) *Helping with Enquiries,* Police Paper No. 12. London: HMSO.

Audit Commission (1996) *Streetwise: Effective Police Patrol.* London: HMSO

Baldwin, J. and Bottoms, A. (1976) *The Urban Criminal.* London: Tavistock.

Bandura, A. (1977) *Social Learning Theory.* New York: Prentice Hall.

Bandura, A. (1983) 'Psychological mechanisms of aggression', in R. Green and E.

Donnerstein (eds) *Aggression: Theoretical and Experimental Reviews,* Volume One. New York: Academic Press.

Bandura, A. (1986) *Social Foundations of Thought and Action.* Englewood Cliffs, NJ: Prentice Hall.

Bannister, J., Fyfe, N. and Kearns, A. (1998), 'Closed Circuit Television and the City', in C. Norris, J. Moran and G. Armstrong (eds), *Surveillance, Closed Circuit Television and Social Control.* Aldershot: Ashgate.

Banton. M. (1964) *The Policeman in the Community.* London: Tavistock.

Barr, R. and Pease, K (1990) 'Crime Placement, Displacement and Deflection', in Tonry, M. and N. Morris (eds) *Crime and Justice,* vol. 12, Chicago: Chicago University Press.

Bayley, D. (1994) *Police for the Future.* New York: Oxford University Press.

Bayley, D. (1996) 'What do police do?' in W. Saulsbury, J. Mott and T. Newburn (eds) *Themes in Contemporary Policing.* London: Independent Inquiry into the Role and Responsibilities of the Police.

Beccaria, C. (1963, first published 1764) *On Crimes and Punishments.* New York: Bobbs Merrill.

Beck, A. and Willis, A. (1999) 'Context-specific Measures of CCTV Effectiveness in the Retail Sector ', in Painter, K. and Tilley, N. (eds) *Crime Prevention Studies*, Vol 10: pp 252–269. Special edition entitled 'Surveillance of Public Space: CCTV, Street Lighting and Crime Prevention'.

Becker, H. (1963) *Outsiders.* New York: The Free Press.

Beirne, P. (1993) *Inventing Criminology.* Albany, NY: State University of New York Press.

Beick, W. and Kessler, D. (1977) *Response Time Analysis in Kansas City.* Mo: Board of Police Commissioners.

Bennett, T. (1990) *Evaluating Neighbourhood Watch.* Aldershot: Gower.

Bittner, E. (1974) 'Florence Nightingale in pursuit of Willie Sutton', in H. Jacob (ed) *Potential for Reform of Criminal Justice.* Beverly Hills, CA: Sage.

Bittner, E. (1975) *The Functions of the Police in Modern Society.* New York: Aronson.

Bittner, E. (1978) 'The function of the police in modern society', in P. K. Manning and J. van Maanen (eds) *Policing: A View from the Street.* Santa Monica, CA: Goodyear.

Bittner, E. and Bayley, D. (1983) *Gauging the Effectiveness of Police Work.* Unpublished manuscript.

Black, D. (1980) *The Manners and Customs of the Police.* London: Academic Press.

Blackburn, R. (1993) *The Psychology of Criminal Conduct.* Chichester: John Wiley.

Blom-Cooper, L. and Drabble, R. (1982) 'Police perceptions of crime', *British Journal of Criminology*, 22: 184–7.

Blumberg, A. (1970) *The Scales of Justice.* Chicago: Aldine.

Bohman, M., Cloninger, C., Sigvardson, S. and von Knorring, A.-L. (1982) 'Predisposition to petty criminality in Swedish adoptees', *Archives of General Psychiatry,* 39: 1233–41.

Bottomley, K. and Coleman, C. (1981) *Understanding Crime Rates.* Farnborough: Gower.

Bottoms, A. and Wiles, P. (1997) 'Environmental criminology', in M. Maguire, R. Morgan, and R. Reiner (eds) *The Oxford Handbook of Criminology,* 2nd edn. Oxford: Clarendon.

Bowlby, J. (1944) 'Forty-four juvenile thieves', *International Journal of Psychoanalysis*, 25: 1–57.

Bowlby, J., Ainsworth, M., Boston, M. and Rosenbluth, D. (1956) 'The effects of mother-child separation: a follow-up study', *British Journal of Medical Psychology*, 29: 211–47.

Bowling, B., Graham, J. and Ross, A. (1994) 'Self-reported offending among young people in England and Wales', in J. Junger-Tas, G. Terlouw and M. Klein (eds) *Delinquent Behaviour among Young People in the Western World*. Amsterdam: Kugler.

Box, S. (1971) *Deviance, Reality and Society*. London: Holt Rinehart and Winston.

Box, S. (1981) *Deviance, Reality and Society*, 2nd edn. London: Holt Rinehart and Winston.

Box, S. (1983) *Power, Crime and Mystification*. London: Tavistock.

Braithwaite, J. (1989) *Crime, Shame and Reintegration*. Cambridge: Cambridge University Press.

Bridges, L. (1983) 'Policing the urban wasteland', *Race and Class*, Autumn.

Bright, J. (1969) The Beat Patrol Experiment. London: Home Office Police Research and Development Branch, Unpublished.

Britton, P. (1997) *The Jigsaw Man*. London: Bantam.

Brody, S. (1976) *The Effectiveness of Sentencing: A review of the literature*, Home Office Research Study No. 35, London: HMSO.

Brown, B. (1995), *Closed Circuit Television in Town Centres: Three Case Studies*, Crime Prevention and Detection Series Paper 73, Home Office: London.

Brown, D. and Hogg, R. (1992) 'Law and order politics, left realism and radical criminology', in R. Matthews and J. Young (eds) *Issues in Realist Criminology*. London: Sage.

Brown, S. (1998), 'What's the Problem Girls? CCTV and the Gendering of Public Safety' in C. Norris, J. Moran and G. Armstrong (eds), *Surveillance, Closed Circuit Television and Social Control*, Aldershot: Ashgate.

Brownmiller, S. (1975) *Against Our Will*. London: Secker and Warburg.

Bulos, M., Chaker, W., Farish, M., Mahalingham, V. and Sarno, C. (1995), *Towards a Safer Sutton? Impact of Closed Circuit Television on Sutton Town Centre*. London: London Borough of Sutton.

Bulos, M. and Grant, D. (eds) (1996), *Towards a Safer Sutton? CCTV One Year On*. London: London Borough of Sutton.

Burgess, A., Hartman, C., Ressler, R., Douglas, J. and McCormack, A. (1986) 'Sexual homicide: a motivational model', *Journal of Interpersonal Violence*, 1: 251–72.

Burgess, R. and Akers, R. (1966) 'A differential association-reinforcement theory of criminal behaviour', *Social Problems*, 14: 128–47.

Burrows, J. (1979), 'The Impact of Closed Circuit Television on Crime in the London Underground' in P. Mayhew, R. Clarke, J. Burrows, M. Hough and S. Winchester, *Crime in Public View*, Home Office Research Study, no. 49. London: HMSO.

Burrows, J. and Tarling, R. (1982) *Clearing Up Crime*, Home Office Research Study No. 73. London: HMSO.

Bursik, R. (1986) 'Ecological stability and the dynamics of delinquency', in A. J. Reiss and M. Tonry (eds) *Communities and Crime*. Chicago: Chicago University Press.

Bursik, R. and Grasmick, H. (1993) *Neighbourhoods and Crime*. New York: Lexington.

Burt, C. (1925) *The Young Delinquent*. London: University of London Press.

Cain, M. (1973) *Society and the Policeman's Role*. London: Routledge and Kegan Paul.

Cain, M. (1986) 'Realism, feminism, methodology and law', *International Journal of the Sociology of Law*, 14: 255–67.

Cameron, D. and Frazer, E. (1987) *The Lust to Kill*. Cambridge: Polity.

Campbell, A. (1984) *The Girls in the Gang*. Oxford: Blackwell.

Campbell, D. and Stanley, J. (1963), *Experimental and Quasi-experimental Designs for Research*. Chicago: Rand MacNally.

Canter, D. (1994) *Criminal Shadows*. London: Harper Collins.

Caputi, J. (1987) *The Age of Sex Crime*. London: The Women's Press.

Carlen, P. (1992) 'Criminal women and criminal justice', in R. Matthews and J. Young (eds) *Issues in Realist Criminology*. London: Sage.

Carlisle, A. (1998) 'The divided self: toward an understanding of the dark side of the serial killer', in R. M. Holmes and S. T. Holmes (eds) *Contemporary Perspectives on Serial Murder*. Thousand Oaks, CA: Sage.

Carrington, K. (1998) 'Postmodernism and feminist criminologies', in P. Walton and J. Young (eds) *The New Criminology Revisited*. Basingstoke: Macmillan.

Chatterton, M. (1976) 'Police in social control', in J. King (ed) *Control Without Custody?* Cambridge: Cambridge Institute of Criminology.

Chatterton, M. (1983) 'Police work and assault charges', in M. Punch (ed) *Control in the Police Organisation*. Cambridge, Mass.: MIT Press.

Clarke, R. and Hough, M. (1984) *Crime and Police Effectiveness*. London: Home Office Research Study 79.

Clarke, R. (1992), *Situational Crime Prevention: Successful Case Studies*. New York: Harrow and Heston.

Cleckley, H. M. (1976) *The Mask of Sanity*, 5th edn. St Louis: C. V. Mosby.

Cloward, R. and Ohlin, L. (1960) *Delinquency and Opportunity*. New York: Free Press.

Cohen, A. K. (1955) *Delinquent Boys*. Glencoe: Free Press.

Cohen, A. K. (1966) *Deviance and Control*. Englewood Cliffs, NJ: Prentice Hall.

Cohen, L. and Felson, M. (1979) 'Social change and crime rate trends: a routine activities approach', *American Sociological Review*, 44: 588–608.

Cohen, S. (ed) (1971) *Images of Deviance*. Harmondsworth: Penguin.

Cohen, S. (1973a) *Folk Devils and Moral Panics*. London: Paladin.

Cohen, S. (1973b) 'The failures of criminology', *The Listener*, 8 November.

Cohen, S. (1985), *Visions of Social Control*. Polity Press: Cambridge.

Cohen, S. (1993) 'Human rights and crimes of the state', *Australian and New Zealand Journal of Criminology*, 26: 97–115.

Cohen, S. (1998) 'Intellectual scepticism and political commitment', in P. Walton and J. Young (eds) *The New Criminology Revisited*. Basingstoke: Macmillan.

Coleman, C. and Moynihan, J. (1996) *Understanding Crime Data: Haunted by the Dark Figure*. Buckingham: Open University Press.

Comrie, M. and Kings, E. (1974) Study of Urban Workloads: Final Report. Home Office Police Research Services Unit, Unpublished.

Connell, R. (1987) *Gender and Power*. Cambridge: Polity.

Connell, R. (1996) *Masculinities.* Cambridge: Polity.

Constant, M. and Turnbull, P. (1994), *The Principles and Practice of CCTV*, Hertfordshire: Paramount Publishing.

Cook, T. D. and Campbell, D. T. (1979), *Quasi-Experimentation: Design and Analysis Issues for Field Settings*, Chicago: Rand McNally.

Cornish, D. and Clarke, R. (eds) (1986) *The Reasoning Criminal.* New York: Springer–Verlag.

Crawford, A., Jones, T., Woodhouse, T. and Young, J. (1990) *The Second Islington Crime Survey.* London: Centre for Criminology, Middlesex Polytechnic.

Critchley, T. (1978) *A History of the Police in England and Wales.* London: Constable.

Currie, E. (1985) *Confronting Crime.* New York: Pantheon.

Damer, S. (1974) 'Wine Alley: the sociology of a dreadful enclosure', *Sociological Review*, 22: 221–48.

Davis, K. (1969) *Discretionary Justice.* Urbana, Ill.: University of Illinois.

Ditton, J. (1998), 'Public Support for Town Centre CCTV Schemes: Myth or Reality', in C. Norris, J. Moran and G. Armstrong (eds), *Surveillance, Closed Circuit Television and Social Control*, Aldershot: Ashgate.

Ditton, J. and Short, E. (1998), 'Evaluating Scotland's First Town Centre CCTV Scheme,' in C. Norris, J. Moran and G. Armstrong (eds), *Surveillance, Closed Circuit Television and Social Control*, Aldershot: Ashgate.

Ditton, J. and Short, E. (1999), 'Yes, It Works, No, It Doesn't: Comparing the Effects of Open CCTV in Two Adjacent Scottish Town Centres,' in Painter, K. and Tilley, N. (eds) *Crime Prevention Studies*, Vol 10: 201–224. Special edition entitled 'Surveillance of Public Space: CCTV, Street Lighting and Crime Prevention'.

Ditton, J., Short, E. Phillips S., Norris, C. and Armstrong, G. (1999), *The Effect of the Introduction of Closed Circuit Television on Recorded Crime Rates and Concern about Crime in Glasgow*, Edinburgh, SCOT: Central Research Unit, Scottish Office.

Dixon, D. (1992) 'Legal regulation and policing pratice', *Social and Legal Studies*, 1: 515–41.

Dixon, D. (1997) *Law in Policing.* Oxford: Clarendon.

Dixon, D. (1999) 'Police investigative procedures', in C. Walker and K. Starmer (eds) *Miscarriages of Justice*, 2nd edn. London: Blackstone.

Downes, D. (1966) *The Delinquent Solution.* London: Routledge and Kegan Paul.

Downes, D. and Rock, P. (1998) *Understanding Deviance*, 3rd edn. Oxford: Oxford University Press.

Drapkin, I. (1983) 'Criminology: intellectual history', in S. Kadish (ed) *Encyclopedia of Crime and Justice.* New York: Free Press.

Duclos, D. (1998) *The Werewolf Complex: America's Fascination with Violence.* Oxford: Berg.

Dunnighan, C. and Norris, C. (1996) 'A risky business: exchange, bargaining and risk in the recruitment and running of informers by English police officers', *Police Studies*, 19: 1–25.

Dunnighan, C. and Norris, C. (1999), 'The detective, the snout, and the Audit Commission: the real costs in using informants', *The Howard Journal*, 38: 67–86.

Durkheim, E. (1952) *Suicide: A Study in Sociology.* London: Routledge and Kegan Paul.

Eaton, M. (1986) *Justice for Women.* Milton Keynes: Open University Press.

Edwards, S. (1984) *Women on Trial.* Manchester: Manchester University Press.

Edwards, S. (1989) *Policing 'Domestic' Violence.* London: Sage.

Egger, S. (ed) (1990) *Serial Murder: An Elusive Phenomenon.* New York: Praeger.

Ekblom, P. (1992), 'The Safer Cities Programe Impact Evaluation: Problem and Progress', *Studies on Crime and Crime Prevention*, Vol. 1. No 1.

Ekblom, P. and Heal, K. (1982) *The Police Response to Calls from the Public.* Research and Planning Unit Paper 9. London: Home Office.

Elliott, D. S., Huizinga, D. and Ageton, S. S. (1985) *Explaining Delinquency and Drug Use.* Beverly Hills, CA: Sage.

Ericson, R. (1982) *Reproducing Order: A Study of Police Patrol Work.* Toronto: University of Toronto Press.

Eysenck, H. (1977) *Crime and Personality*, 3rd edn. London Routledge and Kegan Paul.

Eysenck, H. 'Personality theory and the problems of criminality', in B. J. McGurk, D. M. Thornton and M. Williams (eds) *Applying Psychology to Imprisonment.* London: HMSO.

Farrington, D. (1997) 'Human development and criminal careers', in M. Maguire, R. Morgan, and R. Reiner (eds) *The Oxford Handbook of Criminology,* 2nd edn. Oxford: Clarendon.

Feldman, D. (1964) 'Psychoanalysis and crime', in B. Rosenberg, I. Gerver and F. W. Howton (eds) *Mass Society in Crisis.* New York: Macmillan.

Feldman, P. (1993) *The Psychology of Crime.* Cambridge: Cambridge University Press.

Ferri, E. (1913) *The Positive School of Criminology.* Chicago: Kerr and Co.

Field, S. (1991), *Trends in Crime and their Interpretation: A Study of Recorded Crime in Post War England and Wales*, Home Office Research Study no 119, London: HMSO.

Fielding, N. (1984) 'Police socialisation and police competence', *British Journal of Sociology*, 35: 568–90.

Fielding, N. (1988) 'Competence and culture in the police', *Sociology*, 22: 45–64.

Fielding, N., Kemp, C. and Norris, C. (1989) 'Constraints on the practice of community policing', in R. Morgan and D. J. Smith (eds) *Coming to Terms with Policing.* London: Routledge.

FitzGerald, M. (1993) *Ethnic Minorities and the Criminal Justice System*, Royal Commision on Criminal Justice Research Study No 20. London: HMSO.

Folkard, M., Smith, D. E., and Smith D. D. (1976), *IMPACT Volume 2: The Results of the Experiment*, Home Office Research Study no 36. London: HMSO.

Fox, J. A. (1990) 'Murder they wrote', *Contemporary Psychology*, 35: 890–1.

France, A. and Wiles, P. (1998) 'Dangerous futures: social exclusion and youth work in late modernity', in C. J. Finer and M. Nellis (eds) *Crime and Social Exclusion.* Oxford: Blackwell.

Gabor, T. (1978), 'Crime Displacement: The Literature and Strategies For Its Investigation,' *Crime and Justice*, Vol 6 No 2: 100–107.

Garland, D. (1985) 'The criminal and his science', *British Journal of Criminology*, 25: 109–37.

Garland, D. (1996) 'The limits of the sovereign state', *British Journal of Criminology*, 36: 445–71.

Garland, D. (1997) 'Of crimes and criminals: the development of criminology in Britain', in M. Maguire, R. Morgan, and R. Reiner (eds) *The Oxford Handbook of Criminology*, 2nd edn. Oxford: Clarendon.

Gelsthorpe, L. (1997) 'Feminism and criminology', in M. Maguire, R. Morgan, and R. Reiner (eds) *The Oxford Handbook of Criminology*, 2nd edn. Oxford: Clarendon.

Gelsthorpe, L. and Morris. A. (eds) (1990) *Feminist Perspectives in Criminology*. Buckingham: Open University Press.

Giddens, A. (1990) *The Consequences of Modernity*. Cambridge: Polity.

Giddens, A. (1991) *Modernity and Self-identity*. Cambridge: Polity.

Gill, M. and Turbin, V. (1999) 'Evaluating 'Realistic Evaluation': Evidence from a study of CCTV', in Painter, K. and Tilley, N. (eds) *Crime Prevention Studies*, Vol 10: 225–251. Special edition entitled 'Surveillance of Public Space: CCTV, Street Lighting and Crime Prevention'.

Gilroy, P. (1982) 'The myth of black criminality', *Socialist Register*. London: Merlin.

Glover, E. (1960) *The Roots of Crime*. London: Imago.

Goldstein, J. (1960) 'Police discretion not to invoke the criminal process', *Yale Law Journal*, 69: 543–94.

Goodwin, M., Johnstone, C. and Williams, K. (1998), 'New Spaces of Law Enforcement: Closed Circuit Television, Public Behaviour and the Policing of Public Space', unpublished paper, Aberystwyth: Institute of Geography and Earth Sciences, University of Wales.

Gouldner, A. (1975) *For Sociology*. Harmondsworth: Pelican.

Goring C. (1913) *The English Convict*. London: HMSO.

Gottfredson, M. and Hirschi, T. (1990) *A General Theory of Crime*. Stanford CA: Stanford University Press.

Graham, J. and Bowling, B. (1995) *Young People and Crime*, Home Office Research Study No. 145. London: HMSO.

Graham, S. (1998), 'Towards the Fifth Utility? On the Extension and Normalisation of Public CCTV' in C. Norris, J. Moran and G. Armstrong (eds), *Surveillance, Closed Circuit Television and Social Control*, Aldershot: Ashgate.

Gresswell, D. and Hollin, C. (1994) 'Multiple murder: a review', *British Journal of Criminology*, 34: 1–14.

Hacking, I. (1990) *The Taming of Chance*. Cambridge: Cambridge University Press.

Hagan, J. (1988) *Structural Criminology*. Cambridge: Polity.

Hagan, J., Simpson, J. and Gillis, A. (1979) 'The sexual stratification of social control', *British Journal of Sociology*, 30: 25–38.

Hagan, J., Gillis, A. and Simpson, J. (1985) 'The class structure of gender and delinquency', *American Journal of Sociology*, 90: 1151–78.

Hale, R. and Bolin, A. (1998) 'The female serial killer', in R. M. Holmes and S. T. Holmes (eds) *Contemporary Perspectives on Serial Murder*. Thousand Oaks, CA: Sage.

Hall, S., Critcher, C., Clarke, J., Jefferson, T. and Roberts, B. (1978) *Policing the Crisis*. London: Macmillan.

Hall, S. and Jefferson, T. (eds) (1976) *Resistance Through Rituals*. London: Hutchinson.

Hancox, P. and Morgan, J. (1975), 'The Use of CCTV for Police Control at Football Matches', *Police Research Bulletin*, vol. 25, pp. 41–4.

Harding, S. (ed) (1986) T*he Science Question in Feminism.* Milton Keynes: Open University Press.

Hare, R. D. (1991) *The Hare Psychopathy Checklist – Revised.* Toronto: Multi-Health Systems.

Healy, W. and Bronner, A. F. (1936) *New Light on Delinquency and its Treatment.* New Haven, Conn: Yale University Press.

Heidensohn, F. (1985) *Women and Crime.* Basingstoke: Macmillan.

Heidensohn, F. (1992) *Women in Control? The Role of Women in Law Enforcement.* Oxford: Oxford University Press.

Heidensohn, F. (1996) *Women and Crime,* 2nd edn. Basingstoke: Macmillan.

Henderson. S. K. (1939) *Psychopathic States.* New York: Norton.

Henry, S. and Milovanovic, D. (1996) *Constitutive Criminology.* London: Sage.

Hester, S. and Eglin, P. (1992) *A Sociology of Crime.* London: Routledge.

Hickey, E. W. (1986) 'The female serial murderer', *Journal of Police and Criminal Psychology,* 2: 72–81.

Hickey, E. W. (1990) 'The etiology of victimization in serial murder', in Egger, S. (ed) *Serial Murder: An Elusive Phenomenon.* New York: Praeger.

Hickey, E. W. (1991) *Serial Murderers and Their Victims.* Pacific Grove, CA: Brooks/Cole.

Hickey, E. W. (1997) *Serial Murderers and Their Victims,* 2nd edn. Belmont, CA: Wadsworth.

Hirschi, T. (1969) *Causes of Delinquency.* Berkeley, CA: University of California Press.

Hirschi, T. (1979) 'Separate and unequal is better', *Journal of Research in Crime and Delinquency,* 16: 34–8.

Hirschi, T. (1986) 'On the compatibility of rational choice and social control theories of crime', in Cornish, D. and Clarke, R. (eds) *The Reasoning Criminal.* New York: Springer-Verlag.

Hirst, P. (1975) 'Marx and Engels on law, crime and morality', in I. Taylor, P. Walton and J. Young (eds) *Critical Criminology.* London: Routledge and Kegan Paul.

Holdaway, S. (ed) (1979) *The British Police.* London: Edward Arnold.

Holdaway, S. (1983) *Inside the British Police.* Oxford: Blackwell.

Hollin, C. (1989) *Psychology and Crime.* London: Routledge.

Holmes, R. M. and DeBurger, J. (1988) *Serial Murder.* Newbury Park, CA: Sage.

Holmes, R. M. and Holmes, S. T. (1998) *Serial Murder,* 2nd edn. London : Sage.

Holmes, R. M. and Holmes, S. T. (eds) (1998) *Contemporary Perspectives on Serial Murder.* Thousand Oaks, CA: Sage.

Home Office (1967) *Three Working Parties on Police Manpower, Equipment and Efficiency.* London: HMSO.

Home Office (1993) *Police Reform: A Police Service for the Twenty-first Century.* London: HMSO.

Home Office (1994) *CCTV: Looking Out For You,* London: Home Office.

Home Office (1995) *Review of Police Core and Ancillary Tasks.* London: HMSO.

Home Office (1998) *Criminal Statistics England and Wales 1997.* London: The Stationery Office.

Honess, T. and Charman, E. (1992) *Closed Circuit Television in Public Places, Its*

Acceptability and Perceived Effectiveness, Home Office, Police Research Group, Crime Prevention Unit series, Paper 35, London: Home Office.

Hooton, E. (1939) *The American Criminal: An Anthropological Study.* Cambridge, Mass: Harvard University Press.

Hoyle, C. (1998) *Negotiating Domestic Violence: Police, Criminal Justice and Victims.* Oxford: Clarendon Press.

Huff, R. (1996) *Gangs in America.* Thousand Oaks, CA: Sage.

Hughes, G. (1998) *Understanding Crime Prevention: Social Control, Risk and Late Modernity*, Buckingham: Open University Press.

Jacobs, J. (1962) *The Death and Life of Great American Cities.* London: Jonathan Cape.

James, D. (1979) 'Police-black relations: the professional solution', in S. Holdaway (ed) *The British Police.* London: Edward Arnold.

Jamieson, R. (1998) 'Towards a criminology of war in Europe', in V. Ruggiero, N. South and I. Taylor (eds) *The New European Criminology.* London: Routledge.

Jayewardene, C. (1963) 'The English precursors of Lombroso', *British Journal of Criminology*, 4: 164–70.

Jefferson, T. (1997) 'Masculinities and crime', in M. Maguire, R. Morgan, and R. Reiner (eds) *The Oxford Handbook of Criminology*, 2nd edn. Oxford: Clarendon.

Jefferson T. and Walker, M. (1992) 'Ethnic minorities in the criminal justice system', *Criminal Law Review*, 83–95.

Jefferson, T. and Walker, M. (1993) 'Attitudes to the police of ethnic minorities in a provincial city', *British Journal of Criminology*, 33: 251–66.

Jeffery, C. R. (1965) 'Criminal behavior and learning theory', *Journal of Criminal Law, Criminology and Police Science*, 56: 294–300.

Jenkins, P. (1988) 'Serial murder in England 1940–1985', *Journal of Criminal Justice*, 16: 1–15.

Jenkins, P. (1994) *Using Murder: the Social Construction of Serial Homicide.* New York: Aldine de Gruyter.

Johnston, L. (1992) *The Rebirth of Private Policing.* London: Routledge.

Johnston, L. (2000) *Policing Britain.* Harlow: Longman.

Johnstone, G. (1996) *Medical Concepts and Penal Policy.* London: Cavendish.

Jones, T., MacLean, B. and Young, J. (1986) *The Islington Crime Survey.* Aldershot: Gower.

Jupp, V. (1989), *Methods of Criminological Research*, London: Unwin Hyman.

Kaplan, H. (1980) *Deviant Behaviour in Defense of Self.* New York: Pergamon.

Kaye, T. (1991) *Unsafe and Unsatisfactory? Report of the Independent Inquiry into the Working Practices of the West Midland Serious Crime Squad*, London: Civil Liberties Trust.

Kelling, G., Pate, T., Dieckman, D. and Brown C. (1974), *The Kansas City preventative patrol experiment: a summary report*, Washington D.C.: Police Foundation.

Kemp, C., Norris, C. and Fielding, N. (1992) *Negotiating Nothing: Police Decision-Making in Disputes.* Aldershot: Avebury.

Kiger, K. (1990) 'The darker figure of crime: the serial murder enigma', in Egger, S. (ed) *Serial Murder: An Elusive Phenomenon.* New York: Praeger.

King, M. (1981) *The Framework of Criminal Justice.* London: Croom Helm.

Kinsey, R. (1984) *Merseyside Crime Survey*. Edinburgh: Centre for Criminology, University of Edinburgh.

Kitsuse, J. and Cicourel, A. (1963) 'A note on the uses of official statistics', *Social Problems*, 11: 131–9.

Klein, D. (1973) 'The etiology of female crime', *Issues in Criminology*, 8: 3–30.

Klockars, C. (1985) *The Idea of Police*. Beverly Hills, CA: Sage.

Kohlberg, L. (1964) 'Development of moral character and moral ideology', in M. Hoffman and L. Hoffman (eds) *Review of Child Development Research*, vol 1. New York: Russell Sage Foundation.

Kohlberg, L. (1978) 'Revisions in the theory and practice of mental development', in W. Damon (ed) *New Directions in Child Development: Moral Development*. San Francisco, CA: Jossey-Bass.

Kretschmer, E. (1936) *Physique and Character*. London: Kegan Paul, Trench, Trubner and Co.

Landau, S. and Nathan, G. (1983) 'Selecting delinquents for cautioning in the London Metropolitan area', *British Journal of Criminology*, 23: 128–49.

Lanier, M. and Henry, S. (1998) *Essential Criminology*. Oxford: Westview Press.

Lea, J. (1998) 'Criminology and postmodernity', in P. Walton and J. Young (eds) *The New Criminology Revisited*. Basingstoke: Macmillan.

Lea, J. and Young, J. (1984) *What is to be Done About Law and Order?* Harmondsworth: Penguin.

Lea, J. and Young, J. (1993) *What is to be Done About Law and Order?* 2nd edn. London: Pluto Press.

Lemert, E. (1951) *Social Pathology*. New York: McGraw-Hill.

Lemert, E. (1967) *Human Deviance, Social Problems and Social Control*. Englewood Cliffs, NJ: Prentice Hall.

Leonard, E. (1982) *Women, Crime and Society*. New York: Longman.

Levin, J. and Fox, J. A. (1985) *Mass Murder: America's Growing Menace*. New York: Plenum Press.

Leyton, E. (1989) *Hunting Humans: The Rise of the Modern Multiple Murderer*. Harmondsworth: Penguin Books.

Lilly, J. R., Cullen, F. T., and Ball, R. A. (1995) *Criminological Theory: Context and Consequences*, 2nd edn. London: Sage.

Lombroso, C. (1876) *L'Uomo Delinquente*. Milan: Hoepli.

Loveday, B. (1996) 'Crime at the Core?' in F. Leishman, B. Loveday and S. Savage (eds) *Core Issues in Policing*, Harlow: Longman.

Lundman, R. (ed) (1980) *Police Behaviour*. New York: Oxford University Press.

Lustgarten, L. (1986) *The Governance of Police*. London: Sweet and Maxwell.

Lyon, D. (1999) *Postmodernity*, 2nd edn. Buckingham: Open University Press.

Lyotard, J.-F. (1984) *The Postmodern Condition*. Manchester: Manchester University Press.

MacLean, B. (1992) 'A programme of local crime research for Canada', in J. Lowman and B. MacLean (eds) *Realist Criminology*. Toronto: Toronto University Press.

Macpherson, W. (1999) *The Stephen Lawrence Inquiry*. London: The Stationery Office.

McBarnet, D. (1979) 'Arrest: the legal context of policing', in S. Holdaway (ed) *The British Police*. London: Edward Arnold.

McBarnet, D. (1981) *Conviction*. London: Macmillan.

McCabe, S. and Sutcliffe, F. (1978) *Defining Crime*. Oxford: Basil Blackwell.

McCahill, M. (1998) 'Beyond Foucault: Towards a Contemporary Theory of Surveillance', in C. Norris, J. Moran and G. Armstrong (eds), *Surveillance, Closed Circuit Television and Social Control*. Aldershot: Ashgate.

McCahill, M. (2000) 'The Surveillance Web: The rise and extent of visual surveillance in a Northern City'. Unpublished PhD, Hull: University of Hull.

Maguire, M. (1998) 'Restraining Big Brother? The Regulation of Surveillance in England and Wales', in Norris, C., Moran, J. and Armstrong, G. (eds), *CCTV, Surveillance and Social Control*, Aldershot: Ashgate.

Maguire, M. and Norris, C. (1992) *The Conduct and Supervision of Criminal Investigations*, Royal Commission on Criminal Justice Research Report No. 5. London: HMSO.

Mahalingham, V. (1996) 'Sutton Town Centre Public Perception Survey', in M. Bulos and D. Grant (eds), *Towards a Safer Sutton? CCTV: One Year On*. London: London Borough of Sutton.

Mannheim, H. (1965) *Comparative Criminology*, vols 1 & 2. London: Routledge and Kegan Paul.

Manning, P. (1977) *Police Work*. Cambridge, Mass.: MIT Press.

Manning P. (1982) 'Organisational work: structuration of the environment', *British Journal of Sociology*, 33: 118–139.

Mark, R. (1977) *Policing a Perplexed Society*. London: Allen and Unwin.

Martinson, R. (1974), 'What Works? Questions and Answers about Prison Reform', *The Public Interest*, 35: 22–54.

Masters, B. (1985) *Killing for Company: The Case of Dennis Nilsen*. London: Jonathan Cape.

Matza, D. (1964) *Delinquency and Drift*. New York: Wiley.

Mawby, R. (1979) *Policing the City*. Farnborough: Gower.

Mednick, S., Gabrielli, W., and Hutchings, B. (1987) 'Genetic factors in the etiology of criminal behaviour', in S. Mednick, T. Moffit and S. Stack (eds) *The Causes of Crime: New Biological Approaches*. Cambridge: Cambridge University Press.

Mednick, S. and Volavka, J. (1980) 'Biology and crime', in N. Morris and M. Tonry (eds) *Crime and Justice*, vol 2. Chicago: University of Chicago Press.

Merton, R. (1938) 'Social structure and anomie', *American Sociological Review*, 3: 672–82.

Merton, R. (1957) *Social Theory and Social Structure*. New York: Free Press.

Messerschmidt, J. (1993) *Masculinities and Crime*. Lanham, Md: Rowman and Littlefield.

Messner, S. and Rosenfeld, R. (1994) *Crime and the American Dream*. Belmont, CA: Wadsworth.

Michael, J. and Adler, M. (1933) *Crime, Law and Social Science*. New York: Harcourt Brace Jovanovich.

Mirrlees-Black C., Budd, T., Partridge, S., and Mayhew, P. (1998) *The 1998 British Crime Survey*, Home Office Statistical Bulletin, Issue 21/98, London: Government Statistical Service.

Mischel, W. (1968) *Personality and Assessment*. New York: Wiley.

Moir, A. and Jessel, D. (1995) *A Mind to Crime*. London: Michael Joseph.

Morgan, B. (1990) *The Police Function in the Investigation of Crime*. Aldershot: Avebury.

Morgan, R. and Newburn, T. (1997) *The Future of Policing*. Oxford: Clarendon.

Morris, T. (1957) *The Criminal Area*. London: Routledge and Kegan Paul.

Muir, K. (1977) *Police: Street Corner Politicians*. Chicago: Chicago University Press.

Mullin, C. (1987) *Error of Judgement*. Dublin: Poolbeg.

Muncie, J. (1999)*Youth and Crime*. London: Sage.

Muncie, J. (2000) 'Decriminalizing criminology', in G. Lewis, S. Gewirtz and J. Clarke (eds) *Rethinking Social Policy*. London: Sage.

Muncie, J. and McLaughlin, E. (eds) (1996) *Criminological Perspectives: A Reader*. London: Sage.

Musheno, M., Levine, J. and Palumbo, D. (1978), 'Television Surveillance and Crime Prevention: Evaluation of an Attempt to Create Defensible Space in Public Housing', *Social Science Quarterly*, vol. 58, no. 4, pp. 647–56.

Naffine, N. (1997) *Feminism and Criminology*. Cambridge: Polity.

National Deviancy Conference/Conference of Socialist Economists (eds) (1979) *Capitalism and the Rule of Law: From Deviancy Theory to Marxism*. London: Hutchinson.

Nelken, D. (1997) 'White-collar crime', in M. Maguire, R. Morgan, and R. Reiner (eds) *The Oxford Handbook of Criminology*, 2nd edn. Oxford: Clarendon.

Nicholson, M. (1979) *The Yorkshire Ripper*. London: W. H. Allen.

Norris, C. (1989) 'Avoiding trouble: the patrol officer's perception of encounters with the public', in M. Wetheritt (ed) *Police Research: Some Future Prospects*. Aldershot: Avebury.

Norris, C. and Armstrong, G. (1999) *The Maximum Surveillance Society: The Rise of CCTV*, Oxford: Berg.

Norris, C., Fielding, N., Kemp, C. and Fielding, J. (1992) 'Black and Blue: an analysis of the influence of race on being stopped by the police', *British Journal of Sociology*, 43: 207–24.

Norris, C., Moran, J. and G. Armstrong (1998) 'Algorithmic Surveillance: The Future of Automated Visual Surveillance', in C. Norris, J. Moran and G. Armstrong (eds), *Surveillance, Closed Circuit Television and Social Control*, Aldershot: Ashgate.

Norris, C., Moran, J. and Armstrong, G. (eds) (1998) *Surveillance, Closed Circuit Television and Social Control*, Aldershot: Ashgate.

Norris, J. (1988) *Serial Killers*. London: Arrow.

Norris, J. and Birnes, W. (1998) *Serial Killers: The Growing Menace*. New York: Dolphin.

Nye, R. A. (1984) *Crime, Madness and Politics in Modern France*. Princeton: Princeton University Press.

Packer, H. (1968) *The Limits of the Criminal Sanction*. Stanford, CA: Stanford University Press.

Pahl, J. (1982) 'Police response to battered women', *Journal of Social Welfare Law*, 5: 337–43.

Painter, K. and Tilley, N. (1999), Editors' Introduction: Seeing and Being Seen to Prevent Crime, in K. Painter, and N. Tilley, (eds) *Crime Prevention Studies*, Vol 10 pp. 1–15. Special edition entitled 'Surveillance of Public Space: CCTV, Street Lighting and Crime Prevention'.

Parker, H. (1974) *View From the Boys*. Newton Abbott: David and Charles.

Passas, N. (1990) 'Anomie and corporate deviance', *Contemporary Crises*, 14: 157–78.

Pawson, R. and Tilley, N. (1994), 'What Works in Evaluation Research?', *British Journal of Criminology*, vol. 34, no. 3, pp. 291–306.

Pawson, R. and Tilley, N. (1997), *Realistic Evaluation*, London: Sage.

Pearce, F. and Tombs, S. (1992) 'Realism and corporate crime', in R. Matthews and J. Young (eds) *Issues in Realist Criminology*. London: Sage.

Pease, K. (1997), 'Crime Prevention' in M. Maguire, R. Morgan and R. Reiner (eds) *The Oxford Handbook Of Criminology*, second edition, Oxford: Clarendon Press.

Pease, K. (1999) 'A Review of Street Lighting Evaluations: Crime Reduction Effects', in Painter, K. and Tilley, N. (eds) *Crime Prevention Studies*, Vol 10 pp 47–76. Special edition entitled 'Surveillance of Public Space: CCTV, Street Lighting and Crime Prevention'.

Phillips, C. and Brown, D. (1998) *Entry into the Criminal Justice System: a Survey of Police Arrests and their Outcomes*, Home Office Research Study No. 185. London: Home Office.

Phillips, C. (1999) 'A review of CCTV Evaluations: Crime Reduction Effects and Attitudes Towards its Use' in Painter, K. and Tilley, N. (eds) *Crime Prevention Studies*, Vol 10 pp. 123–156. Special edition entitled 'Surveillance of Public Space: CCTV, Street Lighting and Crime Prevention'.

Plummer, K. (1979) 'Misunderstanding labelling perspectives', in D. Downes and P. Rock (eds) *Deviant Interpretations*. Oxford: Martin Robertson.

Pick, D. (1989) *Faces of Degeneration: A European Disorder*. Cambridge: Cambridge University Press.

Police Foundation/Policy Studies Institute (1996) *The Role and Responsibilities of the Police: Report of an Independent Inquiry*. London: Police Foundation/Policy Studies Institute.

Policy Studies Institute (PSI) (1983) *Police and People in London*, vol IV, D. J. Smith and J. Gray, *The Police in Action*. London: PSI.

Pollak, O. (1961) *The Criminality of Women*. New York: A. S. Barnes.

Poyner, B. (1988) 'Video Cameras and Bus Vandalism', *Journal of Security and Administration*, no. 11, pp. 44–51.

Poyner, B. (1992) 'Situational Crime Prevention in Two Parking Facilities', in R. Clarke, (ed.), *Situational Crime Prevention: Successful Case Studies*, New York: Harrow and Heston.

Prentky, R., Burgess, A., Rokous, F., Lee, A., Hartman, C., Ressler, R. and Douglas, J. (1989) 'The presumptive role of fantasy in serial sexual homicide', *American Journal of Psychiatry*, 146: 887–91.

Punch, M. and Naylor, T. (1973) 'The police: a secret social service', *New Society*, 24: 358–61.

Raine, A. (1993) *The Psychopathology of Crime*. San Diego, CA: Academic Press.

Reckless, W. C. (1961) *The Crime Problem.* New York: Appleton, Century Crofts.

Reeve, A. (1998) 'The Panopticisation of Shopping: CCTV and Leisure Consumption', in C. Norris, J. Moran and G. Armstrong (eds), *Surveillance, Closed Circuit Television and Social Control*, Aldershot: Ashgate.

Reiner, R. (1992) *The Politics of the Police,* 2nd edn. London: Wheatsheaf.

Reiss, A. (1980) 'Police brutality', in R. Lundman (ed) *Police Behaviour.* New York: Oxford University Press.

Ressler, R., Burgess, A. and Douglas, J. (1988) *Sexual Homicide: Patterns and Motives.* Lexington, MA: Lexington Books.

Rice, M. (1990) 'Challenging orthodoxies in feminist theory: a black feminist critique', in Gelsthorpe, L. and Morris. A. (eds) *Feminist Perspectives in Criminology.* Buckingham: Open University Press.

Rock, P. (1973) *Deviant Behaviour.* London: Hutchinson.

Rock, P. (1997) 'Sociological theories of crime', in M. Maguire, R. Morgan, and R. Reiner (eds) *The Oxford Handbook of Criminology,* 2nd edn. Oxford: Clarendon.

Rose, D. (1996) *In the Name of the Law.* London: Vintage.

Roshier, B. (1989), *Controlling Crime: The Classical Perspective in Criminology,* Buckingham, Open University Press.

Rotter, J. B. (1975) 'Some problems and misconceptions related to the construct of internal versus external control of reinforcement', *Journal of Consulting and Clinical Psychology,* 43: 56–67.

Royal Commission on Criminal Justice (1993) *Report.* Cm 2263. London: HMSO.

Rozenberg, J. (1992) 'Miscarriages of Justice' in E. Stockdale and S. Casale (eds) *Criminal Justice Under Stress,* London: Blackstone.

Rubinstein, J. (1973) *City Police.* New York: Ballantine.

Rutter, M. (1972) *Maternal Deprivation Reassessed.* Harmondsworth: Penguin.

Rutter, M. (1981) *Maternal Deprivation Reassessed,* 2nd edn. Harmondsworth: Penguin.

Rutter, M. and Giller, H. (1983) *Juvenile Delinquency: Trends and Perspectives.* Harmondsworth: Penguin.

Rutter, M. Giller, H. and Hagell, A. (1998) *Antisocial Behavior by Young People.* Cambridge: Cambridge University Press.

Sanders, A., Bridges, L., Mulvaney, A. and Crozier, G. (1989) *Advice and Assistance at Police Stations and the 24 Hour Duty Solicitor Scheme.* London: Lord Chancellors Dept.

Sanders, A. and Young, R. (1994) *Criminal Justice.* London: Butterworths.

Sarno, C. (1996), 'The Impact of Closed Circuit Television on Crime in Sutton Town Centre', in M. Bulos and D. Grant (eds), *Towards a Safer Sutton? CCTV One Year On,* London: London Borough of Sutton.

Schulsinger, F. (1977) 'Psychopathy: heredity and environment', in S. Mednick and K. Christiansen (eds) *Biosocial Bases of Criminal Behaviour.* New York: Gardner Press.

Schur, E. (1971) *Labeling Deviant Behavior.* New York: Harper and Row.

Schwendinger, H. and Schwendinger J. (1970) 'Defenders of order or guardians of human rights?' *Issues in Criminology,* 5: 123–57.

Scraton, P. and Chadwick, K. (1991) 'The theoretical and political priorities of critical criminology', in K. Stenson and D. Cowell (eds) *The Politics of Crime*

Control. London: Sage.

Sellar, W. C. and Yeatman, R. J. (1930) *1066 and All That*, 6th edn. London: Methuen.

Sellin, T. (1938) *Culture Conflict and Crime.* New York: Social Science Research Council.

Seltzer, M. (1998) *Serial Killers: Death and Life in America's Wound Culture.* London: Routledge.

Sharp, D. and Wilson D. (2000) '"Household Security": Private Policing and Vigilantism in Doncaster', *The Howard Journal*, 39: 113–131.

Shaw, C. and McKay, H. (1942) *Juvenile Delinquency and Urban Areas.* Chicago: University of Chicago Press.

Shearing, C. and Stenning, P. (eds) (1987) *Private Policing.* Newbury Park, CA: Sage.

Sheldon, W. H. (1949) *Varieties of Delinquent Youth.* New York: Harper.

Short, E. and Ditton, J. (1995), 'Does CCTV Affect Crime?', *CCTV Today*, vol. 2, no. 2, pp. 10–12.

Short, E. and Ditton, J. (1996), *Does Closed Circuit Television Prevent Crime? An Evaluation of the Use of CCTV Surveillance Cameras in Airdrie Town Centre.* Edinburgh: The Scottish Office Central Research Unit.

Short, J. and Strodtbeck, F. (1965) *Group Process and Gang Delinquency.* Chicago: University of Chicago Press.

Sim, J., Scraton, P. and Gordon, P. (1987) 'Introduction: crime, the state and critical analysis', in P. Scraton (ed) *Law, Order and the Authoritarian State.* Milton Keynes: Open University Press.

Skinns, D. (1998), 'Crime Reduction, Diffusion and Displacement: Evaluating the Effectiveness of CCTV' in C. Norris, J. Moran, and G. Armstrong (eds), *Surveillance, Closed Circuit Television and Social Control*, Aldershot: Ashgate.

Skogan, W. (1990) *The Police and the Public in England and Wales: A British Crime Survey Report*, Home Office Research Study No. 117. London HMSO.

Skogan, W. (1994) *Contacts between Police and Public: Findings from the 1992 British Crime Survey*, Home Office Research Study No. 134. London: HMSO.

Slapper, G. and Tombs, S. (1999) *Corporate Crime.* Harlow: Longman.

Smart, C. (1976) *Women, Crime and Criminology.* London: Routledge and Kegan Paul.

Smart, S. (1990) 'Feminist approaches to criminology or postmodern woman meets atavistic man', in Gelsthorpe, L. and Morris. A. (eds) *Feminist Perpectives in Criminology.* Buckingham: Open University Press.

Smith, D. (1997) 'Ethnic origins, crime and criminal justice', in M. Maguire, R. Morgan, and R. Reiner (eds) *The Oxford Handbook of Criminology*, 2nd edn. Oxford: Clarendon.

Smith, H. (1981), *Strategies of Social Research*, New Jersey: Prentice-Hall

Smith, J. (1989) 'There's only one Yorkshire Ripper', in J. Smith, *Misogynies.* London: Faber.

Soothill, K. (1993) 'The serial killer industry', *Journal of Forensic Psychiatry*, 4: 341–54.

South, N. (1998) 'Corporate and state crimes against the environment', in V. Ruggiero, N. South and I. Taylor (eds) *The New European Criminology.* London: Routledge.

Southgate, P. and Ekblom, P. (1986) *Police-Public Encounters*, Home Office Research

Study No. 90. London: HMSO.

Squires, P. (1998a) *The East Grinstead Town Centre CCTV Scheme: An Independent Evaluation.* Brighton: Health and Social Policy Research Centre, University of Brighton.

Squires, P. (1998b) *CCTV and Crime Reduction in Crawley: An Independent Evaluation of the Crawley CCTV System.* Brighton: Health and Social Policy Research Centre, University of Brighton.

Squires, P. (1998c) *CCTV and Crime Prevention in Burgess Hill Town Centre: An Independent Evaluation.* Brighton: Health and Social Policy Research Centre, University of Brighton.

Squires, P. (1998d) *An Evaluation of the Ilford Town Centre CCTV System.* Brighton: Health and Social Policy Research Centre, University of Brighton.

Squires, P. and Measor, L. (1996) *Closed Circuit TV Surveillance and Crime Prevention in Brighton: Half Yearly Report.* Brighton: Health and Social Policy Research Centre, University of Brighton.

Squires, P. and Measor, L. (1997) *CCTV Surveillance and Crime Prevention in Brighton: Follow-up Analysis.* Brighton: Health and Social Policy Research Centre, University of Brighton.

Stanko, E. (1985) *Intimate Intrusions.* London: Routledge and Kegan Paul.

Steer, D. (1980) *Uncovering Crime,* Royal Commission on Criminal Procedure, Research Study No. 7: London: HMSO.

Stevens, P. and Willis, C. (1979) *Race, Crime and Arrests,* Home Office Research Study No. 58. London: HMSO.

Sumner, C. (ed) (1990) *Censure, Politics and Criminal Justice.* Milton Keynes: Open University Press.

Sutherland, E. (1940) 'White-collar criminality', *American Sociological Review,* 5: 1–12.

Sutherland, E. (1945) 'Is "white-collar crime" crime?', *American Sociological Review,* 10: 132–9.

Sutherland, E. (1947) *Principles of Criminology,* 4th edn. Philadelphia: Lippincott.

Sutherland, E. (1949) *White-collar Crime.* New York: Holt Rinehart and Winston.

Sutherland, E. and Cressey, D. (1960) *Principles of Criminology,* 6th edn. Chicago: Lippincott.

Sykes, R. and Brent, E. (1983) *Policing: A Social Behaviorist Perspective.* New Brunswick, NJ: Rutgers University Press.

Tame, C. (1991) 'Freedom, responsibility and justice: the criminology of the "New Right"', in K. Stenson and D. Cowell (eds) *The Politics of Crime Control.* London: Sage.

Tappan, P. (1947) 'Who is the criminal?' *American Sociological Review,* 12: 96–102.

Taylor, I. (1999) *Crime in Context: A Critical Criminology of Market Societies.* Oxford: Polity.

Taylor, I., Walton, P. and Young, J. (1973) *The New Criminology.* London: Routledge and Kegan Paul.

Taylor, I., Walton, P. and Young, J. (eds) (1975) *Critical Criminology.* London: Routledge and Kegan Paul.

Thornton, D. M. and Reid, R. L. (1982) 'Moral reasoning and the type of criminal offence', *British Journal of Social Psychology,* 21: 231–8.

Tilley, N. (1998), 'Evaluating the Effectiveness of CCTV Schemes' in C. Norris, J. Moran and G. Armstrong (eds), *Surveillance, Closed Circuit Television and Social Control*, Aldershot: Ashgate.

Trasler, G. (1962) *The Explanation of Criminality*. London: Routledge and Kegan Paul.

Trasler, G. (1986) 'Situational crime control and rational choice: a critique', in K. Heal and G. Laycock (eds) *Situational Crime Prevention*. London: HMSO.

Waddington, P. (1986) 'Mugging as a moral panic', *British Journal of Sociology*, 37: 245–59.

Waddington, P. (1993) *Calling the Police*. Aldershot: Gower.

Waddington, P. (1999) *Policing Citizens*. London: UCL Press.

Walker, M., Jefferson, T., and Seneviratne, M. (1990) *Ethnic Minorities, Young People and the Criminal Justice System*. Sheffield: Centre for Criminological and Socio-legal Studies, University of Sheffield.

Walklate, S. (1995) *Gender and Crime*. Hemel Hempstead: Prentice Hall.

Walklate, S. (1998) *Understanding Criminology*. Buckingham: Open University Press.

Walton, P. and Young, J. (eds) (1998) *The New Criminology Revisited*. Basingstoke: Macmillan.

Ward Jouve, N. (1988) '*The Street-cleaner': the Yorkshire Ripper Case on Trial*. London: Marion Boyars.

Webster, C. (2000), 'Relegitimating the Democratic Polity: The Closed Circuit Television Revolution in the UK', in Horrocks, I. Moff, J. and Topps, P. (eds) *Democratic Governance and New Technology: Technologically Mediated Innovations in Political Practices in Western Europe*, London: Routledge.

Weiss, R. (1987) 'The Community and Crime Prevention', in E. Johnson (ed.), *Handbook on Crime and Delinquency Prevention*, New York: Greenwood Press.

Werner, E. E. (1989) 'High risk children in young adulthood', *American Journal of Orthopsychiatry*, 59: 72–81.

White, R. and Haines, F. (1996) *Crime and Criminology: An Introduction*. Oxford: Oxford University Press.

Wikström, P.-O. 'Delinquency and the urban stucture', in P.-O. Wikström (ed) *Crime and Measures Against Crime in the City*. Stockholm: National Council for Crime Prevention.

Willis, C. (1983) *The Use, Effectiveness and Impact of Police Stop and Search Powers*, Research and Planning Unit Paper No. 15. London: Home Office.

Wilson, J. (1975) *Thinking About Crime*. New York: Basic Books.

Wilson, J. and Herrnstein, R. (1985) *Crime and Human Nature*. New York: Simon and Schuster.

Woodcock, J. (1992) *Trust in the Police – the search for truth*. International Police Exhibition and Conference (IPEC) Seminar Paper Reprints. London: Major Exhibitions and Conferences Ltd.

Van Maanen, J. (1978) 'The asshole', in P. Manning and J. Van Maanen (eds) *Policing: A View From the Street*. Santa Monica, CA: Goodyear.

Yablonsky, L. (1962) *The Violent Gang*. London: Pelican.

Yochelson, S. and Samenow, S. (1976) *The Criminal Personality.* New York: Jason Aronson.

Young, J. (1971) *The Drugtakers.* London: Paladin.

Young, J. (1981) 'Thinking seriously about crime', in M. Fitzgerald, G. McLennan and J. Pawson (eds) *Crime and Society: Readings in History and Theory.* London: Routledge and Kegan Paul.

Young, J. (1986) 'The failure of criminology', in R. Matthews and J. Young (eds) *Confronting Crime.* London: Sage.

Young, J. (1994) 'Incessant chatter: current paradigms in criminology', in M. Maguire, R. Morgan, and R. Reiner (eds) *The Oxford Handbook of Criminology.* Oxford: Clarendon.

Young, J. (1997) 'Left realist criminology', in M. Maguire, R. Morgan, and R. Reiner (eds) *The Oxford Handbook of Criminology,* 2nd edn. Oxford: Clarendon.

Young, J. (1999) *The Exclusive Society.* London: Sage.

Young, M. (1991) *An Inside Job.* Oxford: Clarendon.

Index